THE GR5 TRAIL
THROUGH THE FRENCH ALPS:
LAKE GENEVA TO NICE

About the Author

Paddy Dillon is an indefatigable long-distance walker who has walked several major European trails. He has written and illustrated almost 40 guidebooks and contributed to more than 20 other books. He lives on the fringes of the English Lake District and has walked, and written about walking, in every county throughout the British Isles. He has led guided walking holidays and has walked throughout Europe, as well as Nepal, Tibet and the Rocky Mountains of Canada and the USA.

While walking his routes, Paddy inputs his notes directly into a palmtop computer every few steps. His descriptions are therefore precise, having been written at the very point at which the reader uses them. He has appeared on television and is a member of the Outdoor Writers and Photographers Guild.

Other Cicerone guides written by Paddy include:

Walking in the North Pennines
The Mountains of Ireland
Walking in the Galloway Hills
Walking in County Durham
The Irish Coast to Coast Walk
Walking on the Isle of Arran
Irish Coastal Walks
Channel Island Walks
Walking in the Isles of Scilly
GR20 Corsica – High Level Route

Walking in Madeira
Walking in the Canaries: Vol 1 West
Walking in the Canaries: Vol 2 East
The South West Coast Path
Walking in Malta
Cleveland Way & Yorkshire Wolds
 Way
The North York Moors
The Great Glen Way
The National Trails

THE GR5 TRAIL
THROUGH THE FRENCH ALPS:
LAKE GENEVA TO NICE

by

Paddy Dillon

2 POLICE SQUARE, MILNTHORPE, CUMBRIA LA7 7PY
www.cicerone.co.uk

First edition 2008
ISBN-13: 978-185284-533-9

Photographs by the author

A catalogue record for this book is available from the British Library

Front cover: Bouquetin high above Pont de la Croé Vie in the Vanoise
(Stage 3, Day 12, GR55)

CONTENTS

International Distress Signal
(*Only to be used in an emergency*)
**Six blasts on a whistle (and flashes with a torch after dark) spaced evenly
for one minute, followed by a minute's pause.
Repeat until an answer is received. The response is three signals per minute
followed by a minute's pause.**

The following signals are used to communicate with a helicopter

Help needed: **Help not required:**

raise both arms
above head to
form a 'V'

raise one arm above
head, extend other
arm downward

**In an emergency the mountain rescue (*secours en montagne*)
can be called on 04 92 22 22 22**
Note: Mountain rescues must be paid for – be insured

Map Key

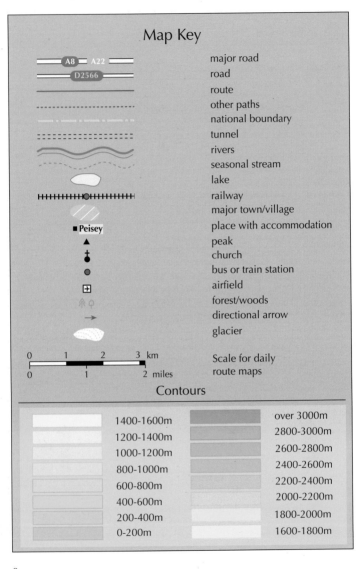

A8 — A22	major road
D2566	road
	route
	other paths
	national boundary
	tunnel
	rivers
	seasonal stream
	lake
++++++●++++++	railway
	major town/village
■ Peisey	place with accommodation
▲	peak
♱	church
●	bus or train station
⊞	airfield
🌲	forest/woods
→	directional arrow
	glacier

0	1	2	3 km	Scale for daily
0		1	2 miles	route maps

Contours

	1400-1600m		over 3000m
	1200-1400m		2800-3000m
	1000-1200m		2600-2800m
	800-1000m		2400-2600m
	600-800m		2200-2400m
	400-600m		2000-2200m
	200-400m		1800-2000m
	0-200m		1600-1800m

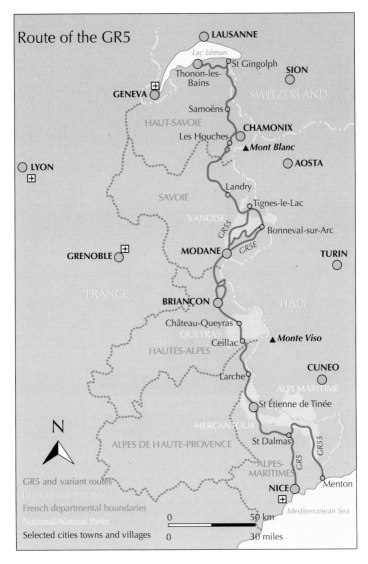

Route of the GR5

LAUSANNE

Lac Léman

St Gingolph

SION

Thonon-les-Bains

SWITZERLAND

GENEVA

Samoëns

HAUT-SAVOIE

CHAMONIX

Les Houches

▲Mont Blanc

LYON

AOSTA

Landry

SAVOIE

Tignes-le-Lac

VANOISE

Bonneval-sur-Arc

MODANE

GR55

GR5E

GRENOBLE

TURIN

FRANCE

ITALY

BRIANÇON

Château-Queyras

QUEYRAS

Ceillac

▲Monte Viso

HAUTES-ALPES

Larche

CUNEO

ALPI MARITIME

St Étienne de Tinée

N

MERCANTOUR

ALPES DE HAUTE-PROVENCE

St Dalmas

GR55

ALPES-MARITIMES

GR5

NICE

Menton

GR5 and variant routes

International frontiers

French departmental boundaries

National/Natural Parks

Selected cities towns and villages

Mediterranean Sea

0		50 km
0		30 miles

The GR5 takes walkers into the heart of the
mountains – the steep slopes of the
Pas de la Cavale (Day 23)

INTRODUCTION

The Glacier de Miage and Dômes de Miage, seen after leaving the Chalets de Miage (Day 7 variant)

Trekking across the French Alps between Geneva and Nice sounds like a daunting task even for experienced long-distance walkers, but let's start by taking a step back to look at the even bigger picture. The GR5 actually starts on the North Sea coast at the Hook of Holland and heads southwards through Belgium and France to end in Nice. This guidebook is concerned only with the celebrated final part of the route, the walkers' 'grand traverse of the Alps' from Lac Léman (Lake Geneva) to the Mediterranean coast.

Every summer, thousands of walkers embark on this trek, either in full or in part, and complete the journey without any problems. Well-graded paths and tracks, the judicious use of strategic cols between the high peaks, and the availability of *refuge* and *gîte* accommodation

ensure that the route is simply a long walk, and one that can be completed by averagely fit, experienced hill-walkers.

People have been crossing the Alps for many centuries, as hunters, traders and warriors, and more recently as travellers and tourists, racers and record-breakers. Your journey should prove much easier than many of those that have gone before, and with some advance thought and planning, coupled with a willingness to adapt and amend those plans on a day-by-day basis, a walk along the GR5 should present a fine challenge, without being too arduous.

It is primarily a summer trek, and a typical Alpine summer will be blessed with plenty of warm, sunny days, tempered by cool breezes on high cols, with views of dazzling snow-capped peaks rising above colourful, flowery slopes. Lodgings, food and drink are available at regular intervals, there is good signposting and waymarking, and the chance to get close to a variety of wildlife – all ensuring that a walk along the GR5 will provide memories that will last for a lifetime.

WALKING THE GR5

Because there are a good many variant and alternative routes available (see Route Outline in this Introduction), the GR5 can measure anything from 645–725km (400–450 miles), and depending on how walkers structure their route, in excess of 40,000m (131,235 feet) could be climbed. But despite its length, and despite the fact that it crosses the mighty Alps, the GR5 is still no more than a long walk.

Paths and tracks are usually well graded, and if they have to climb steep slopes, they do so by means of zigzags, so overall gradients are seldom severe. However, there are some rough and rocky parts, and a few places where walkers who suffer from vertigo might experience problems, but only on a very few occasions is it necessary to use hands to scramble up or down a rocky stretch. Also bear in mind that a sudden snowfall (and it can snow on any day in the summer, although it usually clears very quickly), or ice-crusted rock, could hamper progress.

Walkers with previous experience of the Alps, and of walking long-distance routes, will find a trek along the GR5 well within their ability, and no specialist equipment is required beyond your usual hill-walking kit. Those who have never walked in the Alps, or never attempted a long-distance walk before, should proceed with caution, and preferably gain some experience before tackling the GR5.

Not everyone will wish to walk the whole route in a single trip. Some will be happy to cover a week here and a week there, over a period of a few years, or to split the route into two two-week stages, and as access by public transport is available at many points along the way, it is easy to do this.

In this guidebook, the schedule of seven stages, made up of a total of 31 days, and the breakdown of timings within the days, assumes that the walker is fit, in good health, and has some long-distance walking experience. The GR5 can be covered in three weeks, so a trek of one month would comfortably suit most people. If you prefer to take six weeks, just alter the schedule to suit your needs.

The author has taken careful note of the daily distances covered by other walkers along the GR5, and the day stages given are those that are achievable by someone who is used to long-distance walking, although these timings are easily adapted to match individual requirements. (Also see Timings, in this introduction.)

The GR5 is not simply a linear walk, but bristles with the alternatives and variants described in this guidebook. To begin with, there are two starting points on Lac Léman – either at Thonon-les-Bains or St Gingolph. Then there are two finishing points on the Mediterranean – either at Nice or Menton. The GR5 sometimes splits, with alternative options such as the GR55 and GR5E (Stage 3), and the GR5B and GR5C (Stage 4). These routes may cover several days, such as the GR55 (Stage 3) through the Vanoise, and the GR52 through the Mercantour national park (Stage 7). All these alternatives are described in full, with maps, and are included on the maps for each stage. (The French *grand randonnées*, or GR routes, are administered by the Fédération Française de la Randonnée Pédestre, or FFRP, www.ffrandonnee.fr.)

ALPINE TRAVERSES

People have been crossing the Alps for thousands of years, hunting in the post-glacial forests, herding animals and clearing areas for cultivation. Routes from one valley to another, crossing cols between the peaks, have long been exploited. Perhaps the most famous early mountaineer was 'Otzi', whose mummified corpse was hacked from ice on the border between Austria and Italy in 1991. He lived around 3300BC, wore clothes of leather and woven grass, and was killed and left on the mountainside, to be buried by snow.

The Alps have a bloody history and are shared between countries that were often at war with each other. Celtic tribes occupied many parts, and Roman armies stamped their authority on them. Hannibal famously crossed the Alps to fight the Romans on their own territory. Christianity became the dominant religion (today the religion of the French Alps is overwhelmingly Roman Catholic), although Saracens often raided into the southern Alps.

There was great trade between Alpine valleys, with meat and cheese produced in the mountains finding eager consumers in towns and cities. To assist in the preservation of foodstuffs, mule trains carried salt from the Mediterranean into the mountain valleys, across high cols, to every village, town and city. The backbone trade route was known as the Route du Sel (or Salt Route) and was important throughout medieval times.

Comte Amédée VII of Savoie was known as Le Comte Rouge, or the Red

People once crossed the Alps as traders and warriors, but now do so for enjoyment (Day 18a, GR5C)

Count, as his armour was stained with the blood of his enemies. He annexed Geneva and Nice to Savoie, and so must be credited with making an early bid for the ownership of the GR5, since he took possession of its terminal points! Walkers following the GR5 walk through several former fiefdoms, and not only walk close to Switzerland and Italy, but actually enter those countries briefly. Massive fortifications are seen from time to time in the areas that experienced the most strife, and some roads were built by Napoleonic forces. These days, international frontiers around Europe are very casual, and in the Alps it is possible to pass from one country to another without even realizing.

The notion of making a 'grand traverse of the Alps' has appealed not only to walkers, but also to cyclists and motorists, and routes are available for all. The GR5 used to be called the Grande Traversée des Alpes, or GTA, but that title is more often used for the motoring and cycling route from Thonon-les-Bains to Menton (www.grande-traversee-alpes.com), described for cyclists in Cicerone's guide *Cycling in the French Alps* by Paul Henderson.

<hr>

WHO WALKS THE GR5?

You might think that a trek across the Alps would attract only the hardest of 'he-men', shouldering huge packs and gritting their teeth in the face of adversity, but you would be very wrong. There are indeed plenty of fit walkers on the route, but there are plenty more who are simply average types, and some who are unfit, or carrying injuries, yet they plod on regardless. The author has seen a blind man being led along the route, seen entire family groups with an amazing age range, and seen a couple leading a donkey along the trail. The GR5 attracts all types of walkers, and providing they pitch in at a pace that suits them, they manage fine. You may meet some of the typical characters along the route.

The Flying Dutchman (or Belgian) will scoff at your short walk over the Alps, and tell you that you are doing it all wrong, as you should have started from Holland. The Super-Fit Walker will be trekking solo across the Alps in three weeks or less, and won't have a bead of sweat on them, nor will they be out of breath. They'll pass you with ease, carrying hardly any gear, treating the whole thing as a stroll in the park, being well acquainted with the Alps. The Grossly Overburdened Walker will tell you that they've already posted their excess gear ahead to Nice. The Wild Camper objects to spending money, even begrudging paying for food, and camps in areas where it's forbidden, thinking that anyone spending a night indoors is a softy. The Retired Couple will be taking twice as long as everyone else, having promised themselves this trip for decades, and intend enjoying every minute. The 'Last of the Summer Wine' English party are a threesome, are also retired, but generally have previous Alpine experience, even if they haven't mastered French yet. The Family Group, with mum, dad, the children and maybe the odd aunt or uncle, will be tackling the GR5 over a period of years. The children are beginning to wonder if a beach holiday would be better, but mum and dad say they can have that when they get to the Mediterranean.

You'll be in good company on this trek!

ROUTE OUTLINE

Walking a route as long and as high as the GR5 might appear too difficult for an ordinary walker, but step back and put it into perspective. On a clear day, for example, a half-hour flight between Geneva and Nice reveals the whole route, with its long valleys and convenient passes between high mountains. Some walkers might prefer to drive along the signposted Grande Traversée des Alpes (GTA) motoring route first, between Thonon-les-Bains and Menton, which occasionally crosses the GR5, allows an easy appreciation of the terrain it covers.

It is important to remember that if the whole distance seems too long to contemplate, the GR5 can easily be broken into short stages. Public transport to and from a dozen points along the route is excellent, and many other points also have a reasonably good level of service. In addition, remember that the GR5 isn't simply a linear walk, but has two different starting points, two different finishing points, and on six of the seven stages there are various alternative routes in between. It is entirely up to the individual walker to decide how much of the path is going to be covered, and which alternative routes are to be followed when choices arise.

Read the route outline with reference to the overview map on page 9,

and the maps at the beginning of each of the seven stages.

Stage 1, Days 1 to 6
Starting on the shore of Lac Léman, walkers must decide whether to trek from St Gingolph to La Chapelle d'Abondance in a day (Day 1 (direct)), or start from Thonon-les-Bains and take two days to cover the distance (alternative Day 1 and Day 2). During this first stage the GR5 wanders through the Chablais region, where the pre-Alps give way to the Alps themselves, and it is likely that some of the high passes will be covered in snow. Start too early in the season, and you run the risk of snow being a serious obstacle to progress. As the mountains increase in height, many peaks carrying permanent snow and ice will be seen, culminating in magnificent views of the glaciated summit and flanks of Mont Blanc.

Those who don't want to complete the whole of the GR5 in a single journey could walk for a week and break at Les Houches (Day 6). If a few more days are available, the Chamonix area could be explored before heading home, and if enough of the GR5 has been seen to want to return, it is easy to pick up the route and continue at a later date.

Stage 2, Days 7 to 9
Leaving Les Houches in tandem with the Tour du Mont Blanc, an easy climb onto Col de Voza reveals a choice of routes. The main route simply descends to Bionnassay and Les Contamines, while the higher alternative route climbs up and across the Col de Tricot before dropping to Les Contamines.

Either way, the route then runs up through a long valley on Day 8, with a likelihood of finding snow towards the top of the Col du Bonhomme. Always keep an eye on the weather, since very strong winds, or snow and ice on the path, will render the walk along the Crête des Gittes dangerous, requiring the abandonment of the GR5 and a descent to Les Chapieux. (See Alpine Weather, below, for how to obtain forecasts). Normally, there will be no problem continuing across the lush green mountainsides of the Beaufortain region.

Think ahead when accommodation options become sparse, such as around Plan de la Lai (end of Day 8) and over the Col du Bresson to Valezan (Day 9), and if camping and carrying all supplies, take careful note of the distance between shops where restocking is possible. A bit of advance planning could save a lot of wasted time and frustration.

Again, those who wish to walk just this stage of the GR5 will be looking for options to leave the route easily, and to assist with this approach, there is a variant loop via Landry, which has a railway station (see end of Day 9).

Stage 3, Days 10 to 15 – Three Possible Routes: GR5, GR55 and GR5E

One area that needs a good deal of advance planning is the Parc National de la Vanoise, where the GR5 itself (Days 10–15) takes a very meandering route, while alternatives pursue remarkably different courses. The GR55 high-level route (Days 11–13), for example, runs straight through the heart of the mountains, while the GR5E low-level route (Days 13–15) stays down in the valley of the Arc. Ultimately, all three routes meet in Modane, but only after being apart for several days. Be sure, before leaving Landry on Day 10 and

La Grande Casse, in the heart of the Vanoise, reflected in a lake on the way to the Refuge du Plan du Lac (Day 13)

climbing up through a long valley to the Col du Palet (Day 11), that you are aware of your choices.

On the descent from the Col du Palet to Tignes-le-Lac, the GR5 and GR55 part company. The GR5 runs over to Val d'Isère, then climbs over the Col de l'Iseran (Day 12), which is the highest point on the route at 2770m (9088ft). It then descends towards the valley of the Arc, where at Bonneval-sur-Arc (Day 13) there is an option to take the easy, low-level GR5E to Mondane. Take stock of the time at your disposal, your fitness and energy levels, and the prevailing weather, while juggling these options.

The GR5, after descending to Bessans (Day 12), makes a high-level traverse across the flanks of the mountains overlooking the Arc valley. In doing so, it has to traverse round the rugged gorge of the Doron (Day 13 and Day 14), which pushes into the heart of the Vanoise. Fine *balcon* paths, literally like walking along a balcony, offer splendid views before a descent to Modane (Day 15).

The high-level GR55, meanwhile, runs through the heart of the Vanoise, crossing the broad Col de la Leisse and Col de la Vanoise to reach the village of Pralognan (Day 12). In clear weather the scenery is outstanding, but snow has a habit of lying late into summer on the passes. The Col de Chavière (Day 13) is crossed at 2796m (9173ft), climbing higher than the GR5 before descending to Modane (Day 13).

The low-level GR5E, by complete contrast, simply wanders from Bonneval-sur-Arc (Day 13), down through the valley of the Arc, to join the other two routes at Modane (Day 15).

Stage 4, Days 16 to 20

Modane has excellent transport links and so is a fine place to break the journey if covering the GR5 in stages. Beyond this point, subtle changes to the landscape and weather will make some walkers begin to feel that the Mediterranean is drawing near, but in fact the journey isn't even half completed!

There are two ways out of Modane. One is an old pilgrim route from the town, while the other is a steep, forested ascent from the railway station. The routes reunite near the ski village of Valfréjus to continue towards the Refuge du Thabor near the Col de la Vallée Étroite at the end of Day 16.

In the Vallée Étroite you could be forgiven for thinking that you had strayed into Italy. Signs are in Italian, other walkers are speaking Italian, and when a little village is reached, the food is Italian too. The Vallée Étroite was indeed part of Italy until the mid-20th century, and the nearest big town is Bardonnecchia.

While crossing over the Col de Thures on Day 17, to reach the Vallée de la Clarée, the route splits into a number of alternatives, and walkers are faced with choices.

The main GR5 simply drops down into the Vallée de la Clarée and heads for Plampinet at the end of Day 17. The GR5B (Day 17a), however, stays high after crossing the Col de Thures, and even makes a short incursion into Italy across the flanks of a very rugged mountain. There are no facilities along the GR5B, so anyone following it will almost certainly need to drop down to Plampinet.

A pleasant little lake sits on the grassy Col des Thures high above the Vallée Étroite (Day 17 GR5B)

On Day 18 the GR5 main route leaves Plampinet to cross high cols using relatively easy paths, then drops down to Montgenèvre and uses forest tracks to continue down to Briançon.

Back in the Vallée de la Clarée, meanwhile, the GR5C provides a high-level and at times rough, rocky and exposed alternative (Day 18a) to Briançon. This is fine for walkers who are sure-footed and don't suffer from vertigo, but should be avoided in very strong winds, or if snow and ice cover the paths.

Briançon is the largest town along the course of the GR5, and is rich in military history. The area abounds in fortifications and was a garrison town. Naturally, because of its size, it has excellent transport links, and those who are walking the route in stages can easily break their journey at this point.

Beyond Briançon, the GR5 climbs over the Col des Ayes on Day 19, then enters the well-wooded Parc Naturel Régional du Queyras, traditionally a woodworking and timber-harvesting area, with Ceillac (Day 20) at its heart.

Stage 5, Days 21 to 24
Stage 5 begins at Ceillac, and once over the Col Girardin the route enters the Ubaye region, where it runs concurrently with the GR56 from Fouillouse, passing a series of high-level fortifications on its way to Larche at the end of Day 22.

The northernmost part of the Parc National du Mercantour is entered, where wildlife is given special protection. The scenery is particularly grand on the crossing of the Pas de la Cavale, though this is a remote area, and walkers must rely on tiny hamlets, such as Bousieyas (end of Day 23), or small villages, such as St Dalmas le Selvage (Day 24), to provide food, drink and shelter.

The GR5 is now inside the vast Vallée de la Tinée, but there are still mighty mountains to cross, despite occasional descents into the valley.

St Étienne de Tinée and Auron (end of Day 24) both have regular daily links with Nice, and are therefore ideal start or finish points for those walking the GR5 in stages.

Stage 6, Days 25 to 29

Ahead of Auron, which is at the start of Stage 6, lie the sprawling slopes of Mont Mounier, where at last the distant sheen of the Mediterranean catches the eye. The route makes a long traverse across the deep, forested Vallée de la Tinée, climbing to St Dalmas (Day 26), where there is a major decision to be made. At this point the main GR5 can be followed straight to Nice, or the GR52 offers a longer and much more rugged alternative, finishing on the Mediterranean coast at Menton.

Walkers choosing to stick with the GR5 follow an elevated crest, part-forested but also rocky and arid, with no

food or shelter available, and only one source of water. At the end of this long day (Day 27) is the hilltop village of Utelle, sited defensively against Saracen raiders. Rugged mule tracks cross the deep, forested Gorges de la Vésubie, then easier walking leads from Levens to Aspremont (Day 28), where both villages sit on hilltops. The final stage of the GR5 crosses the arid slopes of Mont Chauve, finally descending from the mountains, before urban walking ends on the shore of the Mediterranean.

Stage 7, Days 27 to 31

The GR52 provides a remarkable alternative ending to this long trek, and is really a splendid route in its own right, allowing the southernmost parts of the Parc National du Mercantour to be explored. Leaving St Dalmas, it heads northwards to cross the Col du Barn, then heads through forested valleys, swinging more southwards to Le Boréon

Splendid views of Menton and the Mediterranean are enjoyed on the final forested descent along the GR52 (Day 31)

(end of Day 27). Some steep, rough and rocky ascents and descents cross boulder-strewn slopes, passing little lakes and passing through the amazing Vallée des Merveilles (Day 29).

There is a long day's walk from the Vallée des Merveilles to Sospel (Day 30), along an arid crest, possibly without water and certainly without food and lodgings. The last day's walk, from Sospel to Menton, stays high, so that the final descent is steep and rugged, landing suddenly on the shore of the Mediterranean at Menton, where this long trek through the Alps clearly reaches its end.

NORTH–SOUTH/ SOUTH–NORTH

The vast majority of walkers follow the GR5 trek from north to south, from Lac Léman to the Mediterranean. There is no reason why the route shouldn't be followed from south to north, but very few go in that direction. Walking north to south means that you are likely to meet the same walkers during your journey. Coming the other way, you will probably walk on your own for most of the time, meeting other GR5 walkers around midday each day, maybe passing only with a nod of the head or a brief, 'Bonjour'.

Starting in the north invariably means there will still be snow lying on the high cols, while starting in the south might mean the trek can commence a couple of weeks earlier. While snow doesn't fall along the Mediterranean shore, it can be a problem further inland if you start too early. Walking southwards does not necessarily mean you will be squinting into the sun, as the sun rides high at these latitudes, and in any case the route is very convoluted in places and takes in every point of the compass. The alternative GR52 (Stage 7), for example, spends a whole morning heading northwards, even though its ultimate destination lies southwards.

The only real difference between walking southwards and walking northwards is the way other people view your progress. Walking southwards, people understand what you are doing and where you are heading. Walking northwards, it seems to take people longer to register what you are doing, and you get the distinct impression that they think you are going the 'wrong' way.

From a practical point of view, the waymarks and signposts work the same both ways, as do all the services and facilities along the route. However, users of this guidebook would find it tedious and occasionally frustrating to have to reverse all the route directions, as well as all the ascents and descents, while following the text. The route summary for the north to south walk can be found in Appendix 1. In addition, to offer some assistance to those walking northwards, a route summary in this direction is provided in Appendix 2.

TIMINGS

In the information box that precedes the route description for each day, a total time for walking that day is given, and the route description for each day is further broken down into sections with timings.

In some ways these timings are meaningless – there will be walkers who go faster than others, and no one is ever

How long will it take to walk? Strong walkers can complete the GR5 in as little as three weeks

going to match every time given for a whole month! Giving precise timings on a route where all kinds of things can affect onward progress is bound to invite criticism, but throughout the Alps people rely on such timings, and they are frequently given on signposts.

Although most walkers trek from north to south, those who go the other way will naturally expect their timings to be different – when a long descent heading southwards becomes a long ascent heading northwards, and vice versa, for example. In Appendix 1 and Appendix 2, timings are given for a north–south trek and a south–north trek respectively.

Don't expect to be able to match any of the timings given, but do take note of them and use them as a guide while assessing your progress. If you keep beating the stated times, then you probably always will, and you might

safely plan to walk longer and further each day as a result. If you keep falling well short, then you probably always will, and you should take careful note and be prepared to split a long day over two shorter days. Some walkers might start quite slowly on the GR5, but pick up speed after a week or so, and if they spot this happening, then they will find it useful when planning ahead.

The timings are purely *walking* times, and do not take any account of time spent resting, stopping for lunch, or taking more than a few snaps with the camera along the way. Any time spent motionless must be added to the time given for each stage. Walkers who like to stop for a few minutes every hour or so, or stop for a couple of beers at every bar, or who take long lunch breaks, might need to allow three or more hours per day!

Occasionally the timings given in this guidebook will vary from those given on signposts along the GR5. In some instances, the author may consider the information on signs to be wrong, and therefore offers an alternative timing. In other cases, information is clearly wrong, and has been corrected. The signposts either side of Modane (Day 15 and Day 16), for instance, are either completely wrong, or have been planted in the wrong order, but either way they are misleading.

WAYMARKING

Waymarking on French GR (or *grand randonnée*) routes is fairly standard. Horizontal red and white paint stripes are used along these routes, with the white stripe always appearing above the red one. Sometimes, little red/white plaques are screwed or glued to posts, rocks, buildings and other immovable objects. The same stripes might appear on signposts after a particular place-name, indicating that the GR route runs there, and by inference, does not run to any other place that might be indicated.

GR5 WAYMARKING SIGNS

Correct direction

Turn left

Turn right

Wrong way

The system is easy to understand, but not entirely foolproof.

The red/white flashes should appear at intervals, either to confirm that the route is still being followed correctly, or to indicate a change of direction. There is an 'official' method of showing whether a left or right turn needs to be made, but this has become corrupted and is rarely used properly, so whenever you see the paint marks clearly bending left or right, assume that a turn needs to be made. If you inadvertently take a wrong turn at a junction, it is usually the case that you will quickly see a red stripe crossed at right angles by a white stripe. The red/white 'X' means that you are going the wrong way and you should immediately turn round and retrace steps.

In some areas, the course of the GR5 intersects other GR routes, or runs in tandem with them. Be very sure to keep following the GR5, but also bear in mind that most variant and alternative routes are also marked with red/white flashes. Anticipate junctions with other trails and double-check that you are following the correct one each time. There are places where the GR5 has been re-routed, and it is usual for old red/white flashes to be painted over with grey paint, or physically removed, but faded markers may remain in place. In national parks, where over-use of paint may constitute an eyesore, some markers have been chiselled off rocks, or re-painted much smaller in size, and therefore aren't quite as obvious.

Waymarking and signposting varies from place to place, and the route description in this guidebook is intended to keep the reader alert when the GR5 switches from track to path, from riverside to forest, or from boulder-scree to grassy slopes. Always keep an eye open for markers and assume that something is wrong if none have been seen for a long time.

IGN maps show the GR routes as slightly bolder red lines than are used for other walking trails, and label them to confirm that they are GR routes. If the map is at odds with what is marked on the ground, then commonsense will have to be used. If the GR5 is found to be at variance with what is described in this guidebook, then the author would welcome news of any changes to the route.

GR5 GEOLOGY

The geology of the whole of the Alps is exceedingly complex, but as the French Alps form only part of the story, the geology of the GR5 is relatively simple to understand. For the most part, walkers tread on a variety of limestones, but in some places crystalline schists and gneisses are prominent. Other notable rock types include shale, sandstone, quartzite and chunky conglomerates.

The geological narrative starts with the break-up of an ancient landmass – a process known as continental drift. The massive 'plates' that carry Europe and Africa parted company, and the gap between them was filled by an ocean that came into being around 140 million years ago. The oldest Alpine rocks are therefore those that were exposed on the ancient seabed.

At different periods through geological time, the ocean was either deep or shallow, depending on the relative positions of the African and European plates. If the sea was shallow, corals colonised the seabed and built up into thick, lime-rich reefs. In deeper water, microscopic plankton thrived near the

Layer upon layer of rock has been folded and faulted to raise the Alps from an ancient ocean

surface of the sea, and their tiny skeletons fell to the seabed to create, over a very long period, thick, limey deposits.

All around the ocean, mountains were being eroded, and rivers carried rubble, sand and mud into the sea, forming alternating beds of sandstone, mudstone and cobbly conglomerates. In some places these became inter-bedded with the limey deposits. At certain times the ocean was as deep as 5km (3 miles) so there was plenty of space to be filled, resulting in a great thickness of rock.

After drifting apart for some considerable time, the African and European plates swung, as if on a pivot, setting them on a collision course, with devastating consequences. The ocean was squeezed out of existence some 60 million years ago, and the accumulated deposits were crushed together, suffering incredible heat and pressure, which often transformed the rock – a process known as metamorphism. With nowhere to go but upwards, the thick, crumpled and contorted beds of rock rose to form the Alps, and on the geological timescale these are very 'young' mountains.

The practical outcome, as far as a walker on the GR5 is concerned, is that a number of rock types can be seen, representing a number of geological periods. The oldest rocks, which have suffered most from metamorphism, are wavy schists and hard, banded gneisses, seen mostly around Mont Blanc, the Vanoise and Mercantour. Triassic rocks include crumbling dolomitic limestones, often pitted with little holes, like a sponge, and soft beds of gypsum. Jurassic limestones are hard and grey, and are the rocks that are encountered most often along the course of the GR5. Upper Jurassic rocks tend to be soft shale and sandstone, often inter-bedded, giving rise to slopes subject to landslip. On top of this series lies hard, dark, durable Cretaceous limestone.

In comparatively recent times – within the past couple of million years – the Alps were heavily glaciated. Monstrous glaciers carved their way through every rock type, tearing some apart with ease, while slowly grinding away at harder bands. Classic U-shaped valleys and bowl-like mountain corries – or 'combes' – abound. Masses of ill-assorted bouldery moraine were dumped as the glaciers melted. Deep hollows ground out by the glaciers filled with water to become lakes. Geologists say that the ice age ended some 10,000 years ago, but of course on the highest Alpine peaks it is still in progress (although those who visit the Alps year after year are well aware that the glaciers are shrinking and may ultimately disappear altogether).

Anyone with a deep interest in geology can obtain geological maps of the Alps from the BRGM, see www.brgm.fr. An easily understood 'crash course' in Alpine geology can be included in a walk along the GR5 by visiting the Espace Géologique at Château-Queyras, on Day 20 of the trek.

ALPINE FLOWERS

The Alps are famous for wildflowers and the colour and interest they lend to a walk is immense. It is simply not possible to do justice to the subject in a short space, but here are a few hints and tips to aid identification. Flower species are

Flowery slopes are a notable feature early in the walking season, fading later into the summer (above Entre Deux Eaux, Stage 3, Day 14, GR5)

divided into 'families' that often exhibit similar characteristics. If a flower looks like a daisy or buttercup, then it is likely to be a member of the daisy or buttercup family. This 'rule' may apply even if colours and shapes are unexpected, such as the purple-petalled aster, which belongs to the daisy family, or the 'unopened' yellow petals of globeflowers, which belong to the buttercup family. If it looks like a tiny pansy, it will doubtless be the mountain pansy, and if it looks like clover, it will doubtless be clover, no matter how big or small or colourful it is.

Some flowers dominate the scene by their sheer size and colour, such as the tall, erect, great yellow gentian. It grows in grassy places, but is toxic and therefore never eaten by grazing animals. Others are noticeable because of their colour and location, such as the blue gentian that grows across high northern cols, whose petals open in full sun but twist tightly together on dull days. Some flowers have distinctive colours and shapes, such as the pink flowers with serrated edges to their petals, known simply as 'pinks'. Bell-shaped flowers, generally in shades of blue, are known as bellflowers. Seasonal variations occur, and the pale-mauve autumn crocus seems to sense when haymaking is over, since it flourishes in fields and pastures in the weeks after mowing.

Alpine rarities abound, of course, but even to shortlist them would be a pointless exercise. On the highest parts of the GR5, *génepy* – better known by its German name, *edelweiss* – can be found, but it suffers at the hands of collectors, and is used to flavour a potent after-dinner *digestif*. Similarly, there are

plenty of humble plants that are common throughout Europe, such as rosebay willowherb, which nevertheless lend colour and interest to the scene. Many plants have short seasons, while others, such as alpenrose and *myrtille*, can always be spotted, since they are perennial and have woody stalks.

To assist identification when flowering plants are coming thick and fast, either carry a comprehensive guide, such as those in the popular Collins series, or look out for large posters showing a range of plants, often displayed along the GR5 by accommodation providers and tourist information centres.

ALPINE WILDLIFE

Anyone finding themselves in Chamonix or Les Houches, either before or during a trek along the GR5, could make a special visit to the Parc de Merlet (www.parcdemerlet.com) to see a range of Alpine animals. Walkers in the Alps may spot some species on a daily basis, while obtaining only the briefest glimpses of other species. Look out for the following:

Marmot These chubby rodents live in colonies in high, grassy areas. Note their habit of standing upright, suddenly dropping into burrows, play fighting and mutual grooming. When disturbed they give a piercing whistle. When you hear this, it may be because of your sudden appearance, but also scan the skies, since it may indicate the presence of a large bird of prey. Marmots hibernate throughout winter, with their body temperature dropping as low as 5°C, and their heart rate dropping to only three or four beats per minute.

Bouquetin These large, sure-footed, goat-like animals often travel in herds. The males have long, thick, curved horns. Young kids emit a heartbreaking bleat, while juveniles can often be seen head-butting each other. Although they are hunted in some areas, they cannot be hunted in the national parks and other reserves, where their numbers are increasing, and where they seem to be more approachable than elsewhere.

Above: *Male bouquetin are sturdy goat-like animals with long, thick, curved horns*

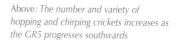

Above: *The number and variety of hopping and chirping crickets increases as the GR5 progresses southwards*

Chamois These dainty, sure-footed, goat-like animals may travel in herds, but are often spotted singly. Their horns are short, straight and slender, curving a little at their very tips. They were almost hunted to extinction, but enjoy protection in

Left: *Dainty chamois are most likely to be seen in the national parks of the Vanoise and Mercantour*

27

many places and their numbers are increasing. They are less likely to be spotted than *bouquetin*, but may tolerate a close approach.

Deer Seldom seen because of their preference for forest cover. Deer tend to graze early and late in the day around the margins of forests, and as most walkers aren't out at those times, they simply don't cross paths. Two types can be spotted – *cerf*, or red deer, and *daim*, or fallow deer.

Sanglier Bristly wild boar are hardly ever seen, as they lie low in forests during the day. However, the damage they do to Alpine pastures alongside forests is often clearly visible. They can literally plough up a pasture overnight while grubbing for food, then vanish at dawn.

Wolf After centuries of persecution, wolves are making a comeback. Since 1992, small numbers have been present in the Parc National du Mercantour, having crossed from Italy. They are unlikely to be spotted. Those wishing to see wolves can visit Alpha (www.alpha-loup.com) at Le Boréon on the GR52 (Day 27/28).

Squirrel Squirrels can be seen in woodlands, but only by walkers who are alert to the sudden sound and sight of them scuttling for cover among the trees. They are dark brown, almost black, with small ears and bushy tails.

Ermine Stoat-like ermine wear their white coats only in the winter, to camouflage themselves against snow. During the summer they wear brown coats, so are difficult to spot in woods or thick vegetation.

Golden Eagle Although seldom seen, gliding silently across ridges, then wheeling out of sight moments later, you can count on the piercing whistle of marmots to indicate when an eagle is present. Golden eagles are very large, so identification should not be a problem, though vultures are also present.

Ptarmigan Ptarmigan are related to grouse and have a preference for high mountains. Their mottled plumage camouflages them on gravelly ground, and they may not be seen even if approached quite closely, unless they move.

Tetras Lyre This black grouse-like bird may not be seen often, but is easily spotted when performing noisy, elaborate mating rituals. They spend most of their time on the ground, preferring forests with well-vegetated clearings.

Fish Many lakes and rivers attract fishermen – ask them what species are in the water. Generally it will be trout. Lac Léman is the largest Alpine lake, and has a long-established fishing fleet, with good stocks of fish that make their way onto restaurant menus. Trout, perch, char and carp are caught. There is a small fishing museum at the start of the GR5 at Thonon-les-Bains.

Insects Lovely butterflies, moths and honeybees flit around flowery *alpages*, while chirping crickets increase in size and number as progress southwards is made. These are the 'benign' insects, but there are also annoying ones. The livestock that grazes Alpine pastures is plagued by flies, and some animals are driven to distraction by the painful jabs of horseflies. Given half a chance, buzzing and blood-sucking insects will pester walkers too. They tend to be worst on hot, still, sunny days, and less troublesome on cold, windy or rainy days. If you are the sort of person who attracts their attention, invest in a strong repellant.

ALPINE FARMING

High Alpine farms are generally no more than *bergeries,* occupied only in the summer months by shepherds who tend flocks of sheep and herds of cattle on flower-rich pastures, or *alpages.* Generally, animals are grazed and fattened, then driven down into the valleys before the onset of winter. Some small farms mow and bale hay for the winter months, even if their fields are tiny. Valley farms do this some weeks in advance of high Alpine farms.

Grazing flowery *alpages* may fatten beef cattle, but dairy cattle are grazed on those slopes to increase the richness of their milk, especially if that milk is to be made into cheese. In some places, rather than driving herds to and from dairy farms, mobile milking machines are parked high on the mountainsides, and can be towed from one area to another as the cattle move from place to place. Sheep and goats are grazed, even to prodigious heights. The goats may be for milking, but the sheep are generally there to be fattened. Freerange grazing animals can travel far in search of good food, and they can disappear from sight on wooded or rocky ground, hence the bongling bells that allow farmers and shepherds to locate their herds by sound.

Flocks of sheep and goats are encountered in many areas and care should be taken not to disturb them

Electric fences are often used to restrict grazing to certain areas. Such fences are not mentioned in the route description, since they are highly mobile and are often shifted across *alpages* from week to week. Usually there is some method of passage, but if not, simply pull one of the slender fenceposts out of the ground and use it to hold the wire down while crossing, then replace the post.

PASTOUS

Huge flocks of sheep, or *troupeaux*, wander apparently untended over extensive *alpages* along the GR5, and signs often warn of their presence. On approaching a flock, walkers may find themselves face-to-face with large white dogs that bark menacingly. These are the famous *pastous*, related to sheepdogs from the Pyrenées. They work unsupervised by man, alone or in pairs, guarding flocks of sheep. *Pastous* are extremely loyal, living and travelling full-time with the sheep, and are fully accepted by the flock.

Pastous are not dangerous, provided that they are treated properly. On approaching a flock, assume that the dogs are somewhere among the sheep, though their white coats make them difficult to spot. Do nothing to alarm the sheep, as the dogs will interpret this as a threat and will react accordingly. The best thing is to make a wide detour around them, if the terrain allows.

If approached by a *pastous*, do not threaten the dog by shouting, or waving arms or sticks. Remain calm and quiet. The dog is simply trying to identify whether you are a 'threat', and while it

may bark, it will not attack without provocation. Once the dog is satisfied that you pose no threat, it will return to the flock. Do not attempt to pet a *pastous*, or feed it, or distract it in any way. It is a working dog whose first responsibility is to the flock it guards.

LANGUAGE

French is spoken from start to finish along the GR5. Local variations in dialect should present no problem, although some people in Nice speak a dialect much closer to Italian. In the Vallée Étroite, north of Briançon, Italian is far more likely to be heard than French, and in any case Italian walkers are likely to be met whenever the route runs close to Italy. In such instances, if your Italian is better than your French, don't hesitate to use it.

Even if you know only a few words of French, be sure to use them, and learn some more. The French appreciate being addressed in their native language, and will render assistance if your command of the language is poor. Don't expect everyone you meet to speak English, because some don't. However, when walkers from many nations land in the same place, English may well become the common tongue.

One of the most challenging times for those with limited fluency in French comes during a communal meal, when every topic under the sun is vigorously discussed, at speed, without a break. At such times, if you contribute nothing, you are quite likely to be ignored, but if you try your best, an effort will be made to include you. Remember that you are walking the GR5, and it is quite likely that others are following the route, so you do have something in common! (A basic set of phrases for use on the GR5 is given in Appendix 4.)

TRAVEL TO THE ALPS

Walkers who live in London or other major European cities will find Eurostar (www.eurostar.com) and TGV trains (www.tgv.com) allow speedy access to the Alps. National Express coaches in Britain link with Eurolines coaches (www.eurolines.com) serving the Alps. There is, for instance, a service billed as linking London Victoria with Chamonix, though in practice it involves a change of coaches. Geneva's tiny coach station has services to and from many parts of Europe, as does the gloomy coach station at Nice.

Those who prefer to fly will find that the most practical airports are Geneva, near the start of the GR5, and Nice at the end of the route. Those who are breaking the trek into stages might also find an approach via the airport at Grenoble useful at some points, with ready access to the valleys around Modane and Briançon. Lyon is convenient for Grenoble, Chambery, etc, in the centre of the route. Easyjet (www.easyjet.com) flies direct from British airports to Geneva, Grenoble and Nice, as does the national carrier, Air France (www.airfrance.com). All three airports have good links with onward buses and trains, allowing many parts of the GR5 to be reached, even if the final link in the chain is little more than an irregular minibus service.

TRAVEL AROUND THE ALPS

Walkers who trek along the GR5 generally leave one village, climb over a high col, then descend to another village. Few have any idea whether public transport links one village with another, and in some cases it will, but in others it won't. If a sudden storm or an unexpected dump of snow effectively closes a stretch of the route, and you want to keep moving, then you need to know what your options are. If you know that a bus is running to your next destination, then you can use it. If you don't have a clue, then you may be seriously inconvenienced. Useful bus or train services are noted throughout this guide, and timetables are often prominently displayed, or they can be obtained from tourist information centres.

SERVICES ON THE GR5

Useful services along the GR5 are noted throughout the route description. Most *refuges* double as restaurants during the day, and almost every restaurant doubles as a bar. Some places dispense only a very limited number of beverages, and these are known as *buvettes*.

Walkers looking for money are directed to banks and ATMs, or *distributeurs de billets*. Some places may have a range of shops, while other may have only a small *épicerie* or *alimentation*, selling basic groceries, or a more specialist *boulangerie* or *patisserie*, selling bread or cakes respectively. Water is of course available at all lodgings along the way, and at all towns and villages. Other isolated sources of drinking water are noted in the text.

If the term 'all services' is used, this means that a town or village has a variety of accommodation options, bank, ATM, post office, and a range of shops, bars and restaurants. Public transport is mentioned, and if there is a tourist information centre, the telephone number and website address is given.

ACCOMMODATION

Lodgings along the GR5 vary in every possible way. Some places boast a range of splendid hotels, while others may have only a single basic *refuge*. Anyone wanting to walk the whole of the GR5 using a specific type of accommodation will find it impossible. In some places there are no hotels, while in other places there are no *refuges*, so overnights will be varied. Accommodation tarifs are often visible while checking into lodgings, or are pinned behind the door of each room. Usually, you can pay for a bed or a room

without taking meals. If you want to pay for dinner, bed and breakfast all together, ask for *demi pension*. See Appendix 3 for an accommodation list.

Campsites

Carrying tents along the GR5 has never really appealed to the French, so campsites are rare, expensive, and pitched more at the car-camper. Where sites exist, they are mentioned. Some *refuges* and *gîtes* may allow an overnight pitch. 'Camping' may be expressly forbidden in many areas, but a bivouac may be tolerated – the difference being that a 'bivouac' is simply an overnight pitch using a small tent. National park regulations may allow a bivouac between 7pm and 7am, but it is wise to check first.

Refuges

These provide basic accommodation. In some areas *refuges* are a few minutes

Some refuges are almost like small hotels, such as the recently renovated Refuge de Péclet-Polset (Stage 3, Day 13, GR55)

apart, while in others they are days apart. The Club Alpin Française runs many *refuges*, while others are privately owned and operated by families or municipal authorities. Sleeping is in mixed dormitories and everyone is usually in bed by 10pm, with a view to rising early. Bunks have mattresses, with duvets or blankets, but you need your own sheets or a sleeping bag or silk liner. Some *refuges* are like small hotels, with hot showers and every comfort, while others are rough-and-ready, without showers or hot water. All *refuges* provide evening meals and breakfast, and usually operate as restaurants during the day. A good site for checking current details of *refuges* is www.refuges.info.

Gîtes d'étape

Gîtes d'étape fulfil a similar role to youth hostels in Britain. They generally offer more facilities than *refuges*, with smaller dormitories. Bunks or beds have mattresses, with duvets or blankets. Some provide sheets, while others require you to provide your own. Some *gîtes* are almost as basic as a good *refuge*, while others are like small hotels. Specific details of *gîtes* along the GR5 can be checked at www.gites-refuges.com.

Chambres d'hôte

These are often high-priced establishments providing individual rooms with all facilities. They are often translated as 'bed and breakfast', but usually offer evening meals too. Some *chambres d'hôte* are quite luxurious, while others are as basic as a good *gîte d'étape*.

Hotels

Hotels may be star-rated or unclassified and standards vary enormously. More stars mean more services and facilities, and a higher price. Most offer a full meals service, but a few offer a basic breakfast and no evening meal, so be sure to check. Whenever there is a choice of hotels in a town or village, some operate under the Logis de France brand, and can be checked at www.logis-de-france.fr.

Advance Booking

Some people like to book all their accommodation in advance, and walk in the knowledge that there is a bed and a meal waiting for them at the end of each day. However, this may be inadvisable on the GR5, where a severe storm or heavy fall of snow could disrupt a carefully planned schedule. The loss of one day's walking could result in a nightmare round of phone calls, trying to cancel bookings and make new ones.

Most walkers will have no problem booking a day or two in advance as they walk, and in the high holiday season weekend, booking a couple days ahead is advised. If language is a problem, *refuge* staff will book ahead on your behalf. Ask staff at *gîtes* or hotels if they will do the same (offering one or two euros for their trouble if they pull a face). In some towns and villages, staff at the tourist information centre (*office de tourisme, maison de tourisme* or *syndicate d'initiative*) will assist. A basic accommodation list is given in Appendix 3.

FOOD AND DRINK

Walkers on the GR5 find plenty of food and drink at regular intervals, though there are odd stages where nothing is available and supplies need to be carried. Shops and restaurants are noted throughout this guide. There may be supermarkets in some places, but only a small *épicerie* in another place, stocking high-priced local specialities.

Refuges operate as restaurants during the day, then provide a set evening meal, or *menu*, for residents. In *refuges* and *gîtes*, it is usual for residents to dine communally, while hotels serve food at individual tables. Evening meals are

substantial and rich in their variety, and provide plenty of energy after the day's exertions. Those with special dietary requirements *must* give plenty of notice! Breakfast, on the other hand, is generally frugal, and may consist of nothing more than bread and jam with coffee or tea. When asked what time you want breakfast, bear in mind that 7am is by no means considered early! You may have to declare, the evening beforehand, what type of hot drink you require for breakfast. A glossary of common terms for food and drink in French can be found in Appendix 4.

Water sources are usually safe to drink, and those that aren't are usually labelled as 'eau non potable'

EAU NON POTABLE

TELEPHONES

Mobile phones do not always get a signal in the Alps. Sometimes, on cresting a col, half the mobiles carried by walkers spring to life, resulting in a string of messages to be answered. Those whose mobiles don't work generally ask the others which provider they are using. The strongest signal may not come from a French mast, but a Swiss or Italian one. Talk to your provider before taking a mobile phone on this trek. Telephone kiosks, or *cabines téléphonique*, are found in all towns and almost every village. They do not take coins, but are operated using a *France Telecom* card. Some hotels provide telephones in rooms, but check the tariff, as some are exorbitant.

PATH CONDITIONS

Some of the mountain paths along the GR5 are steep and rocky, while others were laid centuries ago for mule traffic,

Keep an eye on weather forecasts, or *méteos*, which are posted at frequent intervals along the route

zigzagging uphill rather than climbing straight up. In some places, signs request walkers not to short-cut zig-zags, and as short-cutting makes things more difficult, it should be avoided anyway.

Broad tracks have been made for occasional vehicle use in recent years, often in forests, or to serve high farms and *refuges*. Tracks such as these allow walkers to stride out briskly, at least as far as the next steep slope and zigzag path. The GR5 seldom uses roads, but where it does, walk on the pavement if one is available, or on the left, to face oncoming traffic, unless the nature of the road dictates otherwise. The most awkward roads are those leading into and out of towns, where there are numerous distractions and the red/white route markers are easily missed. To assist walkers, landmarks and street names are noted in this guide.

ALPINE WEATHER

The Alps, being high mountains, are quite capable of generating their own weather, which can be difficult to predict. However, it is well worth getting into a routine of checking weather forecasts, not only for the day, but for the days ahead too. If you have no access to radio or TV forecasts, simply look out for the forecasts, or *météos*, posted at tourist information centres and *refuges*. Most *refuges* will be aware of the *météo*, and most *gîtes* will be happy to find one if they aren't already aware of it. In many places, the forecast is available only in French, but sometimes an English summary is also posted.

Even when you have the most up-to-date forecast, you should still keep a 'weather eye' open, watching especially for the build-up of heavy cloud that often precedes a storm. As far as possible, ensure that you are away from exposed cols and ridges, or better still, safely inside, before a storm breaks. Deep snow can in theory fall on any day in the summer, though it will be rare and should clear quickly.

A typical Alpine summer day will start cool, or even cold, clear and frosty at altitude, and will rapidly warm up as the sun rises. During the afternoon clouds will form, and these may completely obscure the sun, possibly leading to rain or a storm. Often the cloud simply disperses during the night and the next day starts clear again. Most walkers in the Alps start early and finish early, so they avoid being caught in rain later in the day. Sometimes fine weather may last for weeks, while at other times it can rain for weeks, with low cloud wiping out any chance of decent views. Keep a lookout for those forecasts, dress for the prevailing conditions, and be prepared to alter your plans in really nasty weather.

WHEN TO WALK THE GR5

The GR5 is primarily a summer trek. Starting too early or late in the season means that you could have problems with deep snow. Most French people take their holidays between mid-July and mid-August, from Bastille Day to Assumption Day, and this particular time sees the best weather conditions on the GR5, even though there can be stiff competition for beds along the way. Starting in the middle of June will almost certainly mean crossing deep snow on some high cols. Running late into September could mean running into early winter weather. Some *refuges* are open from mid-June to mid-September,

but some are only open in July and August. The more services that close, the more that prospective trekkers must fend for themselves.

KIT CHECK

Some people trek the GR5 carrying full backpacking gear, aiming to camp almost every night along the way. Given the nature of the route, carrying a heavy pack is hard work, but tents and sleeping bags can be lightweight and strong, so pack weight need not be excessive, and certainly no more than 10kg (22lb), with tent, before adding food and water. It will seldom be necessary to pack more than a day's worth of food, and water is available at regular intervals. Only a few people camp along the GR5, and those who do should already be well aware of the kit they need for a successful trek.

Most walkers use *refuges*, *gîtes* and occasional hotels, so aren't burdened with heavy packs. Apart from sheets or sleeping-bag liners (which are more lightweight) or a light sleeping bag, toiletries and a complete change of clothes, nothing else is really essential on top of what you would normally carry on a day's hill walk. When the sun shines strongly at altitude, plenty of sunscreen, a sunhat and sunglasses prove useful. Some people make the mistake of packing far too many clothes, when regular rinsing keeps fewer items fresh. Others take things that may not even be used, thus carrying dead weight along the route.

Refuges and *gîtes* require you to wear 'house shoes' rather than your walking shoes or boots, but you don't need to pack a pair, since these are provided on arrival (although you may prefer to take trainers or sandals). For the actual walking, use whatever shoes or boots you already feel comfortable with, but expect a trek along the whole of the GR5 to cause considerable wear!

To summarise, your normal hill-walking kit should be fine for a trek along the GR5, with the addition of a change of clothes, and basic bedding if staying indoors. Those who intend camping will manage fine with lightweight kit. The GR5 is just a long walk, and so doesn't require any specialist equipment.

MAPS

There are a few walkers, mainly French, who are happy to walk the whole of the GR5 without maps, relying entirely on the red/white route markers and signposts. Many French walkers rely on maps in the FFRP Topoguide series (www.ffrandonnee.fr) that are printed at a scale of 1:50,000, but this means carrying four guidebooks to cover the whole route.

The best maps are the IGN 1:25,000 Serie Bleu, and 21 of these cover the route, numbers 3548 ET, 3528 ET, 3530 ET, 3531 ET, 3531 OT, 3532 OT, 3633 ET, 3534 OT, 3532 ET, 3634 OT, 3535 OT, 3536 OT, 3537 ET, 3637 OT, 3538 ET, 3639 OT, 3640 OT, 3641 ET, 3741 ET, 3742 OT, 3741 OT. These are available along the route, where they can be purchased one at a time, used as required, then posted home at intervals. Alternatively, they can be ordered in advance, either direct from the IGN in France (www.ign.fr) or from British suppliers such as: Stanfords (12–14 Long Acre, London WC2E 9BR, tel 0207 836 1321, www.stanfords.co.uk), The Map Shop (15 High Street, Upton-upon-Severn WR8 0HJ, tel 01684 593146, www.themapshop.co.uk) or Cordee (3a De Montford Street, Leicester LE1 7HD, tel 0116 254 3579, www.cordee.co.uk).

Those who prefer to customise maps on their computers can get IGN 1:25,000 maps of the French Alps on DVD from Memory Map, www.memory-map.co.uk. Google Earth offers detailed aerial photography along the route, www.earth.google.com.

The 1:50,000 Rando Éditions maps of the Tour du Mont Blanc and Vanoise are useful on the earlier stages of the route. Maps at a scale of 1:60,000 are published by Libris (www.libris.fr) but these omit the southern stages around Nice and Menton. Beyond these alternatives, the IGN publish a 1:100,000 series that shows the GR5 on four sheets, and with care these could be used for navigation, but they are more useful to gain an overview of the route.

Look out for the moulded plastic relief maps of various parts of the Alps, produced by the IGN (at the risk of worrying yourself sick!). These are found on walls at *refuges*, *gîtes*, hotels, bars and tourist information centres. While tracing the course of the GR5 on these relief maps, bear in mind that the vertical gradient is hugely exaggerated, and the ascents and descents are nowhere near as steep as they appear!

There are three types of diagrammatic maps in this guidebook, as follows.
• A general map sets the GR5 in its Alpine context, showing the whole route at a glance (page 9).

Many walkers, particularly French, manage fine along the GR5 without maps, relying on signs and markers (Col du Vallonet, Day 22)

- Each of the seven main stages along the route has its own introductory map, so that towns and potential transport links off-route can be seen.
- The daily route maps are at a scale of 1:100,000 and are in the form of a continuous strip running from page to page, covering the entire GR5 and all the variant and alternative routes. While walking north to south, you read these maps from the top of the page to the bottom. Certain placenames in the daily route descriptions have been highlighted in bold and are usually to be found on the maps. An indication of altitude is provided by colour-tinted contours (see map key, page 8). The darker the tint, the greater the altitude, and spot heights are also given. Places offering accommodation along the route are highlighted in yellow, so that it is easy to see at a glance what is available throughout each day.

Route profiles are provided at the rate of one per day, labelled with selected features, so that all the ascents and descents can also be seen at a glance.

CURRENCY AND COSTS

The euro is the currency of the GR5. Large denomination euro notes are difficult to use, so avoid the €500 and €200 notes altogether, and avoid the €100 notes if you can. The rest are fine – €50, €20, €10 and €5. Coins come in €2 and €1. Small denomination coins, while officially termed *cents* around Europe, are referred to as *centimes* in France. They come in values of 50c, 20c, 10c, 5c, 2c and 1c. Prices are written, for example, as 5€20, and spoken as *cinq euro vingt* or *cinq euro vingt centimes*. Even if access is via Geneva in Switzerland, you will find that euros are accepted instead of Swiss francs, generally at a rate of 2 euros to 3 Swiss francs, but it helps enormously if you have the correct change. (Banks and ATMs, or *distributeurs de billets*, are noted along the route.)

Budgeting for a long trek and managing money supplies on the hoof involves a lot of unknown quantities, so you will have to resort to guesswork. The biggest expenses will be accommodation, food and drink, but sometimes these will be available as a 'package' involving a single payment. Expect *demi pension* (dinner, bed and breakfast) in a *refuge* to cost about €30–€35 per person per night. The same deal in a *gîte d'étape* might cost about €35–€45. A single person staying in a hotel might find themselves paying from €45–€100, depending on the quality of the establishment, and this will doubtless include a single supplement for the room. Two or more people sharing a room can expect to pay a little less. At all lodgings the *demi pension* rate will usually state, or at least imply, *boissons non compris*, or drinks not included. If you enjoy a few beers after a day's walk, or a bottle of wine with your meal, then you need to budget separately for it. A simple cup of coffee after a meal might appear as another €2 or €3 on the bill.

During the day, many walkers will take a lunch break at a convenient *refuge* or restaurant if one appears at the right time. Expect small snacks to be quite

The former fortified village of Utelle on a hilltop above the Vésubie valley (Stage 6, Day 27)

pricey, with coffee and a cake maybe costing €5. A full meal might easily set you back €20. Remember that food and drink in the mountains has either been driven up a rugged track, carried in by people or mules, or flown in by helicopter. The convenience of finding food high in the mountains must be balanced against the cost you pay for its transportation. You can of course carry your own food, but stores offering a wide range of goods are sometimes few and far between, and some small shops only offer rather expensive *artisanal* local produce. The longer the gaps between shops, the more you have to carry, otherwise you simply pay the price for someone else carrying it up there.

Surprisingly, some remote *refuges* are equipped to handle payment made with credit cards, using electronic readers, requiring you to enter your PIN. The system, where available, may be entirely operated by radio. However, most remote places will want payment by cash. You will see many French walkers paying by cheque, but unless you have an account with a well-known French bank, this option simply isn't available to you. So cash will do for most things, and a credit/debit card will be accepted on some occasions.

Getting to and from the terminal points of the GR5 from the nearest airports – Geneva and Nice – involves using cheap and regular buses or trains. Bus travel is very cheap, and trains cost only a little more. Depending on your start and finish points, travel between the terminal points and the nearest airports costs something in the region of €5–€15. Avoid using taxis, since they are very expensive by comparison and not at all necessary. Similarly, if bus or train transport is needed to or from other parts of the GR5, expect a bus to be cheaper than a train, expect information to be readily available, expect services to be reliable, and avoid taxis unless you have money to burn.

When cash reserves are running low, you need to be thinking ahead, and you need to know where to find an ATM (*distributeur de billets*) to avoid having to leave the route for a nearby town. Locations of banks and ATMs are mentioned throughout this guidebook. Occasionally an ATM might be inside a building such as a *mairie* or post office, rather than out on a street and available at all hours.

So, how much will it cost per day? If alternating between *refuges* and *gîtes*, with occasional hotels, taking *demi pension*, with perhaps a couple of extra drinks, then a few snack items in the pack from time to time, around €75 per person per day should be ample. If you fancy using a few more hotels, you might expect the daily average to creep up to €100. A hardy backpacker, using a few campsites and several wild pitches, buying food from shops along the way, might get by on as little as €15 per day. The author has seen people settling hotel bills well in excess of €100, as well as others scrimping and saving every cent and spending less than €10 per day.

EMERGENCIES

Anyone walking for a month or so through the Alps can expect to suffer a cut, graze or bruise at some point, and will almost certainly get a jab from a horsefly! A simple first-aid kit will take care of most little problems. Other problems, such as an upset stomach, can often be resolved by visiting a pharmacy, where staff can advise on basic treatment. Beyond that, if medical intervention is required, the European Health Insurance Card, available free to EU residents, could be useful for getting

The Chalets de Bise are tin-roofed buildings, with the Pas de la Bosse rising beyond, to the left (Day 1/Day 2)

KEY POINTS

Advice in a Nutshell

- Don't walk too early or late in the year.
- Make sure you are fit and well prepared.
- Pack light and carry only what you need.
- Don't forget your sheets, sleeping bag or liner.
- Learn some basic French and use it.
- Look out for weather forecasts or météos.
- Take it slow and steady (as the French do).
- Be aware of your options every day.
- Protect against the strong Alpine sun.
- Don't book accommodation too far ahead.

Points to Bear in Mind

- The GR5 is a walk, not a mountaineering expedition.
- Waymarks are usually clear red/white stripes.
- *Refuges* usually operate as restaurants in the day.
- Meals in *refuges* and *gîtes* are usually communal.
- Sleeping arrangements in refuges and *gîtes* are mixed.
- Most people will be asleep in bed by 10pm.
- Mobile phones only rarely get a signal in the Alps.
- *Refuge* staff will help you book a bed ahead.
- 'VTT' (*vélo tout terrain*) means cyclists may be using the path.
- It's fun – enjoy it!

a partial reimbursement of costs. Obtain one from the Post Office before you go. A good insurance policy might also prove useful in this respect.

To summon help, mountain rescue services cover many areas, but need to be contacted using different telephone numbers.

- For police (*gendarmerie*) call 17, and they can contact the mountain rescue if required.
- For ambulance (*samu*) call 15.
- For the fire service (*pompiers*) call 18.

Alternatively any of the emergency services can be summoned using the European emergency number 112. Anyone using a radio can call for assistance on the Emergency Canal E, on 161.300 MHz.

Remember that mountain rescue in France is usually a service that has to be paid for, and if their assistance is needed, they will present you with a bill. A good insurance policy may cover this cost, but check. Better still, walk safely!

STAGE 1
Lac Léman to Les Houches

A distant view of Mont Blanc, as seen from a view indicator on the grassy crest of Tête des Fieux (Day 2)

General Overview Map	IGN 1:100,000 Carte de Promenade 45 Annecy Lausanne.
Alternative Maps	Libris 1:60,000 No 01 Léman (covers route from Lac Léman to the Brévent) and Libris 1:60,000 No 02 Mont Blanc (covers route from Samoëns to Roselend).
	Rando Éditions 1:50,000 A1 Pays du Mont Blanc (covers route from Samoëns to Roselend).

This first, northern stage of the GR5 is quite popular, fitting comfortably into a week. Many walkers use it as a way of reaching Chamonix, where they spend a few more days exploring. Most then go on to plan further trips, even to the extent of completing the whole of the GR5 over a period of years in stages of a few days apiece.

First and foremost, be realistic with your plans. There are two alternative starting points from which to reach La Chapelle d'Abondance, and if you are full of energy, fit and

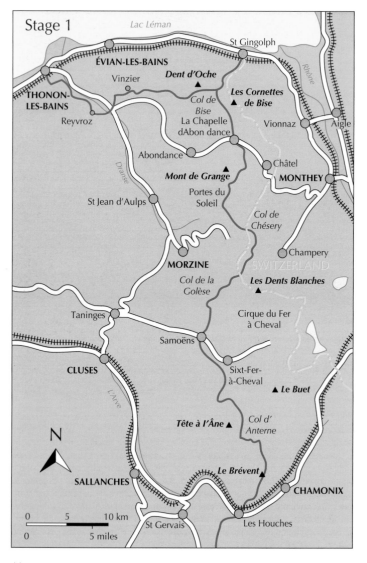

Stage 1

Lac Léman

St Gingolph

ÉVIAN-LES-BAINS

Vinzier

Dent d'Oche ▲

Les Cornettes de Bise ▲

THONON-LES-BAINS

Rhône

Reyvroz

Col de Bise

La Chapelle dAbon dance

Vionnaz

Aigle

Abondance

Mont de Grange ▲

Châtel

MONTHEY

Dranse

St Jean d'Aulps

Portes du Soleil

Col de Chésery

Champery

MORZINE

Col de la Golèse

Les Dents Blanches ▲

SWITZERLAND

Taninges

Cirque du Fer à Cheval

CLUSES

Samoëns

L'Arve

Sixt-Fer-à-Cheval

▲ *Le Buet*

Tête à l'Âne ▲

Col d' Anterne

N

Le Brévent ▲

SALLANCHES

CHAMONIX

0   5   10 km

0   5 miles

St Gervais

Les Houches

44

The rugged limestone cliffs of the Cornettes de Bise loom over the Pas de la Bosse (Day 1/Day 2)

able for the mountains, then by all means start from St Gingolph and walk to La Chapelle d'Abondance on your first day. If you are not so fit, or less confident in your abilities, then consider the gentler approach from Thonon-les-Bains over a period of two days.

Be warned that the Brévent, at the end of this stage, is a huge mountain that can be an obstacle in bad weather. It holds snow well into the summer and is very exposed in storms. In clear weather, there is no finer stance for admiring Mont Blanc. Keep up to date with weather forecasts and ensure as far as possible that your summit bid coincides with optimum conditions to cross in safety and enjoy remarkable views.

The natural arrival and departure airport for this stage is Geneva, which has regular transport links to and from the terminal points of Thonon-les-Bains, St Gingolph and Chamonix, as well as links with other places along the way.

Direct Route to La Chapelle d'Abondance

Travel to St Gingolph

Ferry This is the classic, scenic, but slowest and most expensive approach. Ferries operate from Swiss ports on Lac Léman and it is possible to sail from Geneva to St Gingolph, but allow all day for the journey. Check timetables with the Compagnie Générale de Navigation sur le Lac Léman (CGN), tel 0848 811 848, www.cgn.ch.

Train This is possible only from Switzerland, since the line from France is closed between Évian-les-Bains and St Gingolph, though there is a plan to restore it. Rail approaches are reasonably priced and run via St Maurice and Monthey. Timetables can be checked, tel 027 723 33 30, www.cff.ch.

Bus Bus travel is very cheap. On the Swiss side, CarPostal buses operate in conjunction with trains from Monthey. Details can be checked, tel 027 327 34 34, www.carpostal.ch. On the French side, buses operate from Geneva to Thonon-les-Bains or Évian-les-Bains, where a change of buses links with St Gingolph, except Sundays. Buses are operated by SAT, tel 04 50 26 41 32, www.sat-montblanc.com, or Frossard, tel 04 50 71 85 55, www.frossard.eu.

DAY 1
St Gingolph to La Chapelle d'Abondance

Distance	18 kilometres (11 miles)
Total Ascent	1870 metres (6135 feet)
Total Descent	1225 metres (4020 feet)
Time	7 hours 30 minutes
Map	3528 ET
Food and Drink	Plenty at St Gingolph. Restaurants at Chalets de Bise. Plenty at La Chapelle d'Abondance.
Accommodation	Hotels at St Gingolph. *Chambres d'hôte* at Novel (hotel recently closed). *Refuge* at Chalets de Bise. Hotels and *gîte* at La Chapelle d'Abondance.

The finest way to St Gingolph is to spend most of the day approaching it from Geneva by ferry

47

Only those who arrive fit and seasoned for a mountain walk are likely to cover the distance comfortably from St Gingolph to La Chapelle d'Abondance in a day – there are two steep-sided cols to be crossed. Those who arrive late in the morning could consider walking as far as Novel, and spending the night there. Another approach is to split this long and arduous day at the Chalets de Bise. If in doubt, follow the gentler two-day walk from Thonon-les-Bains to La Chapelle d'Abondance (see two-day alternative, pages 52–64).

St Gingolph

Founded in the year 755 by Gingulf, an officer in the service of Pépin le Bref. From 1204 the area was a property of the Abbaye d'Abondance. The village was divided in 1569 by a treaty between Savoie and Valais. On the Swiss side, the château dates from 1588 and contains a museum, while the church was built in 1677. The French half was burnt in 1944 as a reprisal against *résistance* activities, and most inhabitants lived as refugees in Switzerland. There is a full range of services in St Gingolph and these are mostly concentrated on the French side. The TIC is on the Swiss side, but advises on facilities for the whole village, tel 024 481 84 31, www.st-gingolph.ch.

There are three ways to reach the start of the GR5. If arriving by ferry, at the lake level of 375m (1230ft), walk up the Rue

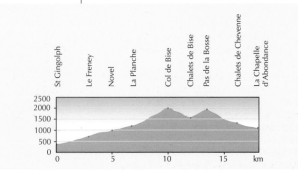

du Lac and cross the frontier bridge, where passports may need to be shown. If arriving by train or bus from Switzerland, walk down from the station and cross the frontier bridge. Walk along the main road and turn left up the Route de Novel, noting the first red/white GR5 marker by a railway bridge. If arriving by bus from France, the terminus is on the Route de Novel. Walk uphill and turn right up the Rue des Gaulles, then walk straight ahead up the Chemin du Cret. Keep left of a water trough and climb to the end of the road.

20min **Cimes Story 550m (1805ft)** *Arboreal adventure site*

Follow a winding track up through the valley of **La Morge Torrente**, enjoying the cascades. The woods are predominantly beech, lush with ferns and mosses. **Le Freney** is signposted to the left, across the river in Switzerland, while the GR5 is signposted to the right. Cross a road at a higher level and continue along a track past a house. A tiny cemetery is reached (water) and a narrow, winding road climbs further uphill to a crumbling village.

1hr 10min **Novel 950m (3115ft)** *Chambres d'hôte*

Back streets and steps lead up to a church. Turn left along a road, but watch for GR5 markers, which later show a short-cut up a track on the right. Pass a road bend and keep right again up a track, passing a wayside **chapel**. Walk further up the road from a bend to find another track climbing to the right. At the next road bend, walk up a narrow road and pass between chalets to continue up a track. At a path junction, turn left for the GR5, passing a sign indicating 'Nice 21 jours – Novel 21 minutes'. Reach a road and turn left to walk downhill a little. A path climbs past trees to reach a car park.

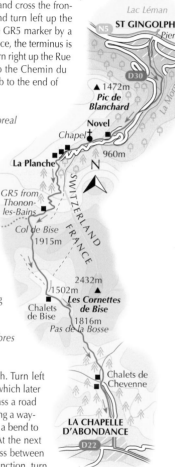

49

45min La Planche 1205m (3953ft) *Water*

Leave the car park and turn left down an undulating forest track. Keep to the right of a meadow, climbing gently until a track allows a left turn back into forest. Emerge close to a stream, **La Morge Torrente**, which marks the Franco–Swiss frontier. Turn right to climb higher through the forest, reaching a steep, open slope with cliffs above. The GR5 exploits a rugged breach in the cliffs. Turn right beyond it to follow a level path, then climb a little to reach a few chalets.

1hr 30min Chalets de Neuteu 1700m (5575ft) *Shelter and water*

Climb a steep path up flowery slopes as marked, reaching a signposted junction at 1834m (6017ft). (**Note** This is the junction with the GR5 from Thonon-les-Bains.) Turn left and climb further to reach a col.

30min Col de Bise 1915m (6283ft) *View of Chalets de Bise Pas de la Bosse, Mont de Grange and higher mountains beyond*

Steep, bouldery, forested slopes are climbed on the way from La Planche to the Chalets de Neuteu

Take care on the initial steep descent, as the path is worn and gritty. It levels out and becomes delightful, crossing a stream and leading directly to some large, tin-roofed buildings beside the **Ruisseau de Bise**. ▸

Nearby Lac de Bise is hardly noticed, being covered in vegetation.

45min Chalets de Bise 1506m (4941ft) *Refuge and two restaurants*

Leave the chalets as signposted and follow a narrow path that winds uphill. ▸

Look for marmots and bouquetin on the steep ascent, while admiring the soaring cliffs of the Cornettes de Bise above.

1hr Pas de la Bosse 1816m (5958ft) *Views of the Vallée d'Abondance, Châtel, Mont de Grange, Dents du Midi and Dents Blanche*

Three paths leave the col, so take the middle one, which descends past the ruined Chalets Cote. Further downhill, the restored **Chalets de la Cheneau** are passed at 1590m (5216ft). Follow the path down a steep, cow-grazed pasture, entering a forest to zigzag down to a junction of tracks.

1hr Chalets de Chevenne 1290m (4232ft) *Water*

Walk down a forest track to reach a road. A left turn along the road leads straight to La Chapelle d'Abondance. The GR5, however, turns right along the road, then almost immediately left to cross a footbridge. Turn left to follow a riverside path, which is part nature trail and part health trail (or *parcours santé*). The path broadens to a track and rejoins the road. All that remains is to walk straight down to a village.

30min La Chapelle d'Abondance 1021m (3350ft) *All services – see end of Day 2, page 64*

The GR5 route description continues at Day 3, page 64.

Alternative Route to La Chapelle d'Abondance

Travel to Thonon-les-Bains

Ferry This is the classic, scenic, but slowest and most expensive approach. Ferries operate from Swiss ports on Lac Léman and in summer it is possible to sail from Geneva to Thonon-les-Bains in an hour by the fastest ferry. Check timetables with the Compagnie Générale de Navigation sur le Lac Léman (CGN), tel 0848 811 848, www.cgn.ch.

Train Rail approaches are reasonably priced, either from the French rail network, or the Gare Eaux-Vives in Geneva in Switzerland – the latter may involve a change at Annemasse. Timetables can be checked – tel 08 91 67 68 00, www.ter-sncf.com.

Bus Bus travel is very cheap. Two companies operate, except Sundays, between Annecy and/or Geneva to Thonon-les-Bains. Check timetables with SAT, tel 04 50 26 41 32, www.sat-montblanc.com, or Frossard, tel 04 50 71 85 55, www.frossard.eu.

DAY 1
Thonon-les-Bains to Chevenoz

Distance	25 kilometres (15½ miles)
Total Ascent	1090 metres (3575 feet)
Total Descent	545 metres (1790 feet)
Time	7 hours
Maps	3428 ET and 3528 ET
Food and Drink	Plenty at Thonon-les-Bains. Shop and hotel/restaurant at Armoy. Cafés at Reyvroz. Bar, supermarket and café off-route at Vinzier. Shop and bar off-route at Chevenoz.
Accommodation	Plenty at Thonon-les-Bains. Hotels off-route at L'Ermitage and Armoy. *Gîte* at Chevenoz.

*Arrival at the harbour at Thonon-les-Bains, with the
Château de Montjoux reflected in Lac Léman*

The GR5 from Thonon-les-Bains takes two longer, but easier, days to reach La Chapelle d'Abondance, compared with the direct one-day approach from St Gingolph. The first day's walk is fairly easy, passing through gentle countryside and woods, with occasional views of the towering peak of Dent d'Oche and maybe distant Mont Blanc. There are steep slopes on either side of the Dranse valley. Little villages offer a small range of services.

Thonon-les-Bains

This Stone Age and Bronze Age lakeside port had its thermal springs developed by the Romans. A fishing museum stands by the Port des Pêcheurs. The 14th-century church dedicated to St Hippolyte stands on the site of an older Roman church. There are several prominent châteaux, including: Montjoux, by the port, with Ripaille along the shore, Sonnaz above the port, and Bellegard in town. Fine belvederes offer good lake views, and a short funicular railway, built in 1888, links the port with the town centre. A full range of services is available. TIC tel 04 40 71 55 55, www.thononlesbains.com.

There are three ways to reach the start of the GR5. If arriving by ferry, passports may need to be shown at the Port des Pêcheurs. The lake level is 375m (1230ft) and there are pedestrian ways (*rues piétonnes*) signposted up from the port

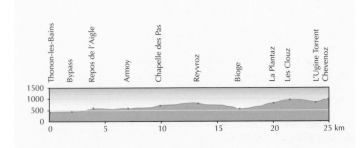

to the town centre. Head straight through the centre to reach the railway station. If arriving by bus, the railway station is a very short walk from the bus station. If arriving by train, the GR5 officially starts outside the railway station at 437m (1434ft). Leave the station and look for the first red/white GR5 markers on Rue Jean Blanchard. Cross a railway footbridge and use an underpass beneath a busy road. Pass the Place de Crête (hotels and café/*boulangerie*) to follow the Chemin des Marmottés. Turn left at a crossroads, up the Chemin de la Vionnaz, to reach the edge of town.

30min **Bridge over bypass 486m (1594ft)**

Cross the bypass and walk straight ahead to follow a track into the **Forêt de Thonon**. This is predominantly oak, with some chestnut and beech. There are many tracks and paths, so watch for red/white GR5 markers. A gentle ascent is followed by a pronounced left turn, then a gentle descent. Later, turn right at a wire-fenced enclosure to walk up to a road. Cross the road and climb to a car park at **L'Ermitage**. (Hotel/restaurant off-route.) Walk through the car park and turn left as signposted for a fitness trail (or *parcours sportif*). The GR5, however, climbs steeply uphill behind a hut to reach a viewpoint.

30min **Repos de l'Aigle 600m (1970ft)** *Views back to Thonon-les-Bains and across Lac Léman to the Jura and Switzerland*

Turn left along a track, then right along the Chemin des Lapins. This path becomes the wider Chemin de Lonnaz, running gently down to a junction at Carrefour du Comte Rouge. Keep straight ahead to curve up round a wooded hollow. Turn right to walk gently down a track to a road near **Le Cornabut**. Cross the road and turn left down a path, then keep right to follow a track to some houses. Turn right, then quickly left to follow the Chemin des Chartreux, which later climbs to a church.

1hr **Armoy 645m (2116ft)** *Hotel, shop, boulangerie/ patisserie, buses to Thonon-les-Bains*

Walk down a track below the church, then turn right up a path. Roughly contour along the top edge of a beech wood, keeping a watch for red/white markers. Turn left after passing a metal barn. There is later an awkward ravine to negotiate, then cross a track to follow a path up to a road. Turn right along the road, but quickly step up to another road and turn left. This is the Route des Champs de Beule, leading to a hamlet.

45min **Les Jossières 722m (2369ft)**

Turn left along the Route de la Capité, then walk up a track called Chemin des Pas, which passes a couple of houses and runs through forest. Pass a wayside shrine, the **Chapelle des Pas**, and follow the track as marked. It undulates, but generally climbs, keeping right to reach 880m (2885ft) before descending. Enjoy a fine view across the Dranse valley to the peak of Dent d'Oche, then head down to a church.

1hr **Reyvroz 776m (2546ft)**

Walk down a road from the church, keeping right as marked down another road looping below a graveyard to reach a crossroads (cafés). Walk down a road sign-posted for Bioge,

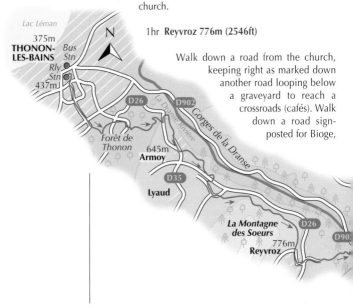

which later becomes a track passing fields. Parts have land-slipped and need care. The track winds down through mixed woods, deep into the valley of the Dranse, landing on a road. Turn right to cross a bridge, then follow a bit of old road to a roundabout on a main road. Turn right as sign-posted for Morzine, passing an adventure centre.

A track leaves a forest and crosses an open slope before descending into the village of Reyvroz

45min **Bioge 550m (1805ft)**
Bar/restaurant, buses to Thonon-les-Bains, Vinzier, Chevenoz and La Chapelle d'Abondance

Follow the main road, but watch for a path down to the left. Cross a bridge dated 1736 over the milky **Dranse Torrente**. Cross a road and walk a short way up a tarmac drive. Turn right up a steep, rough and winding track through mixed woodland. The gradient eases and a right turn is signposted at **Les Chênes**. The track leaves the woods for fields and becomes a tarmac road. Branch right to follow another short track up to a road junction.

45min La Plantaz 774m (2539ft)

Walk straight uphill by road and follow a track straight ahead as marked up a wooded slope. Keep an eye on markers to follow tracks and roads through fields, with a fleeting view of Mont Blanc, to reach a village.

30min Les Clouz 898m (2946ft)

Turn right and walk gently downhill by road, turning left and immediately right as marked, later reaching a bus shelter on the outskirts of another village.

15min Vinzier 870m (2855ft) *15–30min off-route for PO, bar, supermarket with café and ATM, campsite, buses to Thonon-les-Bains, Bioge, Chevenoz and La Chapelle d'Abondance*

Walk down the road from the bus shelter and branch right down a grassy track to a road junction at **Mérou**. Go down the Route de la Dranse, but when the tarmac road bends sharp right, continue straight along a track that winds down through woods to a metal footbridge over **L'Ugine Torrente** at 780m (2560ft). Climb up a steep and rugged path through mixed woods, crossing a road to follow a short, steep path up to another road. Turn right, then left as marked at **Le Cret**, climbing uphill until a junction is reached.

1hr Le Cret 917m (3009ft) *15–30min off-route for gîte d'étape, Chevenoz, bar, shop, buses to Vinzier, Bioge, Thonon-les-Bains and La Chapelle d'Abondance*

DAY 2
Chevenoz to La Chapelle d'Abondance

Distance	22 kilometres (13½ miles)
Total Ascent	1730 metres (5675 feet)
Total Descent	1625 metres (5330 feet)
Time	9 hours
Map	3528 ET
Food and Drink	Restaurants at the Chalets de Bise. Plenty at La Chapelle d'Abondance.
Accommodation	Refuge de la Dent d'Oche lies off-route. *Refuge* at Chalets de Bise. Hotels and *gîtes* at La Chapelle d'Abondance.

After an easy first day, the GR5 climbs high across forested slopes and wanders along grassy, flowery crests. The trail skips from one rugged col to another, passing close to the towering peak of Dent d'Oche. Just before the Col de Bise, it joins the route that climbs more steeply from St Gingolph (see Day 1 (direct)), then a single route proceeds onwards to the Chalets de Bise. Another col is crossed before the descent to La Chapelle d'Abondance.

If a night was spent off-route at **Chevenoz**, there is a choice of ways to return to the GR5. Either retrace steps back up the

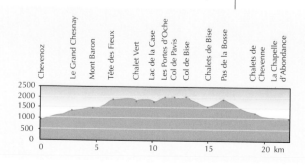

road to **Le Crêt**, or follow a path straight uphill from the *gîte*. The path climbs to a house in a forest, where a track leads up to a junction. Turn right along another track, then left at the next junction, to rejoin the GR5 near a couple of buildings.

If no detour was made, then the GR5 climbs from **Le Crêt**, up a road signposted for **Prébuza**, reaching a few houses at the end of the road. Turn left up a steep and stony forest track, watching for red/white markers at junctions, to emerge into a meadow where the gradient eases. Follow the track to a couple of buildings.

30min **Sur les Trables 1110m (3642ft)**

Cattle graze on a grassy alpage at Le Grand Chenay, high above the village of Chevenoz

The track continues uphill, with views of Lac Léman, then enters forest again. Climb very steeply, then the gradient eases as the track approaches **Le Petit Chesnay**, where a couple of chalets stand at 1336m (4383ft). Follow a path up

60

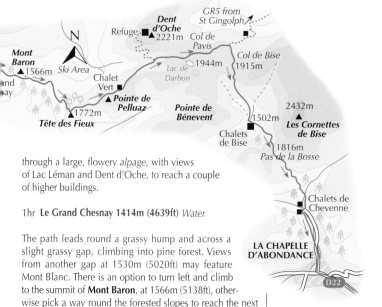

through a large, flowery *alpage,* with views
of Lac Léman and Dent d'Oche, to reach a couple
of higher buildings.

1hr **Le Grand Chesnay 1414m (4639ft)** *Water*

The path leads round a grassy hump and across a
slight grassy gap, climbing into pine forest. Views
from another gap at 1530m (5020ft) may feature
Mont Blanc. There is an option to turn left and climb
to the summit of **Mont Baron**, at 1566m (5138ft), otherwise pick a way round the forested slopes to reach the next
grassy gap.

45min **Les Boeufs 1430m (4690ft)**

Climb into forest and walk through a large clearing, then
back into forest, more or less following a crest. Pass a pylon
at the top of a *télésiège,* then drop down to a gap at **La
Crouaz**, at 1500m (4920ft). Climb a forested slope and
zigzag up to a slight gap at 1600m (5250ft). Pass the top of
another *télésiège* and climb again, steeply at times, up a
well-wooded crest. The path later reaches the open crest of
Tête des Fieux at 1772m (5814ft). There is a splendid
panorama, but follow the undulating crest to a view indicator where all is explained.

1hr 30min **View indicator 1770m (5810ft)** *Views stretch
from the Jura and Lac Léman, past nearby Dent d'Oche, to
Dents du Midi and Mont Blanc*

Drop down to the next gap, at 1750m (5740ft), which is dominated by the hump of Pointe de Pelluaz. Follow a narrow path across a steep and grassy slope, passing under a *télésiège* before entering a combe and dropping down to the ruined **Chalet Vert**. Climb uphill, passing alder scrub, then walk along a flowery crest to the **Col de la Case d'Oche**, at 1812m (5945ft). Drop down to the left to reach a small lake.

30min **Lac de la Case 1750m (5740ft)** *The Refuge de la Dent d'Oche lies well off-route, reached by way of a rocky scramble using a chain and cable*

Keep to the left of the lake to pass between it and a grassed-over lake, then head left to skirt a heap of huge boulders. Keep right while climbing to follow the path marked with red/white flashes. Climb across grassy slopes and scree slopes to the rugged gap of **Les Portes d'Oche** at 1937m (6355ft). ◄ Roughly contour across scree slopes in a boulder-strewn combe high above **Lac de Darbon**. There is a brief glimpse of distant Mont Blanc on the way to another gap.

From Les Portes d'Oche there is a view back to Thonon-les-Bains and Lac Léman.

1hr **Col de Pavis 1944m (6378ft)** *Bouquetin often congregate here*

Turn left to cross the col and follow the path downhill, eventually reaching a point where paths head either side of a large boulder. Turning right short-cuts to the Col de Bise, but the GR5 waymarks lead down to the left, reaching a signpost at another path junction at 1834m (6017ft). (**Note** Junction with the GR5 climbing from St Gingolph.) Turn right to follow the path up to a col.

30min **Col de Bise 1915m (6283ft)** *View of Chalets de Bise, Pas de la Bosse, Mont de Grange and higher mountains beyond*

Take care on the initial steep descent, as the path is worn and gritty. It levels out and becomes delightful, crossing a stream and leading directly to some large, tin-roofed buildings beside the **Ruisseau de Bise**. The nearby Lac de Bise is hardly noticed, being covered in vegetation.

45min Chalets de Bise 1506m (4941ft) *Refuge and two restaurants*

Leave the chalets as signposted and follow a narrow path that winds uphill. ▸

1hr Pas de la Bosse 1816m (5958ft) *Views of the Vallée d'Abondance, Châtel, Mont de Grange, Dents du Midi and Dents Blanche*

Three paths leave the col, so take the middle one, which descends past the ruined Chalets Cote. Further downhill, the restored **Chalets de la Cheneau** are passed at 1590m (5216ft). Follow the path down a steep, cow-grazed pasture, entering a forest to zigzag down to a junction of tracks.

1hr Chalets de Chevenne 1290m (4232ft) *Water*

Walk down a forest track to reach a road. A left turn along the road leads straight to La Chapelle d'Abondance. The

Look for marmots and bouquetin on the steep ascent, while admiring the soaring cliffs of the Cornettes de Bise above.

View of the Chalets de Bise, and back to the Col de Bise, on the ascent towards the Pas de la Bosse

GR5, however, turns right along the road, then almost immediately left to cross a footbridge. Turn left to follow a riverside path, which is part nature trail and part health trail (or *parcours santé*). It broadens to a track and rejoins the road. All that remains is to walk straight down to a village.

30min **La Chapelle d'Abondance 1021m (3350ft)** *All services*

La Chapelle d'Abondance

This village has transformed itself from a quiet farming settlement into a busy ski resort and year-round tourist destination. Old barns made of thick, dark, timber beams and planks recall the days gone by. Modern architecture tries to mirror the old style, but largely fails, and new developments continue to spread. Cattle produce milk for a fine range of cheeses. A full range of services is available. Buses operate to and from Chevenoz, Vinzier, Bioge and Thonon-les-Bains. Check timetables with ColomBus, tel 04 50 71 85 55, www.mobilalp.fr/hautchablais/fr. TIC tel 04 50 73 51 41, www.lachapelle74.com.

DAY 3
La Chapelle d'Abondance to Chésery

Distance	21 kilometres (13 miles)
Total Ascent	1495 metres (4905 feet)
Total Descent	545 metres (1790 feet)
Time	8 hours
Map	3528 ET
Nature of Terrain	Riverside path, followed by steep forest paths, giving way to more open slopes. Easier tracks and paths are used later in the day.

Food and Drink	Restaurant off-route at Trébentaz. Restaurants at Col de Bassachaux and Refuge de Chésery.
Accommodation	Refuge de Trébentaz is off-route. Refuge at Col de Bassachaux. Refuge de Chésery.

Mont de Grange is a large mountain and it takes half a day to trek round its sprawling slopes. Most of the ascent is forested, so views are limited. The higher slopes are open and are grazed by cattle, and a high shoulder above Lenlevay offers an optional ridge-route to the summit, suitable for those with time and energy to spare. The latter half of the route is mostly along good tracks and paths, climbing gradually out of France and into Switzerland.

Leave **La Chapelle d'Abondance** by following the main road in the direction of Châtel, turning right at a metal cow sculpture (shop and hotel) to walk down a track. Turn left to follow a path upstream beside the **Dranse Torrente**. It can be wet and muddy, but continue until a road is reached, and turn right to cross the **Pont du Moulin**, at 1018m (3340ft). Follow a track uphill, passing the waterfall of **La Cascade**. The track climbs steeply to a gate, where a path heads up to the right on a wooded slope, then emerges onto an open slope.

1hr 15min **Sur Bayard 1220m (4000ft)** *View back across the Vallée d'Abondance to Pas de la Bosse. Option to climb off-route to the Refuge de Trébentaz*

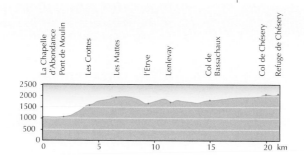

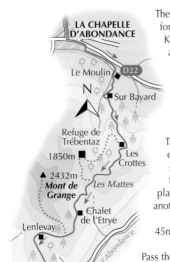

The path runs slightly downhill, then enters a forest and climbs quite steeply at times. Keep an eye open for red/white markers and eventually reach a clearing where there is a chalet.

1hr **Les Crottes 1529m (5016ft)** *Variant route, via Refuge de Trébentaz, to Les Mattes – see page 68 for details*

Take the path as marked back into the forest, though it later begins to follow a broad swathe between the trees, which allows for views. The path is steep and rugged in places, then there is a further clearing at another chalet.

45min **Chalet de la Torrens 1738m (5702ft)**

Pass the chalet on its left-hand side, and watch carefully for markers, as cattle have trodden many paths hereabouts. The GR5 climbs through alder scrub and aims for a prominent stump of rock before crossing a high, grassy, pathless shoulder of Mont de Grange to reach another chalet.

45min **Les Mattes 1930m (6332ft)** *View of Dents du Midi and Dents Blanches, flanked by Mont Blanc and Dent Blanche*

Keep right of the chalet to pick up a trodden path, bending right, then later bending left, making a dramatic loop to negotiate a steep and flowery slope. Head towards a few pines, then zigzag down a steep slope trodden by cattle to reach buildings at **Le Pron**, at 1741m (5712ft). Turn right, then left, keeping an eye open for markers. The GR5 winds down to the foot of a waterfall. Cross the stream and turn left down to a junction of tracks at 1660m (5445ft). Turn right and follow the track up to L'Etrye. Pass a building and keep climbing, enjoying wonderful views along the Vallée d'Abondance. Zigzag up a wooded slope to reach a shoulder at 1840m (6035ft). ▶ The GR5 runs down the track to a huddle of chalets.

There is a view of distant Dent Blanche on the way up, then Mont Blanc on the way down, and an option to climb Mont de Grange, using a waymarked path.

1hr 30min **Lenlevay 1733m (5686ft)** *Water*

Keep straight ahead at a couple of track junctions on a grassy crest at **Les Covagnes**. Roughly contour across shale slopes, then drop while traversing a partly forested slope, with views across the head of the Vallée d'Abondance to peaks on the Franco–Swiss frontier. When a junction of tracks is reached at 1664m (5459ft), follow none of them. Instead, walk up a narrow path and squelch through a marshy area rich in orchids, butterworts and alder scrub. Eventually the path climbs across a road to reach a prominent restaurant.

1hr 15min **Col de Bassachaux 1778m (5833ft)** *Refuge and restaurant*

A level track runs beyond the restaurant, crossing a partly forested slope. The track serves as a nature trail, with information boards about birds. ▶ Keep right at a junction, then right again to pass beneath a *télésiège*. Turn left as signposted for the Col de Chésery, to reach a fork in the path. Keep right and follow the *sentier pieton*, which is for walkers, not the

From here there is a view down to Lac de Motriond, near Morzine.

The broad and grassy Col de Chésery spans an unmarked frontier between France and Switzerland

Piste VTT, which is for cyclists. Both pursue parallel courses and join later.

Continue across a grassy, flowery slope, noting a prominent ski station on top of Pointe des Mossettes. Cross the **Col de Chésery** at 1992m (6535ft), where the GR5 passes from France into Switzerland. ◄ Continue along the path as signposted, aiming for a red-roofed building – but *not* the red-roofed buildings *downhill*.

A nearby building was a customs post, but customs officers are unlikely to be seen.

1hr 30min **Refuge de Chésery 1972m (6470ft)** *Refuge and restaurant*

VARIANT ROUTE

Via Refuge de Trébentaz to Les Mattes

If you spend a night at the Chalets de Bise, before La Chapelle d'Abondance, you could pass through the village and later detour off-route to stay at the Refuge de Trébentaz. The following description leaves the GR5 at the Chalet des Crottes and rejoins the route at Les Mattes.

Leave the **Chalet des Crottes**, at 1529m (5016ft), and follow a track signposted for the Refuge de Trébentaz. This curves round a forested slope, drops downhill, then climbs to a signpost at 1550m (5085ft). Turn left to follow a path uphill, passing a few trees, then rising across steep slopes of grass and limestone scree. The path winds more steeply uphill, keeping well to the left of a ruin, and soon reaches the *refuge*.

1hr 15min **Refuge de Trébentaz 1860m (6102ft)** *Refuge and restaurant*

Turn left to leave the *refuge*, contouring along a narrow path. Later, climb a steep, narrow, winding path up a crumbling shale slope to reach a col. Cross a fence and turn left to follow an easy path down to a chalet.

30min **Les Mattes 1930m (6332ft)** *View of Dents du Midi and Dents Blanches, flanked by Mont Blanc and Dent Blanche*

DAY 4
Chésery to Samoëns

Distance	25 kilometres (15½ miles)
Total Ascent	670 metres (2200 feet)
Total Descent	194 metres (6365 feet)
Time	6 hours 45 minutes
Maps	3528 ET and 3530 ET
Nature of Terrain	*Alpages,* high passes and forest. Mostly along good tracks, giving way to roads at the end. Some linking paths can be rugged.
Food and Drink	Restaurants or *buvettes* on the Swiss stretch at Chaux Palin, Lapisa and La Pierre. Restaurant at Col de la Golèse. Plenty at Samoëns.
Accommodation	*Gîtes* at Chaux Palin and La Pierre on the Swiss stretch. Refuge de Chardonnière off-route. Refuge de la Golèse. Plenty at Samoëns.

Note Signposting and waymarking is different in Switzerland. There are a few red/white paint flashes, but also yellow diamond markers edged in black. Not all signposts mention the GR5, so follow any sign indicating the Col de Cou (or Col de Coux). Euros are accepted in this part of Switzerland (at a rate of around 2 euros to 3 Swiss francs at the time of writing).

The GR5 through Switzerland is mostly along clear and obvious tracks, passing from one col to another before crossing back into France. Most of the route to Samoëns is along tracks, but some of these are very steep, and some linking paths are rugged. However, despite the length, the distance can be covered fairly quickly and easily. At the end of the day, the busy little town of Samoëns offers every comfort for walkers.

Leave the **Refuge de Chésery** and follow a path on the rugged right-hand side of **Lac Vert**, climbing to the gap of

The Dents Blanches look stunning when seen on a clear morning from the Portes de l'Hiver

A track covers the same distance on the other side of Lac Vert.

Portes de l'Hiver at 2096m (6877ft). ◄ Cross the gap and turn left down a track, enjoying magnificent views of the glaciated Dents Blanches. Turn right at a junction of tracks to continue downhill, and the way becomes a little more rugged towards the bottom.

45min **Chaux Palin 1843m (6047ft)** *Gîte d'étape and restaurant, access by road to Les Crosets and Champery*

Turn right to follow a track, keeping left at one junction to head downhill, then right at another to climb uphill a little. The track basically contours from one farmstead to another,

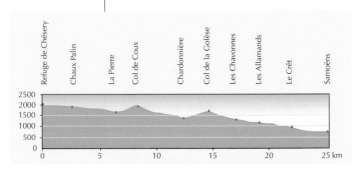

70

passing La Pas to reach **Lapisa** (*buvette*) at 1790m (5870ft). Keep to the left of the farm to find a path running down to another track at **La Pierre** (*gîte d'alpage* and restaurant). Turn right to follow the track uphill a little, then downhill to a hairpin bend.

1hr 15min **La Poyat 1645m (5397ft)**

Turn right up another track at this point. The surface is rugged at times, winding considerably on a slope of shale covered in alpenrose. Eventually a customs post is reached, though customs officers are unlikely to be present.

45min **Col de Coux 1920m (6300ft)**
View indicator split between Switzerland and France; view back to Dents du Midi and Dents Blanches, and ahead to Col de la Golèse, past the curved, boiler-plate slabs of Les Terres Maudites

Cross straight into France, following a steep and winding track downhill, first on an open slope, then past alder scrub and down into pine forest. Avoid all turnings off the main track until close to a river.

45min **Torrente de Chardonnière 1500m (4920ft)**

Refuge de Chésery
1992m 1972m
Col de Chésery
Pointe des Mossettes
2277m

Chaux Palin 1843m

Lapisa
1680m La Pierre

Col de Coux 1920m
Refuge de Chardonnière 1350m

F R A N C E S W I T

Tête de Bostan

Col de la Golèse 1662m
Refuge de la Golèse

Les Chavonnes

N

Les Allamands

Les Suets 1327m Le Pied du Crêt

SAMOËNS

D907

71

Turn left to leave the forest track and ford the river. Follow a pleasant path down through an *alpage,* but keep to the left as marked at Plan des Heures, at 1420m (4660ft), to ford a stream. (Right leads off-route to the **Refuge de Chardonnière**.) A rugged path leads across a steep slope grazed by cattle, then runs back into forest. Cross another steep slope and head back into the forest. (Another path heads off-route to the Refuge de Chardonnière.) Walk up to a track at Bonnevalette, at 1525m (5003ft). Turn left to follow the track up past alder scrub to cross a grassy col overlooked by limestone towers.

1hr 15min **Col de la Golèse 1662m (5453ft)** *Refuge and restaurant*

Immediately on starting the descent, the **Refuge de la Golèse** is seen to the left. Walk down the main track (Samoëns is seen briefly) to **Les Chavonnes** at 1269m (4163ft). The track becomes a road, passing a forest car park at Plan aux Arches, at 1098m (3602ft), and runs down to a small village.

A lovely little chapel stands in the centre of the hamlet of Les Allamands, in a forest clearing

1hr **Les Allamands 1028m (3373ft)** *Water; (the name suggests a German settlement)*

Walk down the road to a car park at 997m (3271ft), then either walk further down the road, which is the 'official' route, or avoid the road using a narrow path off to the right. If using the path, turn left on the well-wooded slope and follow red dots to reach a road bend. The GR5, meanwhile, turns every bend on the road to reach the same point.

Continue down the road, then turn right down a grassy track. Cross a bridge and walk down to the road at **Le Pied du Crêt**, at 900m (2950ft). Turn right to approach a solitary building, which is actually a covered reservoir (water). Just before it, turn left as marked along a woodland path. This is never far from the road and runs parallel to it before joining it again at **Les Fontaines**. Continue onwards (*chambres d'hôte*) to reach a road junction.

45min **Le Chevreret 748m 2454ft**

There appear to be two waymarked routes – one to the *left* and one to the *right* – both following roads. Keep *left* to cross a bridge over the **Clévieux Torrent**. Follow the road roughly parallel to the river to reach a main road on the outskirts of town. Keep *right* to follow a millrace to the **Gîte des Moulins**, then turn left down past more old mill buildings. Turn left at a crossroads and cross the **Clévieux Torrent**, then turn right to reach a main road on the outskirts of town.

15min **Samoëns 703m (2306ft)** *All services*

Samoëns

In 1438 Comte Amédée VIII of Savoie gave people the right to use seven *alpages* to the north, hence the name *septimontains,* from which Samoëns is derived. These days, the old part of the town, clustered round a 500-year old lime tree, is surrounded by new developments. The area attracts outdoor enthusiasts throughout the year, with walking and skiing being popular. Samoëns has a full range of services. Buses run up the valley to Sixt-Fer-à-Cheval and down the valley to Annemasse. Timetables can be checked with SAT, tel 04 50 34 40 09 or see www.sat-montblanc.com. TIC tel 04 50 34 40 28, www.samoens.com.

DAY 5

Samoëns to Refuge de Moëde Anterne

Distance	23 kilometres (14¼ miles)
Total Ascent	1800 metres (5905 feet)
Total Descent	505 metres (1655 feet)
Time	8 hours
Map	3530 ET
Nature of Terrain	Easy riverside walking, then metal ladders in the Gorges des Tines. A climb through forest to *alpages* and high passes on good paths.
Food and Drink	Restaurants off-route at Sixt-Fer-à-Cheval and Selvagny. Also at Cascade du Rouget, Lignon, Refuge d'Anterne and Refuge de Moëde Anterne.
Accommodation	Plenty off-route at Sixt-Fer-à-Cheval. *Gîte* at Selvagny. Refuge d'Anterne and Refuge de Moëde Anterne.

Easy riverside walking leads to a ladder-assisted climb through the Gorges des Tines. More riverside walking leads to the spectacular Cascade du Rouget and the twin falls of Cascade de la Sauffaz and Pleureuse de la Sauffaz. Climbing further, a pleasant *alpage* is passed on the way to the Refuge d'Anterne. Some walkers will be happy to stop, while others will press on across the Col d'Anterne to finish at the Refuge de Moëde Anterne.

Start on the main road on the outskirts of **Samoëns** and walk downstream beside the **Clévieux Torrent** to pass through another crossroads. Follow a dirt road to a footbridge, the **Passerelle de Clévieux**, but don't cross it. Instead, turn left to follow a track away from it, then turn right to reach the banks of the **Giffre Torrent**. Simply follow a well-wooded riverside path upstream until diverted onto the main road at **Le Perret**.

1hr **Pont du Perret 731m (2398ft)** *Water, buses to Samoëns and Sixt-Fer-à-Cheval*

Cross the bridge and follow a road up past a few houses. Continue down a woodland track, and maybe detour left to see the Chapelle de Notre Dame des Grâces. Walk down through a riverside meadow to reach Le Pelly Renadé at 748m (2454ft). Go onto a bridge to see the **Giffre Torrent** in a narrow gorge, but don't cross the bridge (unless to reach the main road, buses and snack bar).

Follow the path up through a beech wood to reach the dramatic **Gorges des Tines**. Climb through using metal ladders: first 24 steps, followed by 12 steps. Follow a winding bouldery path straight past a path junction beside a cliff at **Dessus les Tines**. Climb up 33 steps, then hold onto cables to climb further into the woods. A zigzag descent to Le Bené gives way to an easy path leading through meadows to a bridge.

Deep inside the limestone Gorges des Tines, where ladders are used to make an exit

1hr **Pont des Nants 768m (2520ft)** *Access to Selvagny, gîte and hotel; access to Sixt-Fer-à-Cheval, all services, buses to Samoëns; TIC tel 04 50 34 49 36,* www.sixteracheval.com

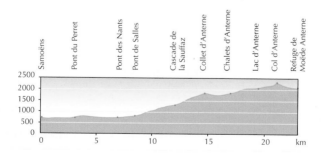

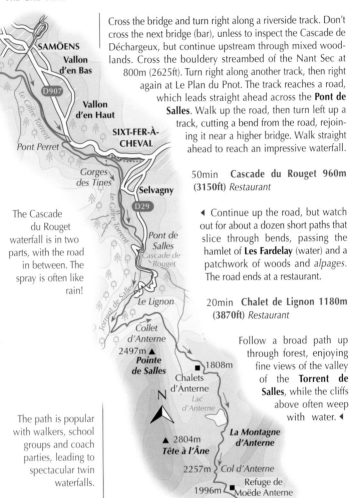

Cross the bridge and turn right along a riverside track. Don't cross the next bridge (bar), unless to inspect the Cascade de Déchargeux, but continue upstream through mixed woodlands. Cross the bouldery streambed of the Nant Sec at 800m (2625ft). Turn right along another track, then right again at Le Plan du Pnot. The track reaches a road, which leads straight ahead across the **Pont de Salles**. Walk up the road, then turn left up a track, cutting a bend from the road, rejoining it near a higher bridge. Walk straight ahead to reach an impressive waterfall.

50min **Cascade du Rouget 960m (3150ft)** *Restaurant*

◄ Continue up the road, but watch out for about a dozen short paths that slice through bends, passing the hamlet of **Les Fardelay** (water) and a patchwork of woods and *alpages*. The road ends at a restaurant.

The Cascade du Rouget waterfall is in two parts, with the road in between. The spray is often like rain!

20min **Chalet de Lignon 1180m (3870ft)** *Restaurant*

Follow a broad path up through forest, enjoying fine views of the valley of the **Torrent de Salles**, while the cliffs above often weep with water. ◄

The path is popular with walkers, school groups and coach parties, leading to spectacular twin waterfalls.

1hr **Cascade de la Sauffaz (left) Pleureuse de la Sauffaz (right) 1450m (4760ft)**

Zigzag uphill and turn left as signposted. The path follows a rugged, partly wooded, inclined terrace, with the cliffs of Pointe de Salles above. The path passes close to a pylon as it crosses a gentle grassy gap.

1hr **Collet d'Anterne 1796m (5892ft)** *View back towards the Gorges des Tines and ahead to Mont Blanc beyond Col d'Anterne*

Drop easily through a boulder-strewn area to cross a footbridge over the **Ruisseau d'Anterne**. The path, which is vague at times, runs through a pleasant *alpage,* with magnificent views of sheer cliffs, to reach a few chalets.

30min **Chalets d'Anterne 1808m (5932ft)** *Refuge and restaurant, named after Alfred Wills, founder of the Alpine Club*

This may be far enough for some, but others may want to press on to the next *refuge* to be closer to the Brévent the next day. Cross the **Ruisseau d'Anterne** beyond the *refuge*, and follow a clear path zigzagging across crumbling banded shale and limestone. The path wanders past limestone outcrops around 2090m (6855ft), then drops down past a signpost at Croisement du Lac. Cross a broad and gentle grassy dip, keeping to the left-hand side of a fine lake, crossing many in-flowing streams.

1hr 10min **Lac d'Anterne 2060m (6760ft)**

The path zigzags uphill across more banded shale and limestone, either crossing snow patches early in summer, or slopes of rubble later in the summer. Look ahead to spot a prominent cross beside a high col, and climb up to it to enjoy magnificent mountain scenery.

40min **Col d'Anterne 2257m (7405ft)** *Views ahead to the Aiguilles Rouge and the Brévent, with Mont Blanc beyond*

Pick a way down a steep and winding path below crumbling banded cliffs, to reach a junction. Turn left to walk down to a track, then head straight for a prominent large building that has been in view throughout the descent.

Be prepared! A sudden summer snowfall changes everything high on the Col d'Anterne

30min **Refuge de Moëde Anterne 1996m (6549ft)** *Refuge and restaurant*

DAY 6
Refuge de Moëde Anterne to Les Houches

Distance	21 kilometres (13 miles)
Total Ascent	1000 metres (3280 feet)
Total Descent	1990 metres (6530 feet)
Time	7 hours
Map	3530 ET
Nature of Terrain	After crossing a wooded valley, an increasingly steep and rugged climb ends on metal ladders high on the Brévent. A long, steep, rugged descent becomes densely forested.
Food and Drink	Restaurants on the Brévent, at the Refuge de Bellachat and off-route at Parc de Merlet. Plenty at Les Houches.
Accommodation	Refuge de Bellachat. Plenty at Les Houches.

Today's objective is to climb the Brévent, but this should be avoided if a storm is imminent, or if there is snow or ice on the steep, rocky slopes. In foul weather, head down the valley to Servoz, where buses and trains run to Les Houches. Once walkers climb towards the Brévent, the only options are to continue or turn back. In clear weather, views of Mont Blanc are without equal, but the summit must be shared with tourists who arrive by *téléphérique*.

Leave the **Refuge de Moëde Anterne** to follow a clear track down towards the huddled **Chalets d'Anterne**. Before reaching them, turn right down a narrow path, crossing squelchy slopes to drop through scrubby woodland. While the Brévent looms large ahead, the path drops deep into a wild valley, becoming firmer underfoot.

45min **Pont d'Arlevé 1597m (5240ft)**

Cross a footbridge and turn right, climbing gradually and fairly easily across a rugged slope covered in alder scrub. For the most part, the path has been built in stone and passes the ruined **Chalets d'Arlevé**. Small streams are crossed on slopes of alpenrose and bilberry, then the path starts zigzagging uphill. There are flights of rough stone steps, as well as airy terrace paths. Tufts of parsley fern grow among hard gneiss blocks. Massive rocky buttresses are circumvented before the path finally climbs past huge boulders to reach a col bearing a tall cairn.

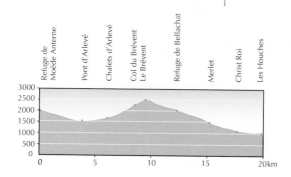

2hr 15min **Col du Brévent 2368m (7769ft)** *Views of Mont Blanc and the Brévent; if the weather is bad, or if the higher slopes are icy, a descent to Planpraz and Chamonix should be considered*

The GR5 turns right on reaching the cairn, but look carefully for the red/white markers, which lead up and down on rugged, bouldery slopes. Several rocky peaks rise ahead, but the route goes down through a small, bouldery valley. Climbing again, a rocky part of the route features two fixed ladders, each with 11 rungs, as well as handrails and metal footplates. Walkers suddenly find themselves on a broad dirt road, and this leads effortlessly onwards. Simply climb to what is actually an artificial summit.

Looking into the heart of the Aiguilles Rouges from the summit of the Brévent

45min **Le Brévent 2525m (8284ft)** *View indicator and restaurant with panoramic terrace facing Mont Blanc; views back to Col d'Anterne and Dents Blanches, and ahead to Col de Voza and Col de Tricot; small display about the Réserve Naturelle des Aiguilles Rouges; téléphérique to Chamonix*

Backtrack down to the dirt road, where a path is signposted for Bellachat. The path has been built with stone, but often crosses hard, bare, banded gneiss. Follow it as it zigzags down a rough and rocky slope overlooking **Lac du Brévent**. A length of rail protects against overshooting a sudden left turn where the path has been cut into a cliff. A fine promenade leads along the top of a steep brow where there are bird's-eye views of Chamonix. As the path drops from this brow, a building appears.

45min **Refuge de Bellachat 2152m (7060ft)** *Refuge and restaurant; views of Mont Blanc, Chamonix and Col de Tricot*

Watch carefully for a signpost for Les Houches and red/white markers, as there is a confusing tangle of paths near the *refuge*. Zigzag down a steep slope and cross a ravine before entering a forest. Keep to the path which, despite being badly worn in places, has been engineered to provide the best passage, with wooden steps in various states of repair. Use metal handrails to cross another ravine and enter another stand of forest. Later, watch for a path junction where there is an option to visit a wildlife park – if you can spare the time and energy.

1hr **Merlet 1562m (5125ft)** *Wildlife park and restaurant – opportunity to see Alpine wildlife at close quarters, tel 04 50 53 47 39, www.parcdemerlet.com*

If not visiting **Merlet**, then keep right as marked for the GR5, which later zigzags down beside the enclosure fence before landing on a road. Turn right down the road, then left as signposted. Keep to the

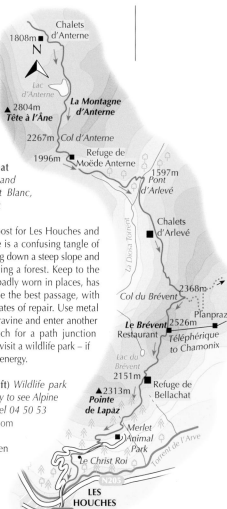

81

red/white marked paths on a forested slope, or follow sign-posts for **Christ Roi** – an imposing statue of Christ built over a small chapel. Watch carefully for more markers, avoiding a very steep track. Later, gentle tracks and roads cross a railway and the **Torrent de l'Arve**. Climb a little by road and turn right into a bustling little town.

1hr 30min **Les Houches 1008m (3308ft)** *All services*

Les Houches

Although forever in the shadow of big, brash Chamonix, Les Houches attracts its fair share of visitors, and is a thriving skiing and outdoor centre. Anyone wanting to visit Chamonix can use the Chamonix Bus, which links Les Houches with Chamonix and Argentière, stopping at numerous points, including all the main lifts up the mountainsides. Timetables can be checked with Transdev, tel 04 50 53 05 55, www.chamonixbus.com. The bus links with Le Mulet, a free bus, or *navette gratuite,* round the centre of Chamonix. SAT buses run between Chamonix, Les Houches and Geneva, tel 04 50 78 05 33, www.sat-montblanc.com. TIC tel 04 50 55 50 62, www.leshouches.com.

Chamonix

A good reason to visit Chamonix is that it is the 'capital of mountaineering', although it is also just a town, like many others, and it's the location that makes it special. Chamonix has a full range of services, and offers the chance to access many scenic, high-level walks using ski lifts. Chamonix TIC, tel 04 50 53 00 24, www.chamonix.com.

STAGE 2
LES HOUCHES TO LANDRY

Mont Joly, seen from a meadow above Bionnassay (Day 7)

General Overview Map	IGN 1:100,000 Carte de Promenade 53 Grenoble Mont Blanc.
Alternative Maps	Libris 1:60,000 No 02 Mont Blanc (covers route from Samoëns to Roselend) and Libris 1:60,000 No 04 Vanoise (covers route from Les Contamines to Valfréjus). Rando Éditions 1:50,000 A1 Pays du Mont Blanc (covers route from Samoëns to Roselend) and Rando Éditions 1:50,000 A2 Beaufortain (covers route from Les Contamines to Val d'Isère).

There are two choices of route for Day 7 – the main route, described first, and the higher-level route, described second.

The main route starts by following the course of the Route du Sel, or Salt Route, over the Col de Voza, through Les Contamines, then continuing over the Col du Bonhomme. The traverse of the Col de Voza is quite easy and would suit walkers who are only just starting this stage from Les Houches.

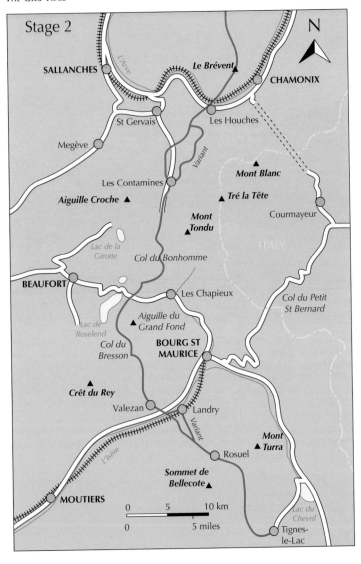

Stage 2

Looking back up the valley after descending from the Refuge de la Balme (Day 9)

Those who already have a taste for the mountains should consider the variant route from the Col de Voza, over the higher Col de Tricot, to Les Contamines.

Bear in mind that the Col du Bonhomme (Day 8) can carry snow late into the summer, and also note that facilities along the first couple of days of this stage come under pressure, because the popular Tour du Mont Blanc follows the same course as the GR5.

Once across the Col du Bonhomme, the departmental boundary is crossed between Haute-Savoie and Savoie. The crowds following the Tour du Mont Blanc are left behind, and more discerning walkers are encountered on the Tour du Beaufortain instead (towards the end of Day 8). If you haven't sampled Beaufort cheese, then you are now in the heartland of its production. As a consequence, expect many paths across *alpages* to be heavily trodden by dairy cattle.

This is only a short stage, and it can be covered in as little as three or four days. Landry is a sensible place to call a halt because it has a railway station offering easy departure and/or arrival for those who are covering the GR5 in easier stages. Those who intend continuing can omit Landry and climb straight back into the mountains from Pont de Bellentre (see end of Day 9).

DAY 7

Les Houches to Les Contamines

Distance	17 kilometres (10½ miles)
Total Ascent	1050 metres (3445 feet)
Total Descent	895 metres (2935 feet)
Time	5 hours 15 minutes
Map	3531 ET
Nature of Terrain	Fairly easy walking, mostly along tracks and minor roads.
Food and Drink	Restaurants at intervals across the Col de Voza, and at Bionnassay and Tresse. Plenty at Les Contamines.
Accommodation	Hotels or *gîtes* at Col de Voza, Bionnassay, Champel and Tresse. Plenty at Les Contamines.

After the increasingly difficult walking of the previous week, this day's walk is relatively easy, mostly along good tracks and paths, though gradients are steep in places. The high point of the day is the Col de Voza, also traversed by the Tour du Mont Blanc and Tramway du Mont Blanc. Expect to see plenty of people throughout the day.

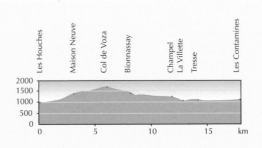

▶ Follow the main commercial road through **Les Houches**, passing the bulk of its businesses and the Téléphérique de Bellevue (linking Les Houches with Bellevue). Turn left before reaching a tunnel to follow a winding road uphill from Les Trabets at 995m (3265ft). Go under a bridge and climb up a dirt road through mixed woodlands, reaching tarmac again at some chalets. Keep right at a road junction, cross a river, then turn left up the Route de Maisonneuve.

Pass more chalets and a *télésiège* at **Maison Neuve**. Continue up the dirt road called Chemin de la Carbotte, winding up through woods and steep meadows, passing a chalet restaurant, followed later by another restaurant. The track finally levels out as it approaches a broad col.

1hr 45min   **Col de Voza 1650m (5413ft)** *Hotel and café/bar; view of the flanks of Mont Blanc; Tramway du Mont Blanc, constructed from 1904 with the original intention of reaching the summit of Mont Blanc* ▶

Cross the tramway line and follow a track heading straight downhill. A steep and winding descent, through forest and meadows, passes the **Refuge du Fioux** (*gîte d'étape* and restaurant) to reach a car park at **Le Crozat**, at 1420m

Those pining for high mountains may consider the alternative route from the Col de Voza over the Col de Tricot – see Day 7a page 90.

Note: Route 7a over the Col du Tricot splits off here.

The Tramway du Mont Blanc climbs from Col de Voza and was originally planned to scale Mont Blanc

(4660ft). Walk down the road, passing an access track for the Ecomusée de la Vieille Maison. Continue down into a quaint village.

45min **Bionnassay 1320m (4330ft)** *Auberge/gîte and café*

Bionnassay

In 1784 and 1785 this was the base camp for expeditions intent on climbing Mont Blanc. A series of information panels titled 'Sur les Pas des Premiers Guides' outline the history and development of mountain guiding in the area. The Ecomusée de la Vieille Maison is an 18th-century farm featuring working demonstrations. On 12 July 1892 the Glacier de Tête Rousse, which contained an enormous mass of water, ruptured with disastrous results. Some 200 million litres (44 million gallons) of water surged down the valley, tearing up mud and rubble, causing devastation all the way to St Gervais, leaving 200 people dead.

Turn left just before the Auberge de Bionnassay, down a track to pass a chapel, then down into mixed woodland in a valley. Cross a footbridge over the milky, glacial **Ruisseau de Bionnassay**, then zigzag up to a forest track at L'Ormey, at 1340m (4395ft). Turn right to follow the undulating track until it leaves the forest and drops down to a village.

45min **Champel 1225m (4020ft)** *Gîte d'étape, water*

Follow the tarmac Route du Champel, with views down the valley to St Gervais, and turn left after a chapel for views up the valley. Go straight down a steep woodland track, the Chemin des Chevruils, to land on a tarmac road in **La Villette**, at 1050m (3445ft). Turn left at a fountain (water) along the Chemin de la Fontaine.

Follow the road uphill, short-cutting the final bends by walking up a track on the left, past an old school and up to **La Gruvaz** (water). Continue up and down the road into a forested valley and cross a river. Turn right down a woodland path, which drops steeply among pines to reach a village, then walk down to a crossroads.

1hr   Tresse 1040m (3412ft) *Hotel and restaurant;
buses to Les Contamines and St Gervais*

Head straight along the Chemin du Quy to
cross a river. The road loops uphill, then continues as a track, becoming a woodland
path. Emerge in a meadow with a view
of Col de Voza and Col de Tricot. Turn
left down a track at Les Meuniers,
cross a stream, then walk down a
road through Les Hoches. This
was the birthplace of Alexis
Bouvard, discoverer of the
planet Neptune. Walk along
a road to each a junction at
Le Molliex. Turn left to
cross a river, then right to
follow a well-wooded
path between the river
and main road,
climbing steeply at
times.   A path
climbs left up to
the centre of a
busy little town.

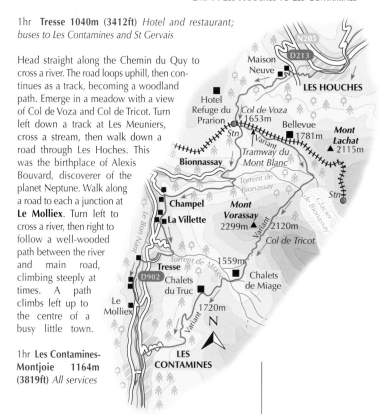

**1hr Les Contamines-
Montjoie   1164m
(3819ft)** *All services*

Les Contamines-Montjoie
Les Contamines is on the Tour du Mont Blanc and
can be very busy, with lots of people coming and
going. Although small, the town offers a full range
of services. Visit the Maison de la Reserve
Naturelle to appreciate the natural history of the
area. SAT buses run to St Gervais and Sallanches
for onward bus and rail travel, tel 04 50 78 05 33,
www.sat-montblanc.com. TIC tel 04 50 47 01 58,
www.lescontamines.com.

DAY 7a

Les Houches to Les Contamines
(high-level route)

Distance	19 kilometres (12 miles)
Total Ascent	1500 metres (4920 feet)
Total Descent	1345 metres (4415 feet)
Time	6 hours
Map	3531 ET
Nature of Terrain	Easy walking at first, mostly along tracks and minor roads. Steep and rugged paths and tracks are used later.
Food and Drink	Restaurants at intervals across Col de Voza, off-route at La Chalette, and at the Chalets de Miage and Chalets du Truc. Plenty at Les Contamines.
Accommodation	Hotel at Col de Voza. *Refuges* at Chalets de Miage and Chalets du Truc. Plenty at Les Contamines.

This variant climbs from the Col de Voza high over the Col de Tricot, offering a longer, tougher alternative to the main route (it is also an alternative on the Tour du Mont Blanc). There is an option to visit the snout of the Glacier de Bionnassay, and no other part of the GR5 runs so close to a glacier. Stunning views take in the flanks of Mont Blanc. There are options to stay or eat at the Chalets de Miage and Chalets du Truc before reaching Les Contamines (see map on page 89).

Follow the main commercial road through **Les Houches**, passing the bulk of its businesses and the Téléphérique de Bellevue (linking Les Houches with Bellevue). Turn left before reaching a tunnel to follow a winding road uphill from Les Trabets at 995m (3265ft). Go under a bridge and climb up a dirt road through mixed woodlands, reaching tarmac again at some chalets. Keep right at a road junction, cross a river, then turn left up the Route de Maisonneuve. Pass more chalets and a *télésiège* at **Maison Neuve**.

Continue up the dirt road called Chemin de la Carbotte, winding up through woods and steep meadows, passing a chalet restaurant, followed later by another restaurant. The track finally levels out as it approaches a broad col.

1hr 45min   **Col de Voza 1650m (5413ft)** *Hotel and café/bar; Tramway du Mont Blanc, constructed from 1904 with the original intention of reaching the summit of Mont Blanc*

Cross the tramway line and turn left up a track, the Chemin de Bellevue, running parallel to the line. Climb steeply at times and cross a hump near the derelict **Hotel Bellevue**. ▶ Here there are views back to Col d'Anterne and the Brévent, as well as the flanks of Mont Blanc. Don't cross the tramway again, unless visiting **La Chalette** (restaurant), but follow a grassy track towards a forest. Take a path across a steep slope, with occasional views down the Bionnassay valley and up towards the Glacier de Bionnassay. The marked route leads down a steep and bouldery path to a suspension footbridge. At the suspension footbridge there is an option to leave the route for the snout of the Glacier de Bionnassay.

This is where route 7 heads down to Bionnassay

45min **Passerelle de Glacier 1600m (5250ft)**

Cross the wobbly footbridge over the milky torrent spouting from the glacier. Climb up to a path junction and keep left (right runs down to Bionnassay). Climb past trees and alder

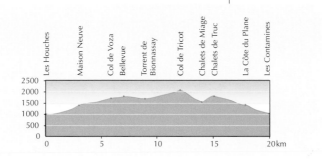

Enjoying a picnic, with a view of the Glacier de Bionnassay, on the way to the Col de Tricot

scrub onto a pleasant flowery *alpage*, then the path is smoother and gentler as it climbs, with fine views on the way to a col.

45min **Col de Tricot 2120m (6955ft)**

Descend from the col along a steep, worn, stony zigzag path. The bottom of the slope is in view all the time, but progress is slow. Eventually reach a group of chalets.

1hr **Chalets de Miage 1550m (5085ft)** *Refuge and restaurant*

Leave the chalets either along a track or a path – both of which meet at a stone bridge. Turn left up a zigzag path to climb through woods, then cross an *alpage*. Keep left at a junction of paths and walk down past another group of chalets.

30min **Chalets du Truc 1720m (5643ft)** *Refuge and restaurant*

Walk down a track into a forest. After taking a sharp right bend, turn left along a rugged forest path, taking care over boulders and tree roots. Watch for a left turn, then later a right turn to reach a track. Turn left down a steep and bendy track, signposted for Les Contamines, to reach a junction at Les Granges de la Frasse. Turn right steeply downhill to reach a road at La Frasse d'en Haut (water, *navette* into Les Contamines). Head left down a road, then turn left to go straight down the Chemin du P'tou, watching for its continuation across road bends, to land beside a church.

1hr 15min **Les Contamines-Montjoie 1164m (3819ft)** *All services – see end of Day 7, main route, page 89*

DAY 8

Les Contamines to Plan de la Lai

Distance:	24 kilometres (15 miles)
Total Ascent	1535 metres (5035 feet)
Total Descent	825 metres (2705 feet)
Time	8 hours
Maps	3531 ET 3531 OT and 3532 OT
Nature of Terrain	The valley walk becomes increasingly wild as roads and tracks give way to rugged paths and maybe snow. After taking a rocky path from col to col, a fine ridge gives way to a long, grassy descent.
Food and Drink	Restaurants on the ascent at Le Pontet, Notre Dame de la Gorge, Chalet de Nant Borrant, Refuge de la Balme and Refuge de la Croix du Bonhomme. Also at Plan de la Lai.
Accommodation	Campsite at Le Pontet. *Refuges* at Nant Borrant, La Balme, Col de la Croix du Bonhomme and Plan de la Lai.

The route from Les Contamines, through the Nant Borrant valley and over the Col du Bonhomme, was for centuries part of the Route du Sel, or Salt Route. It takes the best part of the day to reach the Col du Bonhomme, which holds snow well into summer. Beyond the Refuge de la Croix du Bonhomme, a fine ridge-walk traces the Crête des Gittes, before a descent into Beaufortain, famous for the golden-brown cows that produce rich milk for a fine cheese.

Leave **Les Contamines** by picking up the wooded riverside path. Head upstream to a road bridge, but only cross the road, not the bridge. Cross a footbridge over the river, walk up to the next road bridge, and cross that too. Follow a path upstream to join a road, then following it straight ahead, and keep left of a car park as signposted for the Parc Nordique. A good track continues, often flanked by trees, passing a sporting area (restaurant) and **Le Pontet** (campsite and *gîte*). When a wayside oratory is reached, keep right to continue along the wooded riverside track.

1hr **Notre Dame de la Gorge 1210m (3970ft)** *Restaurant and pilgrim church*

The track climbs steeply, and is either boulder-paved or runs across bare gneiss bedrock. Keep right to cross the Pont Romain (waterfall viewpoint). Climb past a bar/restaurant to reach a *refuge*.

30min **Chalet de Nant Borrant 1459m (4787ft)** *Refuge and restaurant*

Keep climbing up the track, passing Le Rollaz at 1535m (5035ft) (basic bivouac site). Views open out as a fine meadow is entered. There are some chalets down to the left, but stay on the track as it climbs gently onwards (water). Walk up through a little more forest, then cross a bridge over the river beside some enormous limestone boulders.

1hr **Refuge de la Balme 1706m (3970ft)** *Refuge and restaurant; basic bivouac site*

Just above the *refuge*, turn left up a path and climb to a prominent pylon to rejoin the track. Turn left and walk down the track a short way to a concrete bunker.

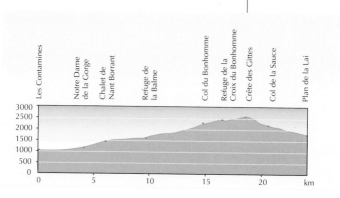

45min Plan Jovet 1920m (6300ft)

Turn right as signposted and follow a path to cross a footbridge over a stream. Climb uphill, later following a path worn into the schist bedrock. Pass a prominent cairn, the Tumulus Plan des Dames at 2043m (6703ft). A little further uphill, note how a small stream is swallowed by a band of limestone. Depending on the season, the path may cross the valley on snow, or on stony ground. Either way, climb more steeply beyond, noting how the badly eroded path traces a junction between flaky slate and crumbling dolomitic limestone. The path finally reaches a col.

1hr 30min Col du Bonhomme 2329m (7641ft) *Shelter; view of Crête des Gittes and Col de la Sauce; departmental boundary between Haute-Savoie and Savoie*

Turn left and climb gradually across a rocky slope, with some short

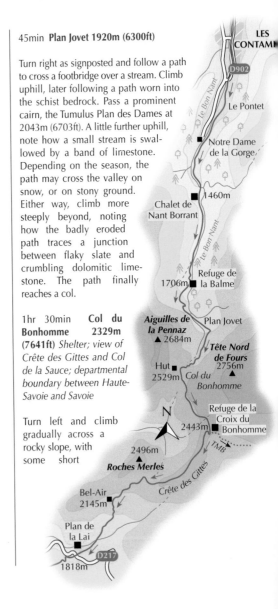

LES CONTAMI

Le Bon Nant

Le Pontet

Notre Dame de la Gorge

1460m

Chalet de Nant Borrant

Le Bon Nant

Refuge de la Balme
1706m

Plan Jovet

Aiguilles de la Pennaz
▲ 2684m

Tête Nord de Fours
2756m ▲

Hut
2529m Col du Bonhomme

Refuge de la Croix du Bonhomme

2443m

TMB

2496m
▲
Roches Merles

Bel-Air
2145m

Crête des Gittes

Plan de la Lai

D217

1818m

N

Snow lies late into the summer across the GR5 as it climbs towards the Col du Bonhomme

Walkers follow a well-trodden path along the Crête des Gittes to reach the Col de la Sauce

descents, as marked. Cross a variety of rock types, and note other types in rockfall debris. After crossing a stream, climb a little round a corner and descend to a *refuge*.

45min Refuge de la Croix du Bonhomme 2433m (7982ft)
Refuge and restaurant; view of the Crête des Gittes and Col de la Sauce, with view indicator available to sort out other features

Don't get mixed up with the Tour du Mont Blanc, which heads down to Les Chapieux, but cross a nearby col at 2408m (7900ft) and climb uphill. A zigzag path crosses crumbling slates, later passing through a notch hammered out of the ridge. A fine stretch leads along the **Crête des Gittes**, but before reaching a pyramidal peak, head down to the right across the flank. Walk along the ridge, then head down to right across the flank again. Cross the ridge, then later cross back again, and finally zigzag down to a col.

Note The walk along the Crête des Gittes is inadvisable in very strong wind, or if snow and ice covers the path. In such conditions, follow the Tour du Mont Blanc down to Les Chapieux, then follow the winding road to Plan de la Lai.

1hr 15min **Col de la Sauce 2307m (7569ft)** *View back to Col du Bonhomme and Mont Blanc, and ahead to La Terrasse and Aiguille de Grand Fond*

The lowest part of the col is on a junction between flaky slate and more durable limestone. Turn left to descend, overlooking steep, grassy, flowery slopes grazed by cattle. The path crosses wet patches and can be muddy. A track is reached at a ruined chalet.

30min **Chalet Bel-Air 2145m (7037ft)**

The track makes sweeping zigzags down a steep, grassy slope, while a path short-cuts through as many bends as possible. The path levels out in pastures dotted with huge boulders. Aim for a footbridge crossing a river then follow a track up to a road. Turn right to reach a *refuge*.

45min **Plan de la Lai 1822m (5978ft)** *Refuge and nearby gîte d'alpage, both with restaurants*

DAY 9
Plan de la Lai to Landry

Distance	29 kilometres (18 miles)
Total Ascent	1075 metres (3525 feet)
Total Descent	2120 metres (6955 feet)
Time	9 hours
Map	3532 OT
Nature of Terrain	Some muddy paths, followed by steep, bouldery slopes. Good tracks and paths towards the end of the day lead deep into a valley.
Food and Drink	Restaurants at Refuge de la Balme, Valezan, Bellentre and Landry.
Accommodation	Refuge de la Balme. *Auberge* and *gîte* at Valezan. Hotel and campsite at Landry.

This long day's walk probably ranks as the muddiest on the GR5. The flaky slate bedrock crumbles to slimy mud, trampled by cattle. When limestone appears on either side of the Col de Bresson, it is often in the form of monstrous boulders. However, things speed up beyond the Refuge de la Balme, when good tracks are used on the way down to the Isère valley. There is no need to walk all the way to Landry if a night at Valezan appeals.

Cross the road from the *refuge* and follow a track up past the Gîte d'Alpage de Plan Mya. Slabs of limestone slope down, and a line of sink-holes is visible where another rock type is encountered. The limestone becomes flaky before the Chalet le Mora is reached. Afterwards, the predominant rock is flaky slate. The track climbs in a sweeping zigzag, so short-cut straight uphill along a path. The bedrock is soft and the path runs through a deeply worn groove. Rejoin the track and turn right to follow it to a solitary building.

40min **La Petite Berge 2070m (6790ft)** *Shelter; view of Mont Blanc beyond Col de la Sauce*

There are views down to Lac de Roselend, an artificial lake created for hydroelectric power.

A muddy path continues across grassy, flowery slopes, with one stretch on duckboards. ◄ Look ahead to spot a gentle col, but don't head directly to it. The waymarked path drifts down to the right to avoid a wet and muddy stretch, then climbs to the grassy col. Pass the ruins of **La Grande Berge** at 2060m (6760ft), then descend past another ruin.

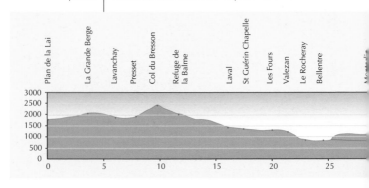

Cross a steep slope covered in alder scrub, where the path is muddy, then cross a grassy slope above a chalet. ▸ Walk down to a track and turn left, then short-cut through a bend as marked. There is one other opportunity to short-cut, otherwise walk round all the bends until the track leads down to a solitary building.

From here there is a view of a valley full of dairy farms, with the prominent rock tower of La Pierra Menta beyond.

50min **Lavachay 1805m (5922ft)**

Before reaching the building, turn left along a narrow path to cross cattle-grazed slopes studded with boulders. Follow the route across a winding track and climb up a path on a slope of alder scrub, passing bouldery rock-fall. Rejoin the track at a waterfall, crossing the flow to continue uphill. There are a couple of short-cut paths, then a signpost stands to the left of the track.

45min **Presset 2000m (6560ft)**

A path climbs up a grassy slope studded with big boulders. ▸ The boulders become bigger further uphill, fallen from two prominent peaks. The one rising left of the path is

Note the rock types, which include a coarse limestone conglomerate and a quartz-rich metamorphic rock.

The Pointe de Presset is a striking feature on the rugged ascent of the Col du Bresson

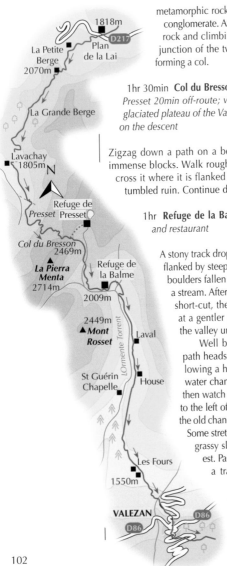

metamorphic rock, while the one to the right is conglomerate. After passing round a buttress of rock and climbing further, it appears that the junction of the two rock types is a weak area forming a col.

1hr 30min Col du Bresson 2469m (8100ft) *Refuge de Presset 20min off-route; view beyond the valley to the glaciated plateau of the Vanoise, view of La Pierra Menta on the descent*

Zigzag down a path on a bouldery slope, passing some immense blocks. Walk roughly parallel to a stream, then cross it where it is flanked by huge boulders to reach a tumbled ruin. Continue downstream to reach a *refuge*.

1hr Refuge de la Balme 2009m (6591ft) *Refuge and restaurant*

A stony track drops from the *refuge* into a valley flanked by steep, grassy slopes. Pass limestone boulders fallen from slabby slopes, then cross a stream. After a bendy stretch, which can be short-cut, the track runs more directly and at a gentler gradient. Walk down through the valley until the first house is seen.

Well before this, but not obvious, a path heads left across a grassy slope, following a horizontal line that was once a water channel. Pass in front of the house, then watch for the continuation of the path to the left of the access track. The course of the old channel is clearer as it enters a forest. Some stretches are wet and muddy, then a grassy slope is reached beyond the forest. Pass a couple of ruins, then follow a track down past a few houses.

2hr Les Fours, at 1550m (5085ft) *Views ahead almost reach the Col du Palet in the Vanoise*

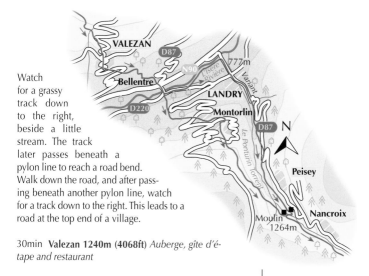

Watch for a grassy track down to the right, beside a little stream. The track later passes beneath a pylon line to reach a road bend. Walk down the road, and after passing beneath another pylon line, watch for a track down to the right. This leads to a road at the top end of a village.

30min **Valezan 1240m (4068ft)** *Auberge, gîte d'étape and restaurant*

Watch for signs reading *passage pieton* for a traffic-free descent past the church. Continue down this back road, and later follow a track beside a field to leave Valezan. Cross a road to pick up a track that was formerly the highway out of the village. When the road is reached again, walk down a little to spot a track heading down from a slope of apple trees. Later, simply cross over the road. One stretch of path offers a fine view of the valley, with Bellentre and Landry in view.

Pass between old buildings at Le Rocheray, at 910m (2985ft), and follow the path downhill. Cross an access road, then later go down steps to follow a road through the hamlet of Le Crey. Step off the road as marked and go down through woods to reach a village, turning left to walk into it.

45min **Bellentre 773m (2536ft)** *Bar/shop and post office*

Take the road to the right of the church, which later leads through a tunnel under a busy road. Follow a path beside a field, dropping down to a bridge over **L'Isère Rivière**.

10min **Pont de Bellentre 719m (2359ft)** *The GR5 main route climbs to Montorlin and Montchavin, but Landry is within easy reach*

If visiting Landry, note that there is no waymarked approach, and walking along the main road is not recommended. A cycleway runs parallel to the river for a safer approach. When a road is reached, turn right into **Landry**.

1hr **Landry 777m (2549ft)** *Hotel, restaurant, shop, bar and campsite; trains to Bourg St Maurice and occasionally to Lyon or Paris; free bus, or navette gratuite to Peisey, Moulin, Nancroix and Rosuel*

The rock tower of La Pierra Menta dominates the descent from the Col du Bresson

STAGE 3
LANDRY TO MODANE

Crossing the Col du Barbier, there is a last view back towards the Dent Parrachée (GR5 Day 15)

General Overview Map	IGN 1:100,000 Carte de Promenade 53 Grenoble Mont Blanc.
Alternative Maps	Libris 1:60,000 No 04 Vanoise (covers route from Les Contamines to Valfréjus).
	Rando Éditions 1:50,000 A2 Beaufortain (covers route from Les Contamines to Val d'Isère) and Rando Éditions 1:50,000 A3 Vanoise (covers route from Rosuel to Valfréjus).

This is the most complex stage along the whole walk, because there are three widely differing possible routes to choose from, which need careful consideration – see the Stage 3 map on the following page.

The **GR5 route** climbs from Landry to Tignes-le-Lac, then heads for Val d'Isère and crosses the Col de l'Iseran, which is the highest point reached on the main route.

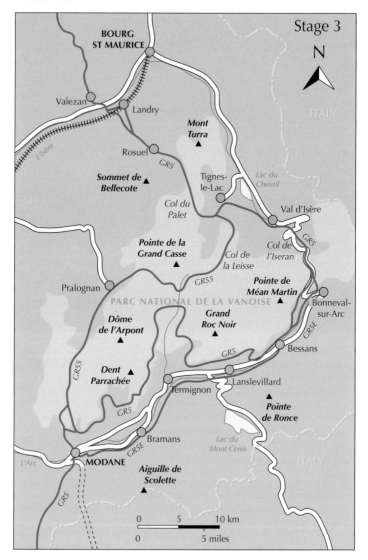

Stage 3

N

BOURG
ST MAURICE

Valezan

Landry

Mont
Turra ▲

Rosuel

GR5

ITALY

Sommet de
Bellecote ▲

Tignes-
le-Lac

Lac du
Chevril

Col du
Palet

Val d'Isère

GR5

Pointe de la
Grand Casse
▲

Col de
la Leisse

Col de
l'Iseran

GR55

Pralognan

PARC NATIONAL DE LA VANOISE

Pointe de
Méan Martin
▲

Dôme
de l'Arpont
▲

Grand
Roc Noir
▲

Bonneval-
sur-Arc

GR55

GR5

GR5E

Bessans

Dent
Parrachée ▲

Termignon

Lanslevillard

Pointe
de Ronce ▲

GR5

Bramans

GR5E

MODANE

Lac du
Mont Cenis

ITALY

L'Arc

Aiguille de
Scolette
▲

GR5

L'Isère

0	5	10 km
0		5 miles

The GR5 crosses a ridge of rubbly moraine to cross the Plan de la Cha on the way to the Refuge du Cuchet (GR5 Day 13)

Descending from the col, the trail heads for Bessans. From Bessans, the GR5 very roughly contours round the high flanks of the Vanoise, often enjoying wonderful views before dropping down to Modane (Day 15).

The **GR55 high-level route** offers a more exciting, remote and scenic experience. It parts company with the GR5 at Tignes-le-Lac (Day 11), climbing high through the wild heart of the Vanoise to reach Pralognan. From there, the route crosses the Col de Chavière, which is the highest point reached on any route in this guidebook. After crossing the col, the route descends and rejoins the GR5 on its way down through forests to Modane. This is quicker than the other two routes and saves two days; pick up the onward route description at Stage 4, Day 16.

The **GR5E low-level variant** can be joined at Bonneval-sur-Arc (main route, Day 12) and followed down through the Arc valley. This route, known as the Chemin du Petit Bonheur, leads from village to village following clear tracks. Walkers who have over-exerted themselves on the early stages of the GR5 might prefer this route, and it could prove useful if really bad weather rules out following either the GR5 or GR55. When the route reaches Modane, it rejoins the main GR5.

There are further options. Walkers can switch easily between the GR5 and GR5E at Bessans on Day 13. There is also a simple link between the GR5 and GR55 via the Refuge d'Entre Deux Eaux (see map on page 151).

GR5 Route – Landry to Modane

DAY 10
Landry to Refuge d'Entre-le-Lac (GR5)

Distance	18 or 21 kilometres (11 or 13 miles)
Total Ascent	1585 metres or 1950 metres (5000 or 6400 feet)
Total Descent	205 metres or 515 metres (675 or 1690 feet)
Time	5 hours 15 minutes or 6 hours 45 minutes
Map	3532 ET
Nature of Terrain	The main route is steeper and tougher than the variant from Landry. Good tracks are used later. Higher paths might be steep and rugged, or almost level and easy in places.
Food and Drink	Restaurants at Montchavin, Peisey, Nancroix, Pont Baudin, Les Lanches (*buvette*), Chalet-Refuge de Rosuel and Refuge d'Entre-le-Lac.
Accommodation	Hotels at Montchavin. Hotels and *chambres d'hôte* at Peisey. *Gîte* and campsite near Pont Baudin. Chalet-refuge de Rosuel and Refuge d'Entre-le-Lac.

Initially there are two routes – the main GR5 route from Pont de Bellentre is steep and tough in places, while the variant from Landry is easier, suiting walkers who arrive by train to complete this stage. Both combine at Moulin to continue up through a valley. Some walkers might spend time exploring villages and stay at the Chalet-Refuge de Rosuel. Strong walkers might climb to the Refuge du Col du Palet (Day 11). In between, a short detour leads to the Refuge d'Entre-le-Lac.

Pont de Bellentre to Moulin
From Pont de Bellentre climb straight uphill from the bridge (for map see page 103), following a track up a wooded slope. Short-cut the bendy track as marked, and do the same when a road bend is reached. The path climbs steeply and

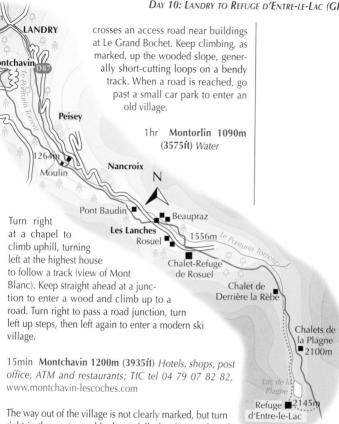

crosses an access road near buildings at Le Grand Bochet. Keep climbing, as marked, up the wooded slope, generally short-cutting loops on a bendy track. When a road is reached, go past a small car park to enter an old village.

1hr **Montorlin 1090m (3575ft)** *Water*

Turn right at a chapel to climb uphill, turning left at the highest house to follow a track (view of Mont Blanc). Keep straight ahead at a junction to enter a wood and climb up to a road. Turn right to pass a road junction, turn left up steps, then left again to enter a modern ski village.

15min **Montchavin 1200m (3935ft)** *Hotels, shops, post office, ATM and restaurants; TIC tel 04 79 07 82 82, www.montchavin-lescoches.com*

The way out of the village is not clearly marked, but turn right in the centre and look carefully for signs and markers. Climb up a stepped street and continue straight up a well-worn path on a grassy slope to leave the village. The path is signposted 'tennis', and once a tennis court is reached, turn left above it. Climb to a road, cross over, then continue up a track through larch forest. Keep climbing along the clearest track, first avoiding a track up to the right, then later avoiding one down to the left, to reach another junction.

30min **La Jacottaz 1500m (4920ft)**

Turn left up a track signposted for Peisey-Nancroix. It levels out briefly under the cables carrying the **Vanoise Express** across the valley. Turn left along a path that undulates across a forested slope (where there are brief glimpses of Peisey, Moulin and Nancroix). Afterwards, it drops in steep and greasy zigzags as it negotiates breaches in rugged cliffs. Hands need to be used, but there is little sense of exposure because of the trees nearby, and one final part is protected with a cable. The path drops to a track near the confluence of two mountain rivers, the Nant Benin Ruisseau and **Ponturin Torrent**. The latter is followed upstream, passing old mill buildings to reach a bridge.

1hr **Moulin 1264m (4147ft)** *Road access to Peisey in 15min for hotels, chambres d'hôte, shops, post office, free bus to Landry and Rosuel; Parc National de la Vanoise information, tel 04 79 62 30 54; TIC tel 04 79 07 88 67; www.peisey-vallandry.com*

VARIANT ROUTE

Landry to Moulin

If starting from **Landry**, leave the centre of the town to follow the road signposted for Peisey-Nancroix, crossing the **Ponturin Torrent**. Follow a path upstream beside the river, rejoining the road. Walk up the road past Les Primaz to find the GR5 on the left. Walk up a track through woods, crossing a stream and the road again at Pont de Chardonnet, at 870m (2855ft). Continue up the path to a higher stretch of road. Turn right, but leave the road at the next hairpin bend.

Follow a track to the right, but almost immediately climb a path to the left and keep climbing. The path is later barred, so turn left and climb steeply to the road again. Turn right to follow it, then later right again to follow a clear track. Continue straight up the Route des Mauilles to reach a road junction at a chapel. (Road access to Peisey in 10min.) Turn right as signposted, then keep left of the Place des Quatre Zoé, and the Route du Vieux Moulin leads to a bridge.

1hr 30min **Moulin 1264m (4147ft)**

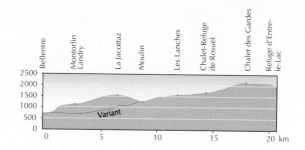

Continue upstream along the track. This is rough and stony in places, climbing steeply at times. Join another track and turn left to walk down to Le Pont Romane (access to **Nancroix** for restaurant and free bus to Peisey and Rosuel). Continue up the track to reach a campsite and sporting area as tarmac appears (*gîte d'étape* and restaurant at end of road). The GR5 steps up to the right to continue, crossing a stream and following a forest track to a large building.

40min **Palais de la Mine 1500m (4920ft)**

Palais de la Mine

L'École Française des Mines was created in Paris in 1783, to regulate the mining industry and to train workers in all aspects of mining. The Corps des Mines was instituted in 1784, consisting of uniformed mining engineers. The Palais de la Mine, now derelict, was the centre of an 18th–19th century lead- and silver-mining site. The ore veins ran through schist and quartzite beds in the mountains. The metal was largely destined for military use, and English and German miners were employed where specialist knowledge was needed.

Pass below the building, then turn right up another track, crossing two rivers using bridges close together. Walk down to a road and turn quickly right and left, then right again at **Les Lanches**, at 1520m (4987ft) (*buvette*). Follow a track past lovely little houses, then turn left to cross a bridge, and right to continue upstream. Follow the track towards farm buildings, enjoying a fine view of the higher valley. Turn right to cross the river to reach a car park and road, then turn left to reach a *refuge*.

20min Chalet-Refuge de Rosuel 1556m (5105ft) *Refuge and restaurant; Parc National de la Vanoise information; free bus to Peisey and Landry; bearded vultures nest nearby*

Just past the *refuge*, turn right along a track, and right again along a path. Pass larches, then climb gently across a flowery slope and continue through tree scrub. Cross a streambed and traverse another open slope, then follow the path up through more extensive tree scrub. Pass beneath a frowning cliff of schist, then the gradient eases among larches, and views stretch back along the valley and up to nearby peaks, while slender cascades pour down the mountainsides. Climb more steeply, and the gradient eases again near a little chalet. Climb again past ice-smoothed gneiss bedrock, on which masses of limestone boulders lie. Cross a stream and head for a signpost.

Direct approach to Refuge d'Entre-le-Lac available from here – see page 113.

1hr 45min Path junction 2050m (6725ft) ◂
Turn left to stay on the GR5, climbing at a gentle gradient on a rugged, boulder-strewn slope. Cross a footbridge over a stream and keep climbing, levelling out on even more boulders (where the Parc National de la Vanoise is entered). Enjoy all-round mountain views, noting the glaciated dome of La Grande Motte, which will be seen over successive days. Boulder-hopping gives way to a cattle-grazed *alpage*, with a farm beyond.

30min Chalets de la Plagne 2100m (6890ft)

Keep right of the chalets to climb round a rocky rib, then climb more gently past the Chalet des Gardes, at 2220m (7283ft), on the **Rocher des Mindières**. There are splendid views down to Lac de la Plagne beneath the cliffs of Mont Blanc de Peisey. The path climbs gently and briefly levels out at a junction.

25min Path junction 2300m (7545ft)

Turn right to leave the GR5 and follow a clear path down across a grassy, bouldery slope. There are fine views of Lac de la Plagne on the way down to the Refuge d'Entre-le-Lac.

15min Refuge d'Entre-le-Lac 2155m (7070ft) *Refuge and restaurant*

Variant Route

Direct approach to Refuge d'Entre-le-Lac

At the path junction at 2050m, turn right at the signpost, as indicated for the Refuge d'Entre-le-Lac, following a bouldery path gently uphill. The route runs upstream beside a river that winds through lush grasslands, with occasional waterfalls. Eventually the path climbs to **Lac de la Plagne**, popular with walkers and fishermen. Although easy at first, the path becomes more difficult while it weaves through massive boulder-scree. Cross a footbridge and stony ground to reach the *refuge*, which overlooks a sloping grassy delta.

1hr Refuge d'Entre-le-Lac 2155m (7070ft) *Refuge and restaurant*

The Refuge d'Entre le Lac is close to a towering cliff and a fine little lake in the Parc National de la Vanoise

DAY 11
Refuge d'Entre-le-Lac to Val d'Isère (GR5)

Distance	19 kilometres (12 miles)
Total Ascent	875 metres (2870 feet)
Total Descent	1220 metres (4005 feet)
Time	5 hours 15 minutes
Maps	3532 ET and 3633 ET
Nature of Terrain	Mostly gently graded ascents and descents, with some short, steep stretches. Good mountain paths with forest paths towards the end.
Food and Drink	Refuge du Col du Palet. Plenty at Tignes-le-Lac and Val d'Isère.
Accommodation	Refuge du Col du Palet. Hotels at Tignes-le-Lac. Hotels and campsite at Val d'Isère.

On today's walk, enjoy crossing the Col du Palet, then make haste through the bizarre high-rise ski development of Tignes-le-Lac. Although every service is available, most walkers prefer to put the town behind them. The GR5 crosses an easy shoulder, offering one last chance to look back at receding Mont Blanc, then drops down to Val d'Isère. This is another ski town that continues to expand apace, but it avoids the worst excesses of Tignes.

Leave the *refuge* and follow the signposted path back uphill, across the slope of grass and boulders, to get straight back onto the GR5.

25min **Path junction 2300m (7545ft)**

Turn right to follow the GR5, looking ahead to spot the white dome of La Grande Motte. Keep to the right of grassy **Plan de la Grassaz**, away from a little stone chalet, and look out for marmots. Cross a streambed and climb more steeply, crossing the outflow and inflow of **Lac de Grattaleu.** Either

keep to the GR5 up to a col, or head left to follow another path, making a short detour to a *refuge*.

1hr 30min **Refuge du Col du Palet 2600m (8530ft)** *Refuge and restaurant*

Leave the *refuge* and either climb straight up a path, or take a slightly longer, easier track uphill. Both cross a high col

Cotton grass grows on the level wet ground close to the shore of Lac de Grattaleu

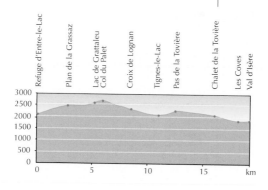

that may be flanked by snow
patches late into summer.

5min **Col du Palet
2652m (8701ft)** *Views
of nearby glaciated
peaks; exit the Parc
National de la Vanoise*

The geology around the
Col du Palet is quite
mixed. On the ascent the
underlying rock is a mixture of
limestone and schist. On the
col itself, both can be found,
while nearby grey, crumbling
humps are rich in gypsum. On the way
downhill, the limestone is dolomitic and
full of tiny holes. Pass a couple of *dolines*,
or solution hollows, one of which contains a
small pool. When a track is reached, climb a
short way up it and go under a *télésiège*, then follow a path
further downhill to a *télésiège* station.

30min **Tichot Télésiège 2468m (8097ft)**

Keep left of the *télésiège* and follow a path across a track.
The Tignes and Val Claret conurbations are evident below,
and seem quite incongruous so close to a national park.
After passing tall poles stuck into the mountainside the route
reaches a viewpoint.

15min **Croix de Lognan 2300m (7545ft)** ◄

Follow the GR5 down into a little valley, the **Combe des
Militaires**. Reach a junction of paths where a left turn is the
GR5 to Tignes-le-Lac. ◄ Follow the path across a track and
zigzag down to a busy road. Cross the road to reach the
shore of **Lac de Tignes** and turn left to follow a lakeshore
path towards town. (The GR55 runs to Val Claret.)

30min **Tignes-le-Lac 2093m (6867ft)** *All services*

The short-cut to the
southern side of Val
Claret links with the
GR55 (for GR55 see
page 141).

The right turn links
with the GR55 at
Val Claret.

2100m
■Chalets de
la Plagne

*Lac de la
Plagne*

■2145m
Refuge
d'Entre-le-Lac

*Plan de
la Grassaz*

*Pointe du
Chardonnet*
▲ 287

*Lac de
Grattaleu*
2550m
Refuge d.
■Col du Pa

2652m
Col du Palet

▲ *Aiguille
de Pran*
2977m

Tignes-le-Lac

This Benidorm-like resort thrives on the fact that it can offer all-year-round skiing, courtesy of the Glacier de la Grande Motte. In the summer months it sells itself as a sporting and family resort. Surprisingly, much of the land nearby is designated as the Réserve Naturelle de la Tignes-Champagny,

and presumably this limits further destruction. A full range of services is available in town, and at nearby Val Claret, with a free bus, or *navette gratuite,* linking both sites. Transdev buses link with Val d'Isère and Bourg St Maurice, tel 04 79 07 04 49, www.altibus.com. TIC tel 04 79 40 04 40, www.tignes.net.

Cross the outflow of the lake and follow a track, watching for red/white markers on *télésiège* supports. Keep off the road and follow the track as it bends left. Continue as marked up a path that crosses a long ridge of rubbly moraine. Watch carefully for markers as the path climbs in a huge zigzag, then proceed over a rough and bouldery slope.

30min **Pas de la Tovière 2252m (7388ft)** *Last view of Mont Blanc*

Walk downhill and keep left of a concrete hut. The land nearby is occasionally used as a landing strip by a local aero club. Signs advise if flights are in progress, but stick to the marked path anyway. A track leads down smooth grassy slopes with a view of Val d'Isère and the mountains flanking

The bouldery slopes of Pas de la Tovière, between Tignes-le-Lac and Val d'Isère

Col de l'Iseran. Zigzag down into larch forest to cross a footbridge. Watch for yellow signs and red/white markers, as there are many other paths and tracks.

Apart from climbing a short way up a track, the route generally runs downhill, and passes an area where springs burst from limestone on the forest floor. When a track is reached, don't follow it, but turn left down a winding path, through a grassy clearing and alongside a hydroelectric station. Cross a bridge over a river and turn right along the main road into the town centre.

1hr 30min **Val d'Isère 1809m (5935ft)** *All services*

Val d'Isère

This is a high-rise ski development, though there are a few old stone buildings near the church. Most GR5 walkers don't visit the roundabout in the middle of the main road in the town centre – those who do will find an announcement that this is the middle of the Grand Traversée des Alpes from Thonon-les-Bains to Menton! Free buses, or *navettes gratuite,* serve different parts of Val d'Isère. Each bus, known as a *train,* is colour-coded as follows: *train rouge* serves Le Fornet and La Daille, *train bleu* serves La Legettaz, *train vert* serves Parc des Sports du Manchet. Transdev buses run to and from Val d'Isère and Bourg St Maurice, tel 04 79 07 04 49, www.altibus.com. From Bourg St Maurice, trains run to Paris and Lyon via Chambéry. TIC tel 04 79 06 06 60, www.valdisere.com.

DAY 12
Val d'Isère to Bessans (GR5)

Distance	25 kilometres (15½ miles)
Total Ascent	1360 metres (4460 feet)
Total Descent	1460 metres (4790 feet)
Time	7 hours 30 minutes
Map	3633 ET
Nature of Terrain	Steep climbing gives way to gentler gradients on the Col de l'Iseran. A steep and rocky descent is followed by a climb to a *balcon* path before a track and rugged path lead down into a valley.
Food and Drink	Restaurant at Col de l'Iseran. Plenty off-route at Bonneval-sur-Arc and at Bessans.
Accommodation	Hotels, *chambres d'hôte* and *refuge* off-route at Bonneval-sur-Arc. Possible *alpage* lodging at Le Vallon. *Gîte* off-route at Le Villaron. Hotels and *gîte* at Bessans.

The road over the Col de l'Iseran was built in 1937 and is one of the highest in France. The old highway survives as a path and the GR5 follows it. The road has to be crossed several times, but little of it is followed. The top of the Col de l'Iseran is the highest point gained on the GR5, and it is often very busy. The descent can include Bonneval-sur-Arc (linking with the GR5E low-level variant), but the main route enjoys a fine *balcon* path before descending to Bessans.

The old church in **Val d'Isère** has a stone steeple, making a fine landmark, and there is a GR5 marker on its wall, indicating a quiet road from the town centre. Walk up the road and branch right along a stone-paved path. Continue up another road and watch for markers showing the way to a field path that runs above a campsite. Pass between buildings at **Le Laisinant,** then head right up a track to pass a building called Les Mélèzes. Watch for markers while passing under a *télésiège* and crossing a stream, being sure to follow a path zigzagging up into a forest, and not some other path. Climb across a ski piste a few times, then the trees thin out on flowery slopes. ◀

Here there is a view back to Val d'Isère and La Grande Motte.

2hr Main road 2310m (7580ft)

Turn left to find the continuation of the path a few paces down the road. Climb again to cross the **Ruisseau de l'Iseran**, which may contain snow into summer. Keep climbing and join a track, crossing the stream at a higher level. Leave the track to follow a path up to the main road. Turn left to walk up the road to a bend, then find the path climbing again. Every time the road is encountered, the path will be found on the other side, eventually reaching a stone hut (shelter). Just beyond is the top of the col.

1hr 30min Col de l'Iseran 2770m (9088ft) *Restaurant, gift shop, possible sweet stall; highest point on the GR5; views of glaciated peaks on the Franco–Italian border*

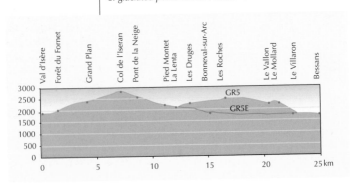

Waterfalls tumble down from Pont de la Neige into the Vallon de la Lenta

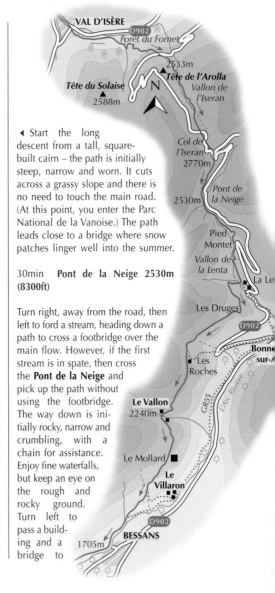

Apart from the former chalet–hotel building on the col, there is a stout little church, Notre Dame de Toute Prudence.

◄ Start the long descent from a tall, square-built cairn – the path is initially steep, narrow and worn. It cuts across a grassy slope and there is no need to touch the main road. (At this point, you enter the Parc National de la Vanoise.) The path leads close to a bridge where snow patches linger well into the summer.

30min **Pont de la Neige 2530m (8300ft)**

Turn right, away from the road, then left to ford a stream, heading down a path to cross a footbridge over the main flow. However, if the first stream is in spate, then cross the **Pont de la Neige** and pick up the path without using the footbridge. The way down is initially rocky, narrow and crumbling, with a chain for assistance. Enjoy fine waterfalls, but keep an eye on the rough and rocky ground. Turn left to pass a building and a bridge to reach a road bend at **Pied Montet**, at 2274m (7461ft). Step onto the road, but look for the path dropping down again, passing bigger waterfalls. One area of smooth outcrops has a boulder-paved path, then a track leads past small farms.

45min **La Lenta 2143m (7031ft)** ▶

Turn right to cross a bridge over the Ruisseau de la Lenta and follow a track uphill. Look out for views of hanging glaciers on the Franco–Italian frontier. Keep right at a track junction at Les Druges, at 2260m (7415ft), then turn left shortly afterwards up a narrow path. This climbs steeply at times up a grassy, flowery slope, offering splendid views of the Arc valley. A few streams have to be crossed, and the more vigorous ones may feature wobbly plank footbridges. Climb to a path junction.

Option to descend to Bonneval-sur-Arc and link with the GR5E low-level route – see page 124. The GR5E route description starts on page 157.

1hr **Les Roches 2440m (8005ft)** ▶

Climb a little to pass a couple of small stone cabins and pass a couple of small pools – if they haven't dried in a hot spell. Reach another cabin and follow the path as it winds down into a valley.

Path off-route to Bonneval-sur-Arc and link with the GR5E in 1hr 15min

45min **Le Vallon 2240m (7350ft)** *Possible alpage lodging*

Small pools of water are passed between Les Roches and Le Vallon, high above Bonneval-sur-Arc

Cattle and sheep graze around **Le Vallon**, which is watered by cascades and has patches of snow lingering through the summer. Cross a bridge and follow an undulating track. Look left later to catch a glimpse of the Chalet des Gardes before passing the ruins of **Le Mollard**. Bessans is in view, but don't follow the track all the way downhill, as it actually runs to Villaron. Go down a track on the left, but leave it to follow a path, which is actually the old way to Bessans. Watch carefully for the old path short-cutting loops on the modern track, as there are few markers. Be sure to spot the last stretch of the old path, leaving a bend and making a beeline for Bessans. ◀ Pass below a cliff to land on a track.

Here you exit the Parc National de la Vanoise.

45min Ruisseau du Pis 1720m (5645ft) *Junction of GR5 and GR5E*

Most walkers will visit the village on the other side.

Turn right and follow the track along **L'Arc Rivière**. This reaches a bridge that the GR5E (but not the GR5) crosses. ◀

15min Bessans 1710m (5610ft) *All services except bank; Transdev buses to Bonneval and Modane; TIC tel 04 79 05 96 52*

VARIANT ROUTE

Link from La Lenta to Bonneval-sur-Arc for the GR5E Low-level Route

Leave the GR5 at **La Lenta** and head for a road bridge. Cross the bridge and follow the road, watching for a path marked down to the left. This is good as far as a concrete hut, then drops in steep and rugged zigzags. Little gates near the bottom lead onto a track and road, winding down past houses to reach the main road just above the *office de tourisme* at **Tralenta**, close to **Bonneval-sur-Arc**.

1hr Tralenta/Bonneval-sur-Arc 1808m (5932ft) *Hotels, chambres d'hôte, refuge, shops, post office and restaurants; morning bus to La Lenta, avoiding need to climb back uphill; Transdev buses to Bessans and Modane, tel 04 79 05 01 32, www.altibus.com; TIC tel 04 79 05 95 95*

DAY 13
Bessans to Refuge du Plan du Lac (GR5)

Distance	30 kilometres (18½ miles)
Total Ascent	1430 metres (4690 feet)
Total Descent	775 metres (2545 feet)
Time	9 hours 15 minutes
Map	3633 ET
Nature of Terrain	Some steep climbs, but mostly gentle gradients along a *balcon* path overlooking the valley.
Food and Drink	Refuge de Vallonbrun and Refuge du Plan du Lac.
Accommodation	Refuge de Vallonbrun, Refuge du Cuchet (unstaffed) and Refuge du Plan du Lac.

After an easy stroll beside L'Arc Rivière, the GR5 climbs back into the mountains. A splendid *balcon* path runs just inside the Parc National de la Vanoise, from the Refuge de Vallonbrun to the Refuge du Cuchet. Fine views take in the peaks along the Franco–Italian frontier, with a peep through the Col du Mont Cenis. The route starts making a long traverse round the deep and rocky gorge of the Doron, penetrating into the heart of the Vanoise.

Leave **Bessans** by crossing the bridge over **L'Arc Rivière**, turning left to follow a track downstream. Turn right at a junction, rising slightly and pulling away from the river to walk between fields. Pass the **Chapelle St Maurice** and head down to a main road.

1hr **Le Chalp 1700m (5575ft)** *Nearby campsite*

Turn right to follow the main road, but as it swings left, watch for a small cairn and marker on the right, which are easily missed. A narrow path rises through woods and continues along an overgrown ridge of rubble, rising through fields to houses and an old chapel.

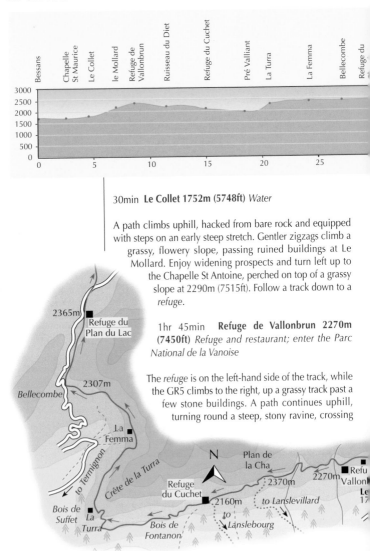

30min **Le Collet 1752m (5748ft)** *Water*

A path climbs uphill, hacked from bare rock and equipped with steps on an early steep stretch. Gentler zigzags climb a grassy, flowery slope, passing ruined buildings at Le Mollard. Enjoy widening prospects and turn left up to the Chapelle St Antoine, perched on top of a grassy slope at 2290m (7515ft). Follow a track down to a *refuge*.

1hr 45min **Refuge de Vallonbrun 2270m (7450ft)** *Refuge and restaurant; enter the Parc National de la Vanoise*

The *refuge* is on the left-hand side of the track, while the GR5 climbs to the right, up a grassy track past a few stone buildings. A path continues uphill, turning round a steep, stony ravine, crossing

the Ruisseau de Burel. Climb parallel to a track, then cross it to follow a signposted path round a ridge of stony moraine to enter a valley.

The Refuge de Vallonbrun sits on a grassy terrace high above the Arc valley

45min Plan de la Cha 2370m (7775ft)

Cross the Ruisseau du Diet and follow the path onwards to reach a junction. (Path off-route to Lanslevillard in 1hr 30min.) The slope steepens, is rugged in places and is grazed by cattle. The path drops and eventually reaches a *refuge* on a scenic perch.

1hr 15min Refuge du Cuchet 2160m (7085ft) *Unstaffed* refuge *with kitchen; if staying, bring your own food supplies; if using water, note the instructions on the purifying system; path off-route to Lanslebourg in 1hr 30min*

127

Don't follow the steep path downhill, but walk along a gentler path, passing well to the right of a couple of chalets. Join a track and turn right to follow it, looping down past a couple more buildings on the way to a forest, the **Bois de Fontanon**. Continue down to a junction with another track.

45min **Pré Valliant 1920m (6300ft)**

Turn right, not up the track, but up a path instead. Turn right at a junction further uphill, and zigzag from the forest onto flowery slopes where the trees thin out and juniper creeps across the ground. Climb round a rocky edge and pass above three little chalets.

1hr **La Turra 2290m (7515ft)** *View of glaciated peaks around the Doron in the heart of the Vanoise*

Follow the path onwards as marked, dropping downhill a little, then climbing easily, keeping above a couple of little dairy farms to reach **La Femma**. Follow a track uphill a little, then downhill past a couple more farms, to reach a road and car park.

1hr 45min **Bellecombe 2307m (7569ft)** *Transdev shuttle-bus to and from Entre Deux Eaux*

Follow a clear path uphill, parallel to the road, but on the other side of a limestone ravine. Pass beside a small lake, and if the air is still, enjoy the mountains reflected in the water. There are magnificent views as the path proceeds across the grassy **Plan du Lac** to reach a *refuge*.

30min **Refuge du Plan du Lac 2365m (7760ft)** *Refuge and restaurant; Parc National de la Vanoise information; Transdev shuttle-bus to Bellecombe and Entre Deux Eaux, as well as early bus from Modane and Termignon, and late bus to Termignon and Modane, tel 04 79 05 01 32, www.altibus.com*

DAY 14

Refuge du Plan du Lac to
Le Montana (GR5)

Distance	31 kilometres (19 miles)
Total Ascent	1305 metres (4280 feet)
Total Descent	1520 metres (4985 feet)
Time	10 hours
Maps	3633 ET and 3534 OT
Nature of Terrain	After crossing a deep valley, a succession of ascents and descents leads across high, boulder-strewn slopes. Later, a fine *balcon* path offers easier walking.
Food and Drink	Off-route at Entre Deux Eaux. Also Refuge de l'Arpont and Le Montana, but note the gap between them.
Accommodation	Refuge d'Entre Deux Eaux and a *gîte d'alpage* lie off-route. Refuge de l'Arpont is halfway through the day. Le Montana and nearby Refuge de Plan Sec are at the end of the day.

This is a long and hard day's walk. Anyone who feels it is too much should break at the Refuge de l'Arpont and cover the distance in two easier days. There are often views of glaciers during the day, and the middle part of the route is surprisingly high. Bear in mind that while paths may be rough and stony at first, traversing high above the Doron, they are much easier later in the day, especially the *balcon* path overlooking the Arc valley.

Leave the **Refuge du Plan du Lac** by walking downhill, roughly parallel to a road. Cross the road beside the **Chapelle St Barthélémy** and walk down a path, crossing a band of quartzite. ▶ The path winds downhill to rejoin the road.

This band of quartzite is prominent and is seen again across the valley.

129

30min **La Renaudière 2045m (6710ft)** *Transdev shuttle-bus to and from Bellecombe, with early and late buses to and from Termignon and Modane; Refuge d'Entre Deux Eaux 15min off-route*

Turn left down the road to cross bridges over two rivers at **Entre Deux Eaux**. There is a *gîte d'alpage* 10min off-route; water drawn from the rivers runs through a tunnel to a reservoir at Plan d'Aval. Follow a track past the Chalets de l'Ile at 2000m (6560ft). Turn left after passing the last building to follow a vague path, as signposted. Pick up and follow a grassy track, zigzagging up a flowery slope with great views of the surrounding mountains. Pass a couple of ruins and avoid a track to the farm of La Para. Eventually a signpost and a path junction are reached.

1hr **Mont de la Para 2300m (7545ft)**
Turn left and keep climbing. Although the bedrock is schist, the mountainside is covered in quartzite fallen from the prominent band above. After passing one huge boulder, quartzite blocks are aligned beside the path. Eventually the path levels out on a boulder-strewn slope, crossing a couple of slight dips. Curiously banded limestone boulders have fallen from an unstable band further uphill. Spend a while gazing at the reflections of mountains in a group of little lakes.

1hr **Lacs des Lozières 2475m (8120ft)** *The lakes fill ice-scooped hollows in the hummocky schist bedrock, and are*

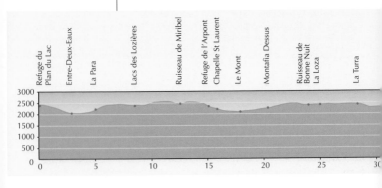

overlooked by the dark peak of Roche Ferran and the glaciated Dôme de Chasseforêt

Cross a stream and follow the path across glacial moraine made largely of quartzite ripped from the valley side. Cross a bridge over a milky glacial stream and follow the path as it winds up a huge tongue of bouldery moraine, this time largely limestone. Climb from the moraine to see the glacier high above. The path turns a corner overlooking a sheep-grazed *alpage*. Further along, the schist bedrock is covered in masses of limestone boulders fallen from a peak above. Follow the path across the mountainside, then cross a broad valley full of slabs and angular boulders.

1hr Ruisseau de Miribel 2530m (8300ft)

The many streams forming the **Ruisseau de Miribel** must be forded, and while gradients are gentle, the going is slow – follow cairns where the line of the path is unclear. After climbing to 2589m (8494ft) the path crosses a rocky slope where *bouquetin* may be seen. ▶ The path eventually descends more steeply and a *refuge* suddenly comes into view, possibly with marmots nearby.

There is a view down the gorge to Termignon, and through the Col du Mont Cenis into Italy.

1hr Refuge de l'Arpont 2309m (7575ft) *Refuge and restaurant*

Follow the path down from the *refuge*, walking on bare schist at times, passing the **Chapelle St Laurent** and old farm buildings. The path crosses streams and passes below a waterfall (some path sections are held in place by girders). Pass through alder scrub woodland, then descend to some ruined buildings.

Path off-route to Termignon in 1hr 30min (for information on Termignon see page 163).

1hr Le Mont 2090m (6857ft) ▶
Climb uphill to cross a rocky ravine, where a very narrow cleft has been plugged with rock to make a footbridge. Zigzag further uphill, then the path runs almost level for a while. There are views of glaciated peaks on almost all sides. The path zigzags down to a solitary building.

Path off-route to Termignon in 1hr 30min

45min Montafia Dessus 2190m (7185ft) ▶

A walker above Montafia, with cloud filling the deep and rocky gorge of the Doron

The GR5 runs downhill and uphill, still on schist, crossing streams before zigzagging up a steep slope to run at a gentler gradient. A fine *balcon* path crosses a vast sandstone scree overlooking Termignon. Reach a junction of paths at 2350m (7710ft), then climb a little to reach a crumbling building and a modern hut.

1hr 45min La Loza 2360m (7743ft) *Path off-route to Sardières in 1hr 30min*

A delightful level grassy track gives way to a gentle climb up across a steep, grassy, sheep-grazed slope overlooking Bramans. The track turns round a huge limestone ravine overlooked by a crumbling rock tower. Sweeping zigzags lead down a steep grassy slope to a grassy col and signpost.

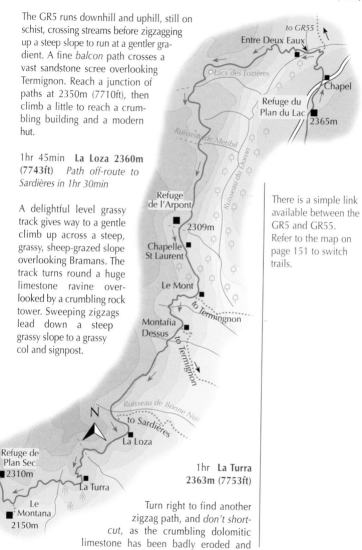

There is a simple link available between the GR5 and GR55. Refer to the map on page 151 to switch trails.

1hr La Turra 2363m (7753ft)

Turn right to find another zigzag path, and *don't short-cut*, as the crumbling dolomitic limestone has been badly eroded and required expensive work to stabilise it. Keep straight ahead at a path junction and follow tight, gravelly zigzags down to a streambed. Cross over and continue along a narrow terrace path, roughly contouring across a steep and grassy slope (exiting the Parc National de la Vanoise) to reach a *télésiège*. Turn left downhill to reach **Le Montana**, or keep straight ahead along the GR5, or follow signs for nearby Refuge de Plan Sec.

1hr **Le Montana 2150m (7055ft)** *Hotel/refuge and restaurant; télésiège link with Aussois for all services; TIC tel 04 79 20 30 80,* www.aussois.co

Tiny walkers follow the GR5 near Le Montana, while dense cloud fills the Arc valley below them

DAY 15
Le Montana to Modane/Fourneaux (GR5)

Distance	21 kilometres (13 miles)
Total Ascent	625 metres (2050 feet)
Total Descent	1675 metres (5495 feet)
Time	7 hours
Map	3534 OT
Nature of Terrain	Good tracks and rugged paths across high, rugged slopes. A long descent through forest, ending with a steep and rugged path and urban road-walking.
Food and Drink	Refuge de Plan Sec, Refuge de la Fournache, Refuge de l'Aiguille Doran, Refuge de l'Orgère and Chalet d'Alpage de Polset are all slightly off-route.
Accommodation	Refuge de Plan Sec, Refuge de la Fournache, Refuge de l'Aiguille Doran, Refuge de l'Orgère and Chalet d'Alpage de Polset are all slightly off-route. Hotels and campsite at Fourneaux, near Modane.

The GR5 finally descends from the Parc National de la Vanoise to Modane. First there is a rugged circuit round a side-valley containing two hydroelectric reservoirs, then a fine *balcon* path offers a bird's-eye view of Modane. A long, convoluted, forested descent is endured before the town is reached. Few walkers have a kind word to say about Modane, and it is by no means a 'tourist' town, but it provides all necessary services in a business-like manner.

If the night was spent at **Le Montana**, then retrace steps back up to the GR5 and turn left. Pass a signposted path junction to reach a junction of two tracks. Cross the first of these and follow the other one gradually up into a valley, with a fine view down to a reservoir. A path up to the right allows a visit to a *refuge*.

The GR5 makes a high-level circuit around the hydroelectric reservoir of Plan d'Amont

20min **Refuge de Plan Sec 2310m (7580ft)** *Refuge and restaurant*

The track eventually leads through a cutting in the quartzite bedrock. Leave it at this point to go down a path on the left to cross a stream. Climb a little and cross another stream, then there is an option to visit another *refuge*.

20min **Refuge de la Fournache 2390m (7840ft)** *Refuge and restaurant*

The GR5 heads down a path, crossing schist bedrock. Keep left at a path junction (the right turn leads off-route up to the Refuge de la Parrachée in 30min). The path enjoys good views of the reservoir and leads down to a bridge, which should be crossed.

20min **Pont de la Sétéria 2206m (7238ft)** *Enter the Parc National de la Vanoise; dirt road off-route to Aussois in 1hr 45min*

Head straight up a winding path on flaky schist bedrock, with great views back to the Dent Parrachée. The path eventually levels out at a junction and signpost. Turn left to descend, then climb gently across a boulder-strewn area where alpen-rose gives way to *myrtille* cover. There are fine views down to both reservoirs and the village of Aussois, then the path zig-zags down a steeper slope before dropping more gently. A gradual ascent crosses slopes of creeping juniper and ankle-twisting quartzite blocks to reach a signpost.

1hr 30min **Col du Barbier 2287m (7503ft)**

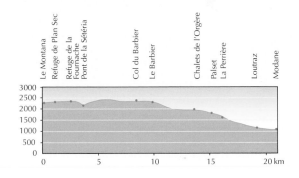

Walkers enjoy an easy balcon path above the Arc valley before a long and convoluted descent

The signpost stands short of the col, but a gentle ascent leads across. The path climbs again, passing a ruin and sheds, then keeps below a new house, and later passes an old building at Le Barbier. A splendid *balcon* path overlooks Modane. The view across the valley is to Valfréjus, Mont Thabor and Col de la Vallée Étroite. Zigzag down through forest (possible water) and follow the path across boulder-scree, where a sign advises against stopping. The path later divides – either head left to the Refuge de l'Aiguille Doran, or right for the Refuge de l'Orgère. The GR5 climbs to the right, then follows a soft, pine-needle path to a few buildings (water) on an *alpage*. Follow a track round a grassy valley to a few chalets near a chapel. (Here you exit the Parc National de la Vanoise.)

Paths to the Refuge de l'Aiguille Doran or Refuge de l'Orgère in 10min

1hr 30min Chalets de l'Orgère 1895m (6217ft) ◄

Beyond the chapel, look for a marked and signposted path climbing into a forest. Contour across the slope, avoiding other paths, to emerge on a track in a clearing near a little house.

Steep and rugged forest short-cut down to Modane, saving 30min

30min Pierre Brune 1800m (5905ft) *Water* ◄

Turn right to find a signpost beside the track. The GR5 follows the track back up into the forest, crossing a road and climbing across chunky quartzite scree. There is a bird's-eye view of Modane, then the track descends gently through denser forest. Watch for a narrow path on the left, down across the forested slope and quartzite scree to land on a track in a charming stone-built hamlet.

30min **Polset 1840m (6035ft)** *Water* ▶

Detour off-route uphill for Chalet d'Alpage de Polset, *refuge* and restaurant

Turn left down a track, which loops down to a road, but which can be short-cut from a sharp right bend by keeping to the left-hand side of a house. Cross the road and walk down a track. The rock alongside is generally hard gneiss, and the track is often flanked by pines, but there are views. This is an old road, partly stone-paved, winding down past a few houses at La Perrière (possible water) before zigzagging down a steep forested slope. A track junction is reached.

1hr 15min **Track junction 1370m (4495ft)**

Continue downhill, and the pines eventually give way to deciduous trees, then the track swings right to cross a bridge over a stream. Turn

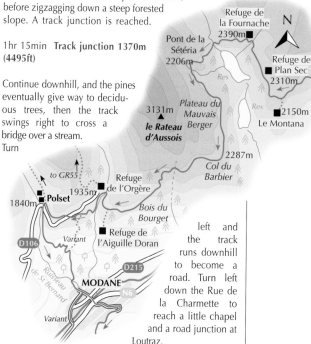

left and the track runs downhill to become a road. Turn left down the Rue de la Charmette to reach a little chapel and a road junction at Loutraz.

30min **Loutraz 1090m (3575ft)** *Signpost and variant routes*

A decision needs to be made: either walk *left* into the centre of Modane, or *right* to the railway station at Fourneaux. Both variants are waymarked, and don't meet again until Valfréjus (Stage 4, Day 16, page 174).

Left leads down the Rue des Chavières, through a staggered crossroads to cross a river. Note La Rizerie, a beautiful building on right. Go under a railway, then straight past a roundabout, then along the Rue Croix Blanche. This leads to the town hall (*hôtel de ville*) in the centre of **Modane**.

Right leads to a gymnasium, where a right turn leads along the Rue de la Vanoise. Continue down to a junction and turn right along the Avenue Emile Charvoz. Cross the Pont Emile Charvoz and turn right to follow the main road into **Fourneaux**.

10min **Modane 1070m (3510ft)**; 15min **Fourneaux 1050m (3445ft)** *All services*

Modane/Fourneaux

Not a 'classic' Alpine town, but a workaday settlement handling road and rail freight in and out of the tunnels between France and Italy. There are some interesting old buildings around town, and a full range of services. Those who start or finish a stage of the GR5 here find rapid access provided by trains to and from Lyon and Paris. Those who need accommodation, trains or tourist information centre should head for Fourneaux rather than Modane. Transdev buses run up the valley to serve many parts of the GR5E (the low-level variant that departs from the GR5 at Bonneval-sur-Arc), as well as a little-known service from the railway station to Entre Deux Eaux, offering a high-level link to both the GR5 and GR55; tel 04 79 05 01 32, www.altibus.com; TIC tel 04 79 05 28 58, www.terramodana.com.

To continue on the GR5, see Stage 4, Day 16, page 169.

DAY 11

Refuge d'Entre-le-Lac to
Refuge d'Entre Deux Eaux (GR55)

Distance	27 kilometres (17 miles)
Total Ascent	1205 metres (3955 feet)
Total Descent	1240 metres (4070 feet)
Time	8 hours 30 minutes
Maps	3532 ET and 3633 ET
Nature of Terrain	Fairly easy paths over high passes, unless covered by snow, in which case attention to route-finding is required.
Food and Drink	Refuge du Col du Palet. Plenty at Val Claret. Refuge de la Leisse. Refuge d'Entre Deux Eaux.
Accommodation	Refuge du Col du Palet. Hotels at Val Claret. Refuge de la Leisse. Refuge d'Entre Deux Eaux.

This alternative route through the Vanoise breaks away from the GR5 on Day 11 at Tignes-le-Lac, via Val Claret. Most of this day's walk is in the Parc National de la Vanoise, the exception being around Val Claret, where the urban intrusion is distracting, but there is an opportunity to stock up on provisions. The scenery is wonderful over the Col de la Leisse and down through the Vallon de la Leisse, but at this altitude snow lies well into summer. The heart of the national park is a wildlife haven, so keep an eye open for *bouquetin*, *chamois*, marmots and golden eagles.

Leave Refuge d'Entre-le-Lac and follow the signposted path back uphill, across the slope of grass and boulders, to get straight back onto the GR5.

25min **Path junction 2300m (7545ft)**

Turn right to follow the GR5, looking ahead to spot the white dome of La Grande Motte. Keep to the right of grassy **Plan de la Grassaz**, away from a little stone chalet, and look out for marmots. Cross a streambed and climb more steeply, crossing the outflow and inflow of **Lac de Grattaleu**. ◀ Either keep to the GR5 up to a col, or head left to follow another path, making a short detour to a *refuge*.

Nodding cotton grass grows along the wet shoreline.

1hr 30min **Refuge du Col du Palet 2600m (8530ft)** *Refuge and restaurant*

Leave the *refuge* and either climb straight up a path, or take a slightly longer, easier track uphill. Both cross a high col that may be flanked by snow patches late into summer.

5min **Col du Palet 2652m (8701ft)** *Views of nearby glaciated peaks; exit the Parc National de la Vanoise*

The geology around the **Col du Palet** is quite mixed. On the ascent the underlying rock is a mixture of limestone and schist. On the col itself, both can be found, while nearby, crumbling grey humps are rich in gypsum. On the way downhill, the limestone is dolomitic and full of tiny holes. Pass a couple of *dolines*, or solution hollows, one of which contains a small pool. When a track is reached, climb a short way up it and go under a *télésiège*, then follow a path

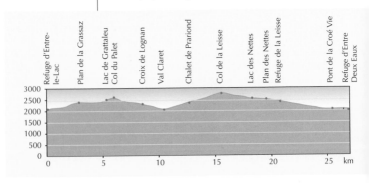

further downhill to a *télésiège* station.

30min Tichot Télésiège 2468m (8097ft)

Keep left of the *télésiège* and follow a path across a track. The Tignes and Val Claret conurbations are evident below and seem quite incongruous so close to a national park. After passing tall poles stuck into the mountainside the route reaches a viewpoint.

15min **Croix de Lognan 2300m (7545ft)** *Short-cut to the southern side of Val Claret links with the GR55*

Follow the GR5 down into a little valley, the **Combe des Militaires**. Reach a junction of paths where a right turn offers a short-cut to Val Claret and the GR55. Keep left, however, to follow the GR5 across a track and zigzag down to a busy road. Cross the road to reach the shore of **Lac de Tignes**, and turn right ▶ to follow a path, the GR55, to a roundabout on the outskirts of **Val Claret**.

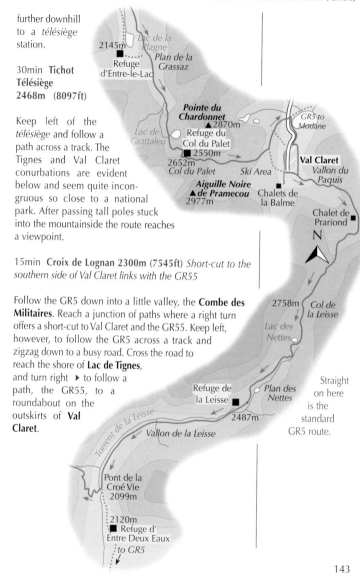

143

Walkers cross snow patches on their way from Val Claret to Col de la Leisse

30min **Val Claret 2100m (6890ft)** *All services*

Val Claret

This high-rise resort thrives on the fact that it can offer all-year-round skiing, courtesy of the Glacier de la Grande Motte. In the summer months it sells itself as a sporting and family resort. Surprisingly, much of the land nearby is designated as the Réserve Naturelle de la Tignes-Champagny, and presumably this limits further destruction. A full range of services is available in town, and at nearby Tignes-le-Lac, with a free bus, or *navette gratuite,* linking both sites. Transdev buses link with Val d'Isère and Bourg St Maurice, tel 04 79 07 04 49, www.altibus.com. TIC tel 04 79 40 04 40, www.tignes.net.

A road curves round the back of **Val Claret**, reaching the tourist information centre, or **Maison de Tignes**. Follow another road up round a bend, then watch carefully to spot a path rising uphill, marked for walkers. Follow the path under a *télésiège*, passing below the **Chalet du Bollin** (restaurant). Go under another *télésiège* and follow the pylons uphill as marked. As height is gained, urban views are lost.

A post bearing rules and regulations is reached (here you enter the Parc National de la Vanoise). The scenery is stunning and the marked path leads gradually uphill – La Grande Motte looks striking with its glacial cap. Snow patches lie well into the summer and may obscure the path, and as the col is broad and hummocky, it could be confusing in mist.

2hr **Col de la Leisse 2758m (9049ft)**

The path wanders through a bleak landscape and is marked by cairns. Lovely lakes come into view and the path stays well to the left of them, descending gently to the outflow of **Lac des Nettes**. The area is strewn with rubble, and only very lightly vegetated, sporting a few brave flowers. Cross a slight hump and head down into a grassier part of the valley. Keep to the right-hand side of a larger lake, crossing extensive scree. Pass

The GR55 crosses a scree slope beside a reservoir on its way down to the Refuge de la Leisse

a small dam and turn round a corner to see the next part of the valley. A *refuge* is reached in a charming situation.

1hr 30min Refuge de la Leisse 2487m (8159ft) *Refuge and restaurant*

The GR55 doubles back from the *refuge* to descend, winding downhill to cross a footbridge (also used by marmots!). There is only one path down through the grassy, boulder-strewn **Vallon de la Leisse**. Simply enjoy the grandeur of the place on a gradual descent to an arched stone bridge.

1hr 15min Pont de la Croé Vie 2099m (6886ft)

The GR55 crosses the bridge, but don't cross if accommodation is required. Instead, follow the path downstream to a couple of nearby lodgings. At a junction, either keep right for the Alpage Christine Richard (*dortoir* and restaurant), or keep left for the Refuge d'Entre Deux Eaux.

30min Refuge d'Entre Deux Eaux 2120m (6955ft) *Refuge and restaurant; 15min to link with GR5; Transdev shuttle-bus to Bellecombe and evening bus to Termignon and Modane, tel 04 79 05 01 32, www.altibus.com*

DAY 12
*Refuge d'Entre Deux Eaux to
Roc de la Pêche (GR55)*

Distance	24 kilometres (15 miles)
Total Ascent	950 metres (3115 feet)
Total Descent	1250 metres (4100 feet)
Time	6 hours 30 minutes
Maps	3532 ET and 3633 ET
Nature of Terrain	A relatively easy climb over a high mountain pass. A steep descent is followed by a long climb on clear tracks.
Food and Drink	Refuge de la Col de la Vanoise. Plenty at Pralognan. Restaurants at Les Prioux and Refuge du Roc de la Pêche.
Accommodation	Refuge de la Col de la Vanoise. Plenty at Pralognan. Refuge Le Repoju at Les Prioux and Refuge du Roc de la Pêche.

The Col de la Leisse and Col de la Vanoise have been used since the Bronze Age for passage though these high mountains. The traverse is wonderfully scenic, and for a high-level route, relatively easy, with *refuges* along the way. The descent from the Col de la Vanoise passes dramatic scenery and eventually leads to the little town of Pralognan. Good tracks lead back into the mountains by way of the Refuge du Roc de la Pêche.

Leave the **Refuge d'Entre Deux Eaux** and retrace steps back into the Vallon de la Leisse, to reach a path junction at an arched stone bridge.

30min **Pont de la Croé Vie 2099m (6886ft)**

Turn left and cross the bridge, then follow a zigzag path up a rough and rocky slope that is covered in patches of alpenrose

A walker crosses stepping stones over the Ruisseau de la Vanoise on the way to the Col de la Vanoise

and juniper. Look out for *bouquetin*, which frequent this area. Schist and quartzite will be noticed, and a path junction is reached at Voûte du Clapier Blanc, at 2300m (7545ft). Turn right to continue uphill, passing a monument to reach a blockhouse.

45min **Blockhouse 2439m (8002ft)**

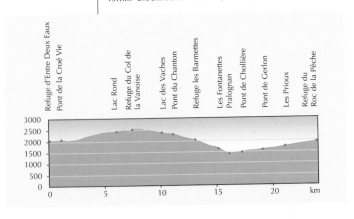

148

The path rises less steeply and soon runs almost level. Cross stepping stones over the **Ruisseau de la Vanoise** and enjoy an easy walk upstream. Pass one shallow lake after another, with views of soaring glaciated peaks all around. All of a sudden, after passing **Lac Rond**, a *refuge* comes into view.

1hr 15min **Refuge du Col de la Vanoise 2517m (8258ft)**
Refuge and restaurant (highest refuge in this guide)

Keep to the right-hand side of the *refuge*, picking up a rugged track and following it past **Lac Long**, admiring rock walls rising nearby. Turn left at a fork, where a short-cut avoids a bend in the track. The descent becomes quite stony and leads to a shallow lake.

30min **Lac des Vaches 2319m (7608ft)**

Walk straight through the middle of the lake using a rock-slab causeway. Descend further, either by following the track or short-cutting the bends when trodden paths allow (here exit the Parc National de la Vanoise). Either way, cross the **Pont du Chanton** over a stream, pausing to admire the mountains rising all round, then continue down past the

Looking back into the mountainous heart of the Vanoise from the Refuge les Barmettes

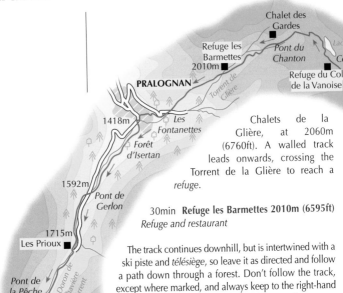

Chalets de la Glière, at 2060m (6760ft). A walled track leads onwards, crossing the Torrent de la Glière to reach a *refuge*.

30min **Refuge les Barmettes 2010m (6595ft)**
Refuge and restaurant

The track continues downhill, but is intertwined with a ski piste and *télésiège*, so leave it as directed and follow a path down through a forest. Don't follow the track, except where marked, and always keep to the right-hand side of the piste. Continue down to a car park.

45min **Les Fontanettes 1650m (5413ft)** *Restaurant*

Keep left of the restaurant, then left again down a rugged 'street' through **Les Fontanettes**. When a road bend is reached, avoid the first path on the left, which leads to the Cascade de la Fraîche, and take the second path down to the left. On the way down the forested slope it is worth stepping left as signposted for a *table d'orientation*, to enjoy a fine view from Rocher de la Fraîche (Pralognan is seen surrounded by mountains).

Zigzag downhill and pass a chapel at Les Bieux, then continue down to another chapel on the Place du Baroz. A hotel is reached further downhill, where the GR55 turns left, while **Pralognan** lies to the right.

30min **Pralognan-la-Vanoise 1418m (4652ft)** *All services; Transdev bus to Moûtiers for rail connections, tel 08 20 22 74 13; TIC 04 79 08 79 08,* www.pralognan.com

Take the left turn at the hotel to leave Pralognan, then turn right at the next junction to cross Dou des Ponts. Turn left as signposted for **Isertan**. Follow the tarmac road to its end and turn right along a track (although a slightly higher forest path could be followed instead). Walk either along the edge of a campsite, or just inside the forest. The track beside the campsite swings right, so turn left up a forest track, climbing beside the **Doron Chavière Torrent** to pass above the Pont de Chollière. The forest track climbs onwards, apart from one downhill stretch, and eventually reaches a car park. Turn right to cross a nearby bridge.

There is an obvious link between the GR55 and GR5. To switch to the GR5, pick up the route description on page 129.

45min **Pont de Gerlon 1592m (5223ft)**

Turn left to continue upstream along another track. Climb past a water intake at the Prise d'Eau de Chavière, where water is piped to a hydroelectric station. The track continues up to a stone-built hamlet.

20min **Les Prioux 1715m (5627ft)** *Refuge and restaurant*

Follow the track straight through to reach the river beyond, but don't cross it. Instead, follow a riverside path upstream to a footbridge, the Passerelle des Anciens, and cross at that point. Turn right to continue along a road to reach a car park. Follow a track onwards, then when it forks, keep right to cross a culvert bridge at **Pont de la Pêche**. Zigzag uphill, climbing steeply at times, until a crest is crossed. Turn left to pass a little chapel and reach a *refuge*.

40min **Refuge du Roc de la Pêche 1911m (6270ft)** *Refuge and restaurant*

DAY 13

Roc de la Pêche to
Modane/Fourneaux (GR55)

Distance	21 kilometres (13 miles)
Total Ascent	950 metres (3115 feet)
Total Descent	1750 metres (5775 feet)
Time	7 hours
Map	3633 ET
Nature of Terrain	A long track and rugged path lead to a high col. A descent from mountains to pasture gives way to forest and urban road-walking.
Food and Drink	*Buvette* at Alpage de Ritord. Restaurants at Refuge de Péclet-Polset and Chalet d'Alpage de Polset. Plenty at Modane/Fourneaux.
Accommodation	Refuge de Péclet-Polset. Chalet d'Alpage de Polset. Hotels and campsite at Fourneaux, near Modane.

The Col de Chavière is the highest point on the GR55 and features extensive views. The steep and stony slopes may be covered with extensive patches of snow, even late into summer. A gradual descent to Modane sees the mountainsides give way to pleasant pastures at Polset, then there is a steep and convoluted descent through forest. Modane has a full range of services and is an important transport hub in the Arc valley.

At Chavière you enter the Parc National de la Vanoise. Views of Péclet-Polset are lost, but an impressive saw-tooth range of peaks rises across the valley.

The track beyond the **Refuge du Roc de la Pêche** undulates across an *alpage*, with a view of the glaciated peak of Péclet-Polset. When a fork is reached, a detour left leads to the **Alpage de Ritord,** at 1971m (6467ft) (*buvette*). Keep right to stay on the GR55, which climbs past ruins at **Chavière**. ◄ Pass the Mollaret d'en bas cabin, then later pass a ruin and keep climbing. The track turns round a hollow, then zigzags uphill past a small pool. Watch out on

the right for the appearance of a *refuge* from behind a rock bar.

2hr 15min Refuge de Péclet-Polset 2474m (8117ft) *5min off-route, refuge and restaurant*

The GR55 follows a narrow path heading left before the *refuge*. It meanders up and along a grassy, bouldery moraine

The Refuge de Péclet-Polset sits in a remote area of the Vanoise and is passed closely by the GR55

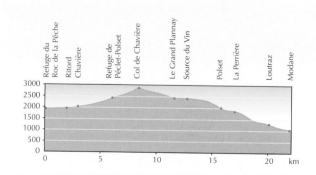

and proves reasonably easy underfoot. Later, it climbs on crumbly schist and there are fine views back down the valley. Broken, barren limestone slabs come next, and cairns help determine the route, but bear in mind that large snow patches lie late into summer in this area. Broken quartzite forms a boulder-scree, then more schist proves loose on the final steep climb to a col.

1hr Col de Chavière 2796m (9173ft) *View back to Mont Blanc and ahead to Monte Viso (highest point on the GR55)*

The far side of the col is steep and stony, but less likely to carry large snow patches. The path winds about as it descends, and eventually levels out before climbing gently onto a grassy hump studded with huge boulders.

45min Path junction 2504m (8215ft) ◄

Variant route to the Refuge de l'Orgère – see page 156 for details

The path splits, with the GR55 going right, and a variant route to the Refuge de l'Orgère going left. Turn right to follow the GR55 down through the boulder-strewn *alpage* of **Le Grand Plannay**. ◄ Pass a restored cabin and enjoy a view of three waterfalls side-by-side across the valley. (The Source du Vin beside the path turns out only to dispense water!) Enter a forest where the path contours across steep and flowery slopes, then drop downhill to emerge in a pleasant valley dotted with restored buildings.

1hr Polset 1840m (6035ft) *Water; detour off-route as marked for Chalet d'Alpage de Polset, refuge and restaurant*

Le Grand Plannay wasn't always this peaceful, as the shattered, rusting remains of military shell-cases testify.

Turn left down a track, which loops down to a road, but which can be short-cut from a sharp right bend by keeping to the left-hand side of a house. Cross the road and walk down a track. The rock alongside is generally hard gneiss, and the track is often flanked by pines, although there are still views. This is an old road, partly stone-paved, winding down past a few houses at La Perrière (possible water) before zigzagging down a steep forested slope. A track junction is reached.

1hr 15min Track junction 1370m (4495ft)

Continue downhill, and the pines eventually give way to deciduous trees, then the track swings right to cross a bridge over a stream. Turn left and the track runs downhill to become a road. Turn left down the Rue de la Charmette to reach a little chapel and a road junction at **Loutraz**.

30min Loutraz 1090m (3575ft) *Signpost and variant routes*

A decision needs to be made here: either walk *left* into the centre of Modane, or *right* to the railway station at Fourneaux. Both variants are waymarked, and don't meet again until Valfréjus (Stage 4, Day 16, page 174).

Left leads down the Rue des Chavières, through a staggered crossroads to cross a river. Note La Rizerie, a beautiful building on right. Go under a railway, then straight past a roundabout, then along the Rue Croix Blanche. This leads to the town hall (*hôtel de ville*) in the centre of **Modane**.

Right leads to a gymnasium, where a right turn leads along the Rue de la Vanoise. Continue down to a junction and turn right along the Avenue Emile Charvoz. Cross the Pont Emile Charvoz and turn right to follow the main road into **Fourneaux**.

10min Modane 1070m (3510ft);
15min Fourneaux 1050m (3445ft)
All services – see end of Day 15, page 140

To continue on the GR5, see Stage 4, Day 16, page 169.

Refuge du Roc de la Pêche 1911m

Alpage de Ritord 1971m

Le Doron de Chavière Torrent

2474m

Refuge de Péclet-Polset

Col de Chavière

2796m

2504m

Lac de la Partie

Le Grand Plannay

Plannay

Variant

Ruisseau de Povaret

2673m ▲ **Tête Noire**

N

Refuge de l'Orgère 1935m

→ GR5

Ruisseau de St Bernard

■ **Polset** 1840m

Refuge de l'Aiguille Doran

D106

Variant

Ruisseau de St Bernard

D215

MODANE

N6

Variant

The path is often quite easy as it descends from the Col de Chavière towards the hamlet of Polset

VARIANT ROUTE

Refuge de l'Orgère

From the path junction at 2504m (8215ft), turn left and climb a little past some big boulders. The path descends gently across the flank of **Tête Noire**, then climbs gently along a broad, inclined grassy terrace. Descend again and pass ruins at **L'Estiva**. Zigzag down through forest to land on a road at the **Refuge de l'Orgère** (*refuge* and restaurant; here you leave the Parc National de la Vanoise). Walk down the road and turn left down a path to link with the main GR5 to continue to Modane.

GR5E Low-Level Route – Bonneval-sur-Arc to Modane

DAY 13
Bonneval-sur-Arc to Lanslevillard (GR5E)

Distance	20 kilometres (12½ miles)
Total Ascent	250 metres (820 feet)
Total Descent	530 metres (1740 feet)
Time	5 hours
Map	3633 ET
Nature of Terrain:	A gentle valley walk along easy riverside tracks, forest tracks and field tracks.
Food and Drink	Plenty at Bessans and Lanslevillard.
Accommodation	*Gîte* at Le Villard. Hotels and *gîte* at Bessans. Hotels and campsite at Lanslevillard.

The GR5E leaves Bonneval-sur-Arc along an easy riverside track, pulling away from the river to pass through fields, woods and the hamlet of Le Villaron. After exploring Bessans the route often follows forest tracks, climbing high past Chantelouve. After descending through fields the trail reaches Lanslevillard and Lanslebourg. The day's walk is fairly short and easy, allowing time to appreciate the typical Haute Maurienne villages, with their heavy stone roofs.

Tralenta/Bonneval-sur-Arc 1808m (5932ft) *Hotels, chambres d'hôte, refuge, shops, post office and restaurants; Transdev bus to Bessans, Lanslevillard and Modane, tel 04 79 05 01 32, www.altibus.com; TIC tel 04 79 05 95 95* ▶

Follow a narrow road straight through rustic **Bonneval-sur-Arc**, admiring old buildings and passing the church to leave the village. A clear track heads to the right through hay meadows, running roughly parallel to **L'Arc Rivière**, though little is seen of it due to trees and bushes alongside. The track

For the link from La Lenta on the GR5 to Bonneval-sur-Arc for the GR5E, see page 124.

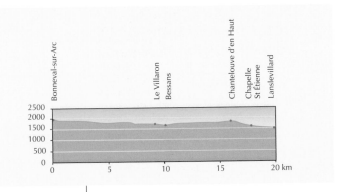

Neolithic art is present on the Rocher du Château but is difficult to discern.

eventually leads to a few stone cabins, then a short, rugged path crosses a hump to reach the overhanging Rocher du Château. ◀ Another track continues through meadows to reach a road at Chapelle St Bernard. Walk up the road into a little hamlet.

1hr 30min **Le Villaron 1740m** (5710m) *Gîte d'étape, water*

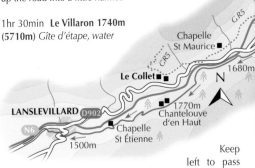

Keep left to pass the *gîte*, where the road gives way to a track through fields, later running close to **L'Arc Rivière**. Pass the trickle of the **Ruisseau du Pis** (junction of the GR5E and GR5) and continue downstream to a bridge. The GR5E crosses the bridge, but the GR5 doesn't.

45min **Bessans 1710m (5610ft)** *All services except bank; Transdev bus to Bonneval-sur-Arc, Lanslevillard and Modane; TIC tel 04 79 05 96 52*

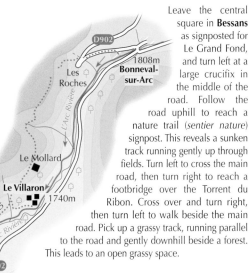

Leave the central square in **Bessans** as signposted for Le Grand Fond, and turn left at a large crucifix in the middle of the road. Follow the road uphill to reach a nature trail (*sentier nature*) signpost. This reveals a sunken track running gently up through fields. Turn left to cross the main road, then turn right to reach a footbridge over the Torrent du Ribon. Cross over and turn right, then turn left to walk beside the main road. Pick up a grassy track, running parallel to the road and gently downhill beside a forest. This leads to an open grassy space.

45min Les Chardonnettes 1680m (5510ft) *Nearby campsite*

Turn left to follow a gravel track through mixed forest, staying on the main track at all times and avoiding all others. This later climbs through the forest, passes through a meadow and reaches a few little houses.

1hr Chantelouve d'en Haut 1770m (5805ft)

A track descends steeply from Chantelouve d'en Haut, taking the GR5E down towards Lanslevillard

159

Drop steeply downhill beside the houses and follow the track back into forest. Keep right at junctions as signposted. After turning right at Le Châtel, the track leaves the forest and winds down past the **Chapelle St Étienne**. Keep following the track through fields to reach a junction, then keep left to reach the top end of a large village. Simply follow a road down through the centre to reach a church.

1hr **Lanslevillard 1500m (4920ft)** *All services, plus the services of nearby Lanslebourg; Transdev bus to Bessans, Bonneval-sur-Arc and Modane, tel 04 79 05 01 32, www.altibus.com; TIC tel 04 79 05 99 15, www.valcenis.com*

DAY 14
Lanslevillard to Bramans (GR5E)

Distance	17 kilometres (10½ miles)
Total Ascent	180 metres (590 feet)
Total Descent	430 metres (1410 feet)
Time	4 hours 15 minutes
Maps	3633 ET & 3634 OT
Nature of Terrain	An easy valley walk from village to village using forest and field tracks.
Food and Drink	Plenty at Lanslebourg and off-route at Termignon. Restaurant at Bramans.
Accommodation	Plenty at Lanslebourg and off-route at Termignon. Hotel at Bramans. Campsites at Lanslebourg, Termignon, Sollières-Envers and Bramans.

After an urban start on roads through Lanslevillard and Lanslebourg, the GR5E follows forest tracks up and downhill towards the lovely village of Termignon, which lies just off-route. A couple more small villages are passed on the way to Bramans. Again, a short and easy day, allowing plenty of time to explore charming stone-built villages. Some walkers might wish to continue straight to Modane, but that would make it a long trek.

To leave **Lanslevillard** follow the Rue des Rochers away from the church. When the main road is reached, there is no alternative but to follow it a short distance down to Les Champs, where a quieter road on the left can be followed. Developers seem keen to close the green space between Lanslevillard and Lanslebourg, but at the end of the road a short forest track remains in place. This leads to a road running beside **L'Arc Rivière**, which in turn leads to a bridge. Only cross the bridge if visiting the town centre.

30min **Lanslebourg-Mont Cenis 1400m** (4595ft) *All services*

Lanslebourg-Mont Cenis
Hannibal is reputed to have passed through here in AD218, crossing the Col du Mont Cenis to fight the Romans on their own soil. For centuries the col was a major transport route between France and the Piémont, and Napoleon had the first real road over it constructed in 1805. Traffic is much reduced these days, following the construction of rail and road tunnels between Modane and Bardonecchia. Since 1967, Lanslebourg and Lanslevillard have been referred to as the Station de Val Cenis, offering a full range of services.

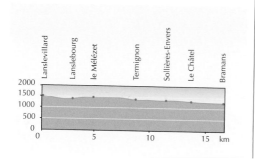

The busy little town of Lanslebourg lies along the opposite bank of the Arc, but is easily visited

Transdev buses run to Modane and Bonneval-sur-Arc, linking most villages along the way. TIC tel 04 79 05 23 66, www.valcenis.com.

Cross the Mont Cenis road and follow a minor road under a nearby *télésiège*. Walk down the road until a signpost at 1390m (4560ft) marks a forest track climbing to the left. There are a couple of sharp bends, otherwise keep straight ahead at all junctions. The track climbs gently at Carrefour du Revet, at 1495m (4905ft). Keep straight ahead at Le Mélézet, at 1500m (4920ft). ◄ Keep right at a track junction at 1490m (4890ft) and turn round a couple of sharp bends on

At Le Mélézet there is a view of glaciated Dent Parrachée.

TERM

N6

L'Adroit

D83

S
1290m E

✚ Airfield

Le Châtel
1265m

D83

L'Arc Rivière

1222m
Le Verney

N6

BRAMANS
1250m

the descent. The track leaves the forest to descend gently through fields. Turn right down a road to reach a large car park.

1hr 30min **Termignon 1350m (4430ft)** *5min off-route – all services except bank; Transdev bus to Modane and Bonneval-sur-Arc, as well as early and late bus to Entre Deux Eaux for the GR5 and GR55, tel 04 79 05 01 32, www.altibus.com; TIC tel 04 79 20 51 67, www.3petitsvillages.com*

If not visiting **Termignon**, turn left along a track through fields, looking down on a gravel pit beside the river. The track runs through forest and more fields, then passes beneath a marble cliff where there is a prominent tower of

A track runs through fields between Termignon and Sollières-Envers

rock, with a small lake nearby at **Grotte des Balmes**. Follow the road past a campsite and turn left up into a village.

45min   **Sollières-Envers   1290m   (4230ft)** *Musée archéologique*

Walk straight through the village by road and out the other side. After passing the Chapelle St Claude, at 1300m (4265ft), turn left up a track. This rises through cereal fields, passing a small **airfield**. Head down through a patch of forest towards a quarry, but as soon as a road is reached, turn left uphill. Pass **Le Châtel**, at 1265m (4150ft), and continue along a walled track with good views of the valley. Continue along a road called the Chemin du Châtel to reach the little hamlet of **Les Hauts du Verney** at 1240m (4070ft). Walk down the Route du Mont Froid and turn left down the Route des Chasseurs Alpins. Turn left again to enter a village.

A track crosses a gentle col beyond Bramans, then runs through forests

1hr 15min **Le Verney 1222m (4009ft)** *Boulangerie/patisserie, Transdev buses*

Follow the Rue des Diligences all the way through the village, but keep off the main road to climb uphill. Take a short-cut through a bend to reach a church (campsite). Head straight along a road to Le Moulin, and note a mill wheel in passing. Cross a girder-work bridge over a river, looking upstream to see a ravine cut into the marble bedrock. Walk straight along the road into a village.

15min **Bramans 1250m (4100ft)** *Hotel, gîte d'étape, restaurant, shop, post office; Transdev buses to most villages between Modane and Bonneval-sur-Arc, tel 04 79 05 01 32, www.altibus.com; TIC tel 04 79 05 03 45 or www.3petitsvillages.com*

DAY 15

Bramans to Modane/Fourneaux (GR5E)

Distance	13 kilometres (8 miles)
Total Ascent	350 metres (1150 feet)
Total Descent	500 metres (1640 feet)
Time	3 hours 14 minutes
Map	3534 OT
Nature of Terrain	Easy roads and tracks through fields and forest, ending with a steep descent on a forest path, then urban road walking.
Food and Drink	Restaurant at Fort Marie-Thérèse. Plenty at La Norma and Modane.
Accommodation	Hotels and campsite at Fourneaux, near Modane.

This short day's walk could see the GR5E completed in a morning, leaving the afternoon free to follow the GR5 to Valfréjus (Stage 4, Day 16). After climbing from Bramans and entering forest, there are glimpses of Fort Victor-Emmanuel across the valley. Closer to hand and much easier to visit is the Redoute Marie-Thérèse. The GR5E climbs up to the resort of La Norma before descending to Modane. Modane can either be avoided, or visited for its full range of services.

Leave the *mairie* in **Bramans** and walk straight through the village. The **Rue du Canton** leaves the village and walkers climb until the tarmac ends. Follow a **track** cut into the marble bedrock on a gentle **col**.

15min **Croix du Mollard Chez Nous, 1300m (4265ft)**

The track runs down through an open space, then there are more and more trees. Keep right at a junction as marked, passing a few small clearings. The track undulates, with a few mountain and valley views, before running down to a busy main road.

A view of Fort Victor Emmanuel from a point above the Fort Marie-Thérèse

1hr Fort Marie-Thèrése 1258m (4127ft) *Restaurant in early 19th-century fort, with views of Fort Victor-Emmanuel; Transdev buses to Modane, tel 04 79 05 01 32*

Cross the Pont du Nant Ste Anne, then follow a zigzag track uphill. Keep right along a fairly level track, with views between trees of Fort Victor-Emmanuel. When the track descends steeply from a junction, keep left as signposted (right leads 30min off-route to Avrieux). Later, keep left at another junction, as signposted for La Norma. The track climbs and undulates, passing a marble sculpture to reach a

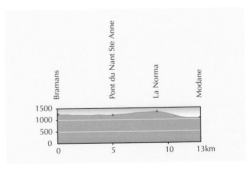

road. Follow the road uphill to a sharp bend and continue straight ahead along another road. When this road makes a sharp bend at another marble sculpture, continue up a forest track. The track becomes a road at some chalets and heads down into a village.

1hr **La Norma 1370m (4495ft)** *ATM, shops, restaurants*

> **La Norma**
>
> This is primarily a family sport resort, but also provides for passing walkers. The GR5E is not marked through the village, but if in doubt, ask someone the way to the *aquapark* to get back on course. There is a *navette* service to Modane, which needs to be arranged through the *office de tourisme* in the village centre (TIC tel 04 79 20 31 46, www.la-norma.com).

To pick up the GR5E, find the *télécabine* station, then head straight across the grass to a forest and pick up a track. This leads past marble sculptures to an *aquapark* enclosed by a fence. Turn right alongside the fence, then right again as signposted for Modane, down a forest path. Unseen cliffs are protected by a wooden fence, and there is a sudden view of the town deep in the valley.

Do not take the steep path down to the left, but walk down a more gently graded forest path. Later, watch on the left for a path short-cutting out of the forest onto a track. Turn left to follow this delightful, flowery, partly forested route down through a rock cutting into a ravine. Cross a concrete ford and skirt past a marble

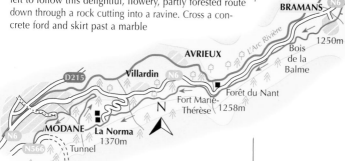

After descending through forest from La Norma, the GR5E finally approaches Modane

quarry, following the track to join a road. Continue down past allotments to reach a junction.

45min Modane Pâquier 1110m (3640ft) *Junction of the GR5E and the GR5*

Turning left at this point avoids Modane entirely and offers walkers an opportunity to climb directly to Valfréjus. To enter the town, however, walk down the road, the Rue de Frejus, through a crossroads, and down the Rue du Charmaix. Turn left along the Rue de la Liberté and later turn right to reach the town hall (*hôtel de ville*) in the centre of **Modane**.

15min Modane 1070m (3510ft); **30min Fourneaux 1050m (3445ft)** *All services – see end of Day 15, page 140*

The main GR5 route continues from Modane – see Stage 4.

STAGE 4
MODANE TO CEILLAC

Walking along a clear track across gentle grassy slopes towards La Replanette (Day 16)

General Overview Map	IGN 1:100,000 Carte de Promenade 54 Grenoble Gap.
Alternative Maps	Libris 1:60,000 No 06 Queyras Ubaye (covers route from Montgenèvre to St Étienne de Tinée). Rando Éditions 1:50,000 A3 Vanoise (covers route from Rosuel to Valfréjus) and Rando Éditions 1:50,000 A6 Ecrins (covers route from the Vallée Étroite to Col des Ayes).

On the Col de la Vallée Étroite (Day 17), the departmental boundary is crossed between Savoie and Hautes-Alpes, and Mediterranean influences begin to impinge on the senses.

Once over the Col des Thures, also on Day 17, there are two variant routes to consider. The main route of the GR5 simply drops into the Vallée de la Clarée for an easy interlude. The alternative, the GR5B, stays high and makes a rugged foray into Italy, linking with the main GR5 route again above Plampinet.

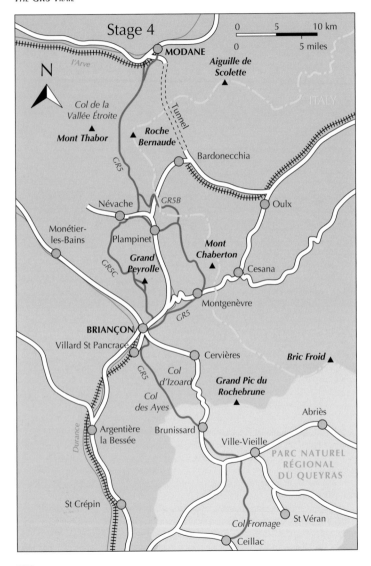

Grassy slopes gradually give way to forest on the way down from Col de la Lauze to Montgenèvre (Day 18)

On Day 18 the GR5 continues to Briançon, but another variant, the GR5C, climbs from the Vallée de la Clarée, and follows a rugged ridge before dropping to Briançon. If it proves difficult to choose between these variants, good bus services allow keen walkers to follow them all without having to retrace steps!

There are few big towns along the course of the GR5, but Briançon is well worth exploring if time can be spared. The GR5 leaves Briançon and climbs to the Col des Ayes, where it enters the Parc Naturel Régional du Queyras. This well-forested region specialises in the production of woodwork crafts and timber. Fine villages and the iconic Fort du Queyras are passed, before the route crosses the Col Fromage and descends to Ceillac in the heart of the park. This entire stage is never very far from the Franco–Italian frontier, while valleys head west to converge on the distant town and transport hub of Gap.

Those walkers tackling the GR5 over a series of holidays should check transport details carefully on the latter part of this stage. While Modane and Briançon are excellent transport hubs, Brunissard and Ceillac have limited bus links to nearby towns. If planning to break your trek along the GR5, or joining at such places, check transport details well in advance.

DAY 16
Modane/Fourneaux to Refuge du Thabor

Distance	13 or 16 kilometres (8 or 10 miles)
Total Ascent	1500 metres (4920 feet)
Total Descent	50 metres (165 feet)
Time	5 hours 45 minutes or 6 hours
Map	3535 OT
Nature of Terrain	A choice of forested ascents, then a long walk up through a valley, where a steep track and easier paths cross grassy slopes.
Food and Drink	Restaurants at Valfréjus. Refuge du Thabor.
Accommodation	Hotels at Valfréjus and *gîte* nearby. Refuge du Thabor.

There are two ways up to Valfréjus: the main route from Modane and a variant route from Fourneaux. The route from Modane is longer in terms of distance and time, but more gently graded than the steep climb from Fourneaux. Either way, the GR5 continues up to the Col de la Vallée Étroite, and is quite gentle towards the top. Some will be happy to cross the col and keep walking, while others divert a little off-route to the Refuge du Thabor.

Main Route from Modane
Start at the town hall (*hôtel de ville*) in the centre of **Modane,** at 1070m (3510ft), where a signpost is laden with walking destinations. Face the building, keep to the right-hand side and follow a road up to a junction. Turn left along the Rue de la Liberté, which becomes a back street leading close to a church. Turn right up the Rue du Charmaix, which is the start of a pilgrim route, the Pélerinage du Charmaix. Keep left up the Rue du Fréjus, through a cross-roads to pass some allotments.

15min **Modane Pâquier 1110m (3640ft)** *Junction of the GR5 and GR5E*

Turn right along a track to pass above a railway tunnel. Climb past the first of several pilgrimage 'stations' and follow the track up to a road bend. Walk up the road and watch for a path climbing from the next bend. Steep, narrow, gritty paths climb a forested slope crisscrossed by storm drains. Walk beside the main road serving the Tunnel de Fréjus. A narrow tarmac road goes under the main road, later turning left and right to give way to a forest track.

Follow the track uphill, climbing steeply to a road bend. Walk up the road, turning left and right at other hairpin bends. Follow another forest track from the next bend, climbing steeply to rejoin the road at a higher level. Follow yet another track, which crosses a bridge over a gorge to reach a chapel.

2hr Sanctuaire Notre Dame du Charmaix 1506m (4941ft)
Chapel dating from 1401, built to house a fifth-century statue of the Virgin

The Sanctuaire Notre Dame du Charmaix is at the end of a pilgrimage trail climbing from Modane

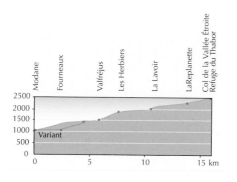

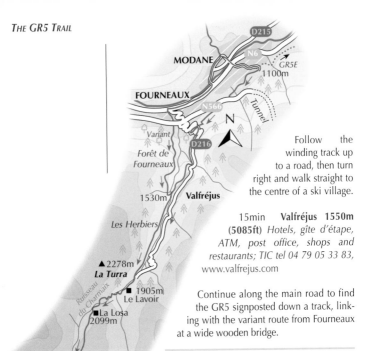

Follow the winding track up to a road, then turn right and walk straight to the centre of a ski village.

15min **Valfréjus 1550m (5085ft)** *Hotels, gîte d'étape, ATM, post office, shops and restaurants; TIC tel 04 79 05 33 83, www.valfrejus.com*

Continue along the main road to find the GR5 signposted down a track, linking with the variant route from Fourneaux at a wide wooden bridge.

VARIANT ROUTE

From Fourneaux

Start from the *mairie* in the centre of **Fourneaux**, at 1050m (3445ft), where a signpost lists walking destinations. Walk straight up a road towards the railway, turning right to find a footbridge. Cross over the line and turn right along a road, then left up the Rue des Cités Moulin to reach a car park by a church (water). Follow a winding track up to the towering supports of a road bridge, the Viaduc de Charmaix. Turn left along a path, under the bridge and into woodland.

Climb straight through an intersection of paths, into mixed forest. Keep climbing and branch left at a path junction. The path climbs steeply to a track, where another left turn is made. Another path heads up to the left, and as more height is gained, there are views back to Fourneaux and across the valley to Valfréjus. When a higher track is reached, turn left and follow it downhill, crossing a wide wooden bridge over the Ruisseau du Charmaix.

At the Ruisseau du Charmaix the GR5 main route is rejoined.

2hr 15min **Ruisseau du Charmaix 1530m (5020ft)** *5min off-route to Valfréjus*

Continue upstream as signposted across a footbridge. Follow a narrow forest path up steep zigzags. Join a track in a clearing and follow it up past a few houses at **Les Herbiers**. The track climbs though a forest and eventually crosses a bridge to reach a dirt road beneath the imposing Fort du Lavoir. Walk up the road and keep straight ahead at a junction to reach a car park beside a hydroelectric intake dam.

1h 30min **Le Lavoir 1905m (6250ft)**

Follow a winding track up a slope of alder scrub woodland to reach a higher hydroelectric intake dam. Branch left at a track junction at **La Losa**, as signposted for the GR5. The

The path easily negotiates a bouldery patch on the way towards the Col de la Vallée Étroite

There is a view of Mont Thabor at the head of the valley and part of the Vanoise beyond the valley mouth. Little buildings and ruins dot the landscape, and the highest building in view is the Refuge du Thabor.

track gives way to an easy path climbing gently across grassy slopes, passing **La Replanette**. ◄ The best way to approach it is to walk almost to the top of the **Col de la Vallée Étroite**. Turn right just before reaching the col and follow a clear path that skirts round the foot of a bouldery quartzite scree. A short climb leads to the *refuge*.

2h **Refuge du Thabor 2502m (8209ft)** *Refuge and restaurant*

DAY 17
Refuge du Thabor to Plampinet

Distance	21 kilometres (13 miles)
Total Ascent	525 metres (1720 feet)
Total Descent	1545 metres (5070 feet)
Time	6 hours 30 minutes
Map	3535 OT
Nature of Terrain	Gentle walking down through a valley, with increasing forest cover. A steep climb to a grassy col, then a rugged descent to valley tracks.
Food and Drink	Restaurants in the Vallée Étroite, off-route around Névache, and at Plampinet.
Accommodation	*Refuges* in the Vallée Étroite. Plenty off-route around Névache. *Auberges* and *chambres d'hôte* at Plampinet.

The main GR5 route crosses the Col de la Vallée Étroite, leading from Savoie to Hautes-Alpes, and this valley was until the mid 20th century the frontier between France and Italy. Despite France's annexation of the Vallée Étroite, the easiest road access is from Italy, and Italian is usually spoken in the valley. A forested climb leads to the broad, grassy Col des Thures, where the GR5 descends to Plampinet in the Vallée de la Clarée. The alternative routes for Day 17 and Day 18 (GR5B and GR5C) both climb high into the mountains.

Leave the **Refuge du Thabor** and retrace steps along the path skirting the foot of a bouldery quartzite scree. Turn right to cross a gentle col.

The Col de la Vallée Étroite was the frontier between France and Italy in the mid 20th century

15min **Col de la Vallée Étroite 2434m (7986ft)** *Italian – Passo di Valle Stretta; former Franco–Italian frontier, now the departmental boundary between Savoie and Hautes-Alpes*

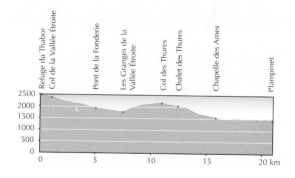

177

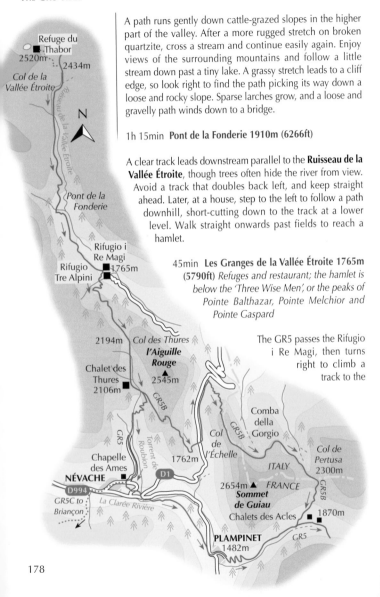

A path runs gently down cattle-grazed slopes in the higher part of the valley. After a more rugged stretch on broken quartzite, cross a stream and continue easily again. Enjoy views of the surrounding mountains and follow a little stream down past a tiny lake. A grassy stretch leads to a cliff edge, so look right to find the path picking its way down a loose and rocky slope. Sparse larches grow, and a loose and gravelly path winds down to a bridge.

1h 15min **Pont de la Fonderie 1910m (6266ft)**

A clear track leads downstream parallel to the **Ruisseau de la Vallée Étroite**, though trees often hide the river from view. Avoid a track that doubles back left, and keep straight ahead. Later, at a house, step to the left to follow a path downhill, short-cutting down to the track at a lower level. Walk straight onwards past fields to reach a hamlet.

45min **Les Granges de la Vallée Étroite 1765m (5790ft)** *Refuges and restaurant; the hamlet is below the 'Three Wise Men', or the peaks of Pointe Balthazar, Pointe Melchior and Pointe Gaspard*

The GR5 passes the Rifugio i Re Magi, then turns right to climb a track to the

Refuge du Thabor
2520m 2434m

Col de la Vallée Étroite

N

Ruisseau de la Vallée Étroite

Pont de la Fonderie

Rifugio i Re Magi
Rifugio Tre Alpini 1765m

2194m *Col des Thures*
l'Aiguille Rouge ▲ 2545m

Chalet des Thures 2106m

GR5B

GR5

Comba della Gorgio

GR5B

Col de l'Échelle

Col de Pertusa 2300m

GR5B

Chapelle des Ames
NÉVACHE
D994
GR5C to Briançon

Torrent de Roubion

1762m

D1

La Clarée Rivière

2654m ▲ *FRANCE*
Sommet de Guiau
Chalets des Acles

ITALY

1870m

GR5

PLAMPINET 1482m

Rifugio Tre Alpini. Turn right to climb straight up a field track, turning left across a streambed to enter a forest. Zigzag uphill, passing from limestone to quartzite, and views become splendid as the larches thin out, giving way to grassy slopes. Cross over a gentle col to pass a small lake.

1h 30min Col des Thures 2194m (7198ft) *Former Franco–Italian frontier; view of the Vallée de la Clarée and mountains beyond*

Grooved paths leave the col, heading gently down to the solitary **Chalet des Thures**, at 2106m (6909ft) (water). Turn left before reaching the building and walk to a fork in the path.

30min Path junction 2100m (6890ft) ▶

Fork right to follow the GR5, which is a level path along the top of crumbling cliffs of coarse conglomerate. Drop suddenly down a winding path on those same cliffs into a pine forest. Keep right at a path junction to pass the imposing rock tower of **La Demoiselle**. The path joins a track running downhill, but soon afterwards watch for another path heading off to the right. After climbing a little, then zigzagging downhill, the path rejoins the track at small building.

45min Chalet Forestier des Combes 1750m (5740ft) *Water and shelter*

The track leads through a forested, crumbling marble ravine. Pass a barrier at a small car park and follow the track down through terraced fields. Continue along a road from some houses to reach a road junction near a tiny chapel.

30min Chapelle des Ames 1623m (5325ft) ▶

Turn left to leave the chapel and continue along the GR5 main route, towards the large circular Centre de Vacances. Just before reaching it, head left along a track and cross a bridge over a river. Turn right down a track, passing terraced hayfields to reach St Hippolyte Chapelle. Turn right to walk down to the main road. (Nearby Roubion has hotels, restaurants and a shop.)

Junction of GR5 main route and GR5B high-level variant – see Day 17a on page 181

Turn right to access a range of services in Névache or to link with the GR5C high-level variant (see Day 18a, page 191).

Crumbling slopes of conglomerate have to be crossed on the way down into the Vallée de la Clarée

Cross the main road to follow a track towards a campsite. Turn right to cross the Pont des Armands and follow a track downstream beside the **Clarée Rivière**. The track climbs gently through a 'natural' forest campsite at Les Arras, then descends gently through fields to reach a road bend near a village.

1hr **Plampinet 1482m (4414ft)** *Auberges and chambres d'hôte; Resalp bus to Névache and Briançon, tel 04 92 20 47 50,* www.autocar-resalp.com

DAY 17a
La Vallée Étroite to Plampinet (GR5B)

Distance	22 kilometres (13½ miles)
Total Ascent	1315 metres (4315 feet)
Total Descent	1600 metres (5250 feet)
Time	7 hours 30 minutes
Map	3535 OT
Nature of Terrain	Paths vary from being gentle and easy to steep and stony. The Sommet de Guiau features crumbling rock and its slopes should not be traversed in very bad weather.
Food and Drink	Restaurants at Plampinet.
Accommodation	*Auberges* and *chambres d'hôte* at Plampinet.

The GR5B is a fine, high-level variant, traversing rugged mountains to make a short incursion into Italy. The route avoids the Vallée de la Clarée and so avoids lodgings and services, thus creating a problem. Unless walkers trek a long and hard day from the Vallée Étroite to Montgenèvre, they will have to descend to Plampinet for the night, climbing back in the morning. Parts of this variant feature unstable rock, so it is best avoided in very bad weather. (See map on page 178.)

The GR5 leaves **La Valleee Étroite** by climbing from the Rifugio i Re Magi to the Rifugio Tre Alpini. Turn right to climb straight up a field track, turning left across a streambed to enter a forest. Zigzag uphill, passing from limestone to quartzite, and views become splendid as the larches thin out, giving way to grassy slopes. Cross over a gentle col to pass a small lake.

1h 30min   **Col des Thures 2194m (7198ft)** *Former Franco–Italian frontier; view of the Vallée de la Clarée and mountains beyond.*

Grooved paths leave the col, heading gently down to the solitary **Chalet des Thures,** at 2106m (6909ft) (water). Turn left before reaching the building and walk to a fork in the path.

Junction of GR5 main route and GR5B variant

30min **Path junction 2100m (6890ft)** ◀

For the GR5B, fork left to follow a narrow path climbing easily across a flowery slope, with limestone scree and larches. The path zigzags uphill and weaves between limestone humps dotted with sparse pines. Stay on the most well-trodden path to reach a prominent junction, where the GR5B heads downhill to the right. ◀ The path zigzags down among thickening pines to reach another junction (where the GR57 offers a short-cut down to Plampinet, if needed). The GR5B turns left and zigzags further down a forested slope to reach a road.

From here there is a view of the Sommet de Guiau's rugged slopes.

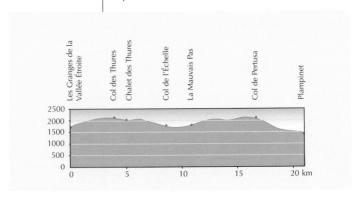

182

1hr **Col de l'Échelle 1762m (5781ft)** *Italian – Colle della Scala; Resalp bus to Névache, in France, and Bardoneccia, in Italy, tel 04 92 20 47 50,* www.autocar-resalp.com

While some walkers turn left and follow the road downhill, the GR5B crosses the road and runs parallel, weaving between forested and grassy areas. Pass an old customs post and keep an eye on the red/white markers. The road is a linear car park and picnic site on summer weekends. Reach the first of a series of bends where the road begins its descent towards Bardonecchia.

30min **La Mauvais Pas 1779m (5837ft)**

A signpost on the right indicates the path climbing from the road. Watch for markers, as the way is indistinct at first, passing old concrete bunkers. A clear and obvious stony path later zigzags up a forested slope. The trees thin out and the path picks its way along a crumbling slope overlooking Bardonecchia in Italy. Look for stone frontier markers bearing the letters 'F' and 'I', along with more concrete bunkers.

The path crosses into Italy at 2266m (7434ft), then runs down into the **Comba della Gorgio**, a vast scree-filled amphitheatre fringed by crumbling buttresses and towers of rock. Stay on the clearest path to climb beneath cliffs and

The GR5B briefly enters Italy as it traverses the rugged northern slopes of the Sommet de Guiau

monstrous stumps of rock. Zigzag steeply downhill from a shoulder, then watch carefully for markers as the path wanders among pines and climbs past larches to reach a col.

2hr 15min Col de Pertusa 2300m (7545ft) *Franco–Italian frontier*

The col isn't crossed at its lowest point, nor should walkers follow the clearest path. Red/white markers indicate a lesser path leading to derelict military buildings. Zigzag down grassy slopes into a forest and continue downhill. The path becomes a track leading down to a junction with a broader track.

Junction of GR5B and GR5 main route

45min Track junction 1846m (6056ft) ◄

Unless continuing straight to Montgenèvre, turn right to follow the GR5 down to Plampinet, bearing in mind that steps will need to be retraced the following day. Pass a wayside shrine and brush past cliffs to leave the high valley. Enjoy fine views over the Vallée de la Clarée and follow the track as it winds downhill with ease on a steep and rugged forested slope. A tarmac road is reached on entering a village.

Boulder-strewn areas of limestone are crossed on the slopes of the Sommet de Guiau

1hr Plampinet 1482m (4414ft) *Auberges and chambres d'hôte; Resalp bus to Névache and Briançon, tel 04 92 20 47 50,* www.autocar-resalp.com

DAY 18

Plampinet to Briançon

Distance	27 kilometres (17 miles)
Total Ascent	1350 metres (4430 feet)
Total Descent	1650 metres (5415 feet)
Time	8 hours 45 minutes
Maps:	3535 OT and 3536 OT
Nature of Terrain	Good forest tracks and gentle mountain paths on the ascent. Good paths and lengthy forest tracks on the descent.
Food and Drink	Plenty at Montgenèvre and Briançon.
Accommodation	Plenty at Montgenèvre. *Gîtes* off-route at Les Alberts, Vachette and Le Fontenil. Plenty at Briançon.

On the main route of the GR5 from the Vallée de la Clarée, height is easily gained by following a forest track up from Plampinet, then up again from the Chalets des Acles. Easy paths cross the Col de Dormillouse and Col de la Lauze, then the descent to Montgenèvre uses good paths and forest tracks. Continue gradually down through forest to Briançon. Anyone with an interest in military history would enjoy exploring Briançon.

Walk past two *auberges* to reach the top end of **Plampinet**, where the road gives way to a winding forest track. Climb a steep and rugged slope with relative ease and enjoy fine views of the Vallée de la Clarée. Brush past cliffs to enter a high valley, passing a wayside shrine and the junction with the GR5B. Follow the track to a large clearing dotted with chalets.

1hr 45min **Chalets des Acles 1870m (6135ft)**

Turn right to cross the **Torrent des Acles** and follow a track up a steep, forested slope. After passing a boulder-scree, watch for a path branching right from the track. Ahead, on the right, are extensive steep screes, but the path stays clear and follows a gentle grassy swathe up from the forest to a high col.

1hr 45min Col de Dormillouse 2445m (8020ft)

Enjoy views both ways from the col, but don't go down the other side. Instead, head left to traverse round a hummocky, sheep- and goat-grazed combe to reach a higher col. ◀

Here there is a view of the Crête de Peyrolle and GR5C.

30min Col de la Lauze 2529m (8363ft)

The col is on a well-defined ridge. No sooner do walkers step up to it, than they step down the other side! Follow the clearest path downhill, round another hummocky, grassy combe near Clot des Fonds. The path runs at a gentler gradient and passes beneath the Télésiège du Rocher Rouge. Drop steeply down a track, and while the sensible thing would be to continue down the track, the GR5 turns left up another track, then right along a grassy path that becomes steep, loose and stony, before rejoining the track. (**Note** Coming the other way, both the track and path are signposted as the GR5!)

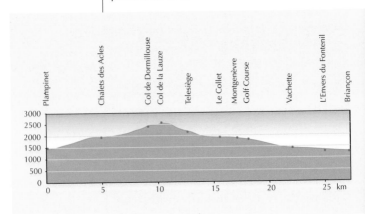

186

The Chalets des Acles are passed on the long and gradual climb from Plampinet to Col de Dormillouse

45min Vallon des Baisses 2050m (6725ft)

Continue down the track on the forested slopes of the **Vallon des Baisses**. Follow a grassy path parallel to the track for a while as marked, then later stick exclusively to the track, which is the Chemin des Baisses. The first houses glimpsed are actually in Italy, then the track swings right to join a road near Village du Soleil. Walk straight ahead, then follow a path parallel to the road, especially when a busier road appears, full of trucks running between France and Italy. Continue towards a prosperous-looking town.

1hr 15min Montgenèvre 1849m (6066ft) *All services, but some are closed in summer*

Montgenèvre

The Col de Montgenèvre has always been strategically important – Caesar, Charlemagne, Charles VIII and Napoléon I marched their armies back and forth across it. Napoléon has a monument raised in his memory, and he had the route improved. Fleets of trucks cross the col these days, but it is also used by the Chemin de Compostelle – a pilgrim trail signposted for Rome and Santiago. Modern Montgenèvre owes its fame and fortune to staging the first military skiing event in 1907, and for many years it was considered the best winter sports venue. Resalp bus to Briançon in France, and Oulx in Italy, tel 04 92 20 47 50, www.autocar-resalp.com; TIC tel 04 92 21 52 52.

Pass the *office de tourisme*, avoid the main road, and follow the quiet Rue de l'Église past the church in the town centre. At the end of this road, turn left and quickly right to walk beside the main road a short way. When the road bends left, keep straight ahead along an old road running parallel. Use a pedestrian crossing to reach the Télécabine de Chalmettes and walk down beside the main road with care, passing a golf course.

15min Golf course 1781m (5843ft)

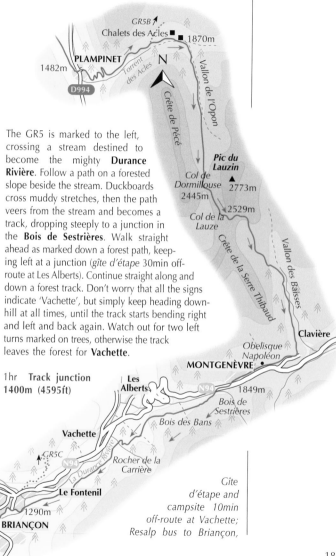

The GR5 is marked to the left, crossing a stream destined to become the mighty **Durance Rivière**. Follow a path on a forested slope beside the stream. Duckboards cross muddy stretches, then the path veers from the stream and becomes a track, dropping steeply to a junction in the **Bois de Sestrières**. Walk straight ahead as marked down a forest path, keeping left at a junction (*gîte d'étape* 30min off-route at Les Alberts). Continue straight along and down a forest track. Don't worry that all the signs indicate 'Vachette', but simply keep heading downhill at all times, until the track starts bending right and left and back again. Watch out for two left turns marked on trees, otherwise the track leaves the forest for **Vachette**.

1hr Track junction
1400m (4595ft)

Gîte d'étape and campsite 10min off-route at Vachette; Resalp bus to Briançon,

189

Montgenèvre and Névache in France, and Oulx and Bardonecchia, in Italy

Follow a forest track climbing gently and signposted for Briançon. It runs gently up and down, then when rising towards a bend, watch for red/white markers showing a right turn down a broad and stony path. Keep to the most obvious path, slicing across another path to pass between terraced fields. A road leads down into a small village.

45min **L'Envers du Fontenil 1300m (4265ft)** *Gîte d'étape 5min off-route at Le Fontenil*

Turn left along a road before reaching the river, and the tarmac gives way to a track passing fields. Turn right and left as marked to find a path climbing from a field into mixed woodland. Walk down a track to cross a stone bridge.

15min **Pont d'Asfeld 1290m (4232ft)** *Early 18th-century bridge spanning a deep gorge; note the pre-metric measurements for the span of 120 'pieds' and height of 168 'pieds'*

Climb up a track to a viewpoint, then go through a stone gateway into the well-fortified **Cité Vauban** (all services, being part of Briançon). Walk down a winding road, the Rue Aspirant Jan, which stays on the ramparts all the way down through the **Porte d'Embrun**. The walled city is left behind after passing a series of gates and deep ditches. Turn left down the Chemin Vieux, then left again after a school, down a stepped path on a well-wooded slope. Watch for red/white markers, or if a wrong turning is made, simply follow the **Durance Rivière** downstream.

Enter a dirt car park and turn left to cross a bridge. Turn right through another car park to reach a road junction and roundabout. Turn left to start climbing the Col de l'Izoard road, but after the footway runs out, turn right down another road, which leads to a road junction and roundabout near the railway station.

30min **Briançon 1180m (3870ft)** *All services*

Briançon
The Guigues family, who were the first to use the name (later title) Dauphin, dominated a fortified hilltop site from the 11th century, but lost power in the 15th century. The town of Briançon is known from the 13th century and appears to have been planned and built with its regular street pattern in one fell swoop. Massive fortified walls were built in the late 17th century under the direction of Sébastien le Prestre de Vauban. Forts continued to be built after his death, into the 18th century, and Briançon became a major garrison town. It is one of the highest towns of its size in Europe, surpassed only by Davos in Switzerland. A full range of services are available, and the town is a transport hub with bus and rail services to Gap and Valence, for Paris. Direct bus services run to Grenoble and Marseille. TIC 04 92 21 08 50 www.briancon.com.

DAY 18a
Névache to Briançon (GR5C)

Distance	27 kilometres (17 miles)
Total Ascent	1380 metres (4530 feet)
Total Descent	1825 metres (5990 feet)
Time	8 hours 30 minutes
Maps	3535 OT and 3536 OT
Nature of Terrain	A forested ascent to a lake, a climb to a rugged col, then easy walking along tracks. A rough and exposed ridge leads to a steep and rocky descent, giving way to zigzag forest paths.
Food and Drink	Café at Col de Granon. Plenty in Briançon.
Accommodation	Plenty in Briançon.

The GR5C, which leaves the main GR5 at the Chapelle des Ames, strives to stay high in the mountains. While much of it is easy, one stretch is exposed and unsuitable for use in very windy weather, or if snow and ice covers the path. This variant route even includes a 'variant' of its own to outflank the rocky crest of the Crête de Peyrolle, but it still leaves a rugged descent. In clear weather this is a splendid walk, highly recommended when compared to the main route, with wonderful and extensive views. A head for heights is an advantage.

Névache is the name for Sallé, Le Cros and other small, conjoined settlements in the Vallée de la Clarée.

Leave the GR5 main route at the **Chapelle des Ames** and follow the GR5C along a road though Sallé (*chambres d'hôte* and restaurant). Turn right along the main road (hotel) to reach Le Cros (hotel). Turn left across the Pont de Fortville and walk straight ahead on a track, then climb through terraced fields into forest. Watch for a path marked to the right, which soon starts zigzagging uphill.

Wider bends feature as the trees thin out, with views of the Vallée de la Clarée. Limestone gives way to quartzite before a junction is reached. Here the GR57 heads left, and the GR5C heads right, so keep right, to cross a shoulder and drop gently among larches to reach the **Ruisseau de Cristol** and a footbridge. Do not cross, but follow the path upstream, leaving dense forest to climb gentle, grassy, sparsely forested slopes to a lovely lake.

2hr **Lac de Cristol 2245m (7365ft).**

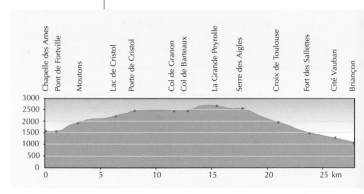

Watch carefully for markers, as the route does *not* follow the lakeshore path, but instead turns left just before reaching the lake. Follow the GR5C for the best conditions underfoot, climbing across grassy slopes and a variety of hard sandstone and gritstone to reach a rugged col.

The GR5C follows a fine ridge path along the Crête de Peyrolle

45min **Porte de Cristol 2483m (8146ft)** *View back across the Vallée de la Clarée to the distant Vanoise*

Drop down a short, rugged path and continue straight ahead along a track, signposted for the Col de Granon. Keep left at a junction with another track and climb gently round the slopes of **La Gardiole**. When another junction is reached, keep right and start descending gently. ▶ Pass above a few buildings to reach a road near a col.

Here there is a view from the glaciated Ecrins, to Briançon deep in the valley, with the Col des Ayes framing distant peaks either side of the Ubaye valley.

45min **Col de Granon 2413m (7917ft)** *Café; nearby barracks once housed soldiers training for mountain warfare*

Walk down the road past old barracks (water), then turn left down a track signposted for the Crête de Peyrolle. Briefly pass the upper part of a forest, then keep right at a track

(**Note** Before reaching the col look out for a variant route signposted to the right – see 'Variant Avoiding Crête de Peyrolle', page 196.)

From Croix de la Cime there is a view of the Ecrins, distant Vanoise, and Monte Viso in Italy.

junction. Climb gently towards a col, where the track ends in a turning circle. ◄

30min **Col de Barteaux 2380m (7810ft)**

A well-worn, crunchy quartzite path climbs steeply uphill. Walk along the rugged crest of the **Crête de Peyrolle** – or alongside it, either as the path dictates, or your ability permits. Pass a cross on Croix de la Cime at 2603m (8540ft). ◄ Walk down to a col, still on quartzite, then climb uphill and outflank a dramatic overhanging crest of limestone. The narrow path heads from col to col, rather than summit to summit. After passing **La Grande Peyrolle** and dropping to a col, note the variant route zigzagging up from a steep-sided combe. Keep close to the rocky crest, or even walk along it, to reach the final summit on the ridge, and the last of the extensive views.

1hr 45min **Serre des Aigles 2567m (8422ft)**

The descent is very steep and rocky, so follow the red/white marked path faithfully. The path surface can be bare rock, or loose stones, so take care throughout. After this initial nasty stretch, a better path zigzags down past a few pines to reach a col and a derelict **blockhouse**. Climb past the building on its left-hand side, then follow a well-engineered path downhill. Sometimes it has been cut into the limestone and sometimes it features a built-up edge. The gradient is gentle, but pines press in on both sides at times. Zigzag downhill to a track near a wooden building and transmitter mast. Follow the track down to some ruined stone buildings, then turn left up to a viewpoint.

1hr 15min **Croix de Toulouse 1973m (6437ft)** *View of forts around Briançon, along the valley and up to the Col des Ayes.*

A *via ferrata* drops straight down towards Briançon, but ordinary walkers will follow the path signposted 'Briançon par le Fort des Salettes'. Zigzag downhill, passing the Font de Bon Repos on one bend (water). One minute there are views to the Col de Montgenèvre, then there are views between the pines of Briançon. Eventually the zigzag path lands beside a fort.

45min Fort des Salettes 1452m (4764ft) *Occasionally open for visits; view of other forts around Briançon*

Walk down a track towards a cliff used by rock climbers. Watch for a path down to the left, then continue straight down a track. Walk down a minor road to reach a busy main road. Cross over to reach fortified ramparts near the Porte de Pignerol.

15min Cité Vauban 1330m (4365ft) *All services, being part of Briançon*

The GR5C doesn't pass through the ramparts, but turns right and follows them downhill to the **Porte d'Embrun**, where it rejoins the main GR5. Continue down the Chemin Vieux, then left again after a school, down a stepped path on a well-wooded slope. Watch for red/white markers, or if a wrong turning is made, simply follow the **Durance Rivière** downstream. Enter a dirt car park and turn left to cross a bridge. Turn right through another car park to reach a road junction and roundabout. Turn left to start climbing the Col de l'Izoard road, but after the footway runs out, turn right down another road, which leads to a road junction and roundabout near the railway station.

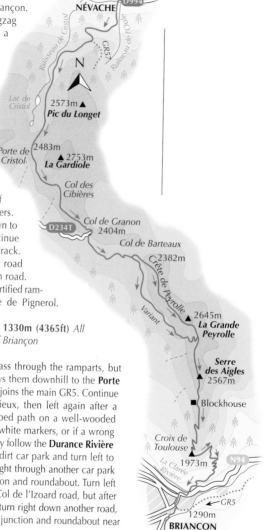

30min **Briançon 1180m (3870ft)** *All services – see page 191*

VARIANT ROUTE

Avoiding Crête de Peyrolle

This variant avoids *most* of the exposed ridge, but not *all* of it, and there is no avoiding the steep descent to Briançon. It leaves the GR5C near the **Col de Barteaux**, running gently down a grassy slope, crossing hard sandstone, gritstone and quartzite, with creeping juniper scrub appearing later.

A path junction is reached at Les Sagnes. Keep left to climb gently to Croix du Pied, where a cross stands beside a forest. Climb uphill and cross a slope, then keep left at another path junction. Climb across a slope of quartzite boulders and pass the top edge of a forest. Turn a corner later to drop into a little valley, where quartzite gives way to limestone. A gently graded path rises across limestone scree, and later turns a rocky corner to enter a steep-sided combe. Drop downhill a little and link with a path that zigzags up a grassy slope to reach a col. Turn right to continue along the GR5C towards **Serre des Aigles**, and from there follow the route description on page 194.

DAY 19

Briançon to Brunissard

Distance	22 kilometres (13½ miles)
Total Ascent	1425 metres (4675 feet)
Total Descent	860 metres (2820 feet)
Time	5 hours 30 minutes
Maps:	3536 OT and 3537 ET
Nature of Terrain	City suburbs give way to fields and forest, with a long and gradual climb to a high col. Good paths and tracks lead downhill.

Food and Drink	*Buvette* at Chalets des Ayes. Restaurants at Brunissard.
Accommodation	*Gîte* off-route at Villard St Pancrace. Campsite near Brunissard. *Gîte* in Brunissard.

The GR5 is anything but direct as it leaves Briançon, striving to avoid busy roads in the suburbs. A forested valley is visited on the way to Villard St Pancrace, then a lengthy dirt road leads through a forested valley to the Chalets des Ayes. A forest path climbs higher, then trees give way to open slopes on the final approach to the Col des Ayes. The GR5 enters the Parc Naturel Régional du Queyras, enjoying remarkable scenery to Brunissard.

If starting from the railway station at **Briançon**, follow the road signposted for Villard St Pancrace. Take the next turning right from a roundabout, which is the GR5. Walk up the road, but watch for a path climbing left, between a small field and a large building. Continue straight up a road to reach a village and a prominent church tower.

15min **Pont de Cervières 1229m (4032ft)**

Turn left and immediately right to follow the Chemin du Canal du Four away from the village. A level path passes

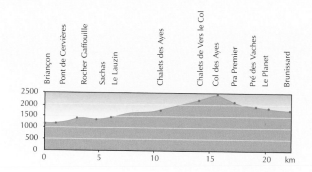

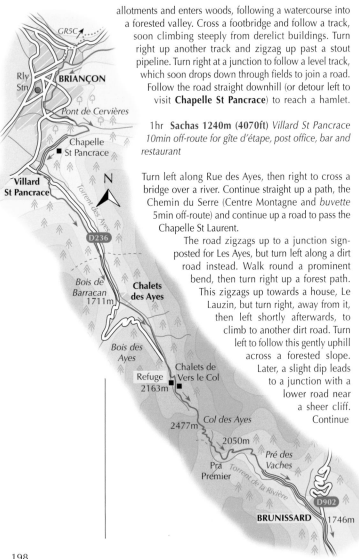

allotments and enters woods, following a watercourse into a forested valley. Cross a footbridge and follow a track, soon climbing steeply from derelict buildings. Turn right up another track and zigzag up past a stout pipeline. Turn right at a junction to follow a level track, which soon drops down through fields to join a road. Follow the road straight downhill (or detour left to visit **Chapelle St Pancrace**) to reach a hamlet.

1hr **Sachas 1240m (4070ft)** *Villard St Pancrace 10min off-route for gîte d'étape, post office, bar and restaurant*

Turn left along Rue des Ayes, then right to cross a bridge over a river. Continue straight up a path, the Chemin du Serre (Centre Montagne and *buvette* 5min off-route) and continue up a road to pass the Chapelle St Laurent.

The road zigzags up to a junction signposted for Les Ayes, but turn left along a dirt road instead. Walk round a prominent bend, then turn right up a forest path. This zigzags up towards a house, Le Lauzin, but turn right, away from it, then left shortly afterwards, to climb to another dirt road. Turn left to follow this gently uphill across a forested slope. Later, a slight dip leads to a junction with a lower road near a sheer cliff. Continue

198

along a tarmac road, following a river upstream to a little chapel, keeping right to pass a few chalets.

1hr 30min Chalets des Ayes 1711m (5614ft) *Buvette*

Turn left off the road to go up a track, then take a path to the left of the highest chalet. Walk up through a field and climb steeply into the **Bois des Ayes**. The trees are mixed and dense at first, dominated by larch later, but there are views as height is gained, and the gradient eases. Turn left up a track, and as the last few pines thin out, grassy slopes rise around a handful of chalets.

1hr 15min Chalets de Vers le Col 2163m (7096ft) *Basic unstaffed refuge*

Just before the end of the track, a path climbs to the left. Follow it up grassy slopes, crossing limestone and quartzite scree, aiming for a high col.

45min Col des Ayes 2477m (8127ft) *View back to the suburbs of Briançon and the Ecrins; view ahead as far as Monte Viso, in Italy; enter the Parc Naturel Régional du Queyras*

Chalets des Ayes, on the way to the Col des Ayes

Zigzag down a path on a slope covered in wiry tufts of grass, noting a transition underfoot from quartzite back to limestone. The path overlooks a lovely grassy valley containing a few chalets overlooked by mountains. Land on a dirt road beside some sheds and turn left downhill. The scene changes dramatically, revealing a looming cliff overlooking a flat grassy area and small lake. The dirt road zigzags down a scree slope, but walkers can short-cut part way down, reaching a car park beside the grass.

45min **Pra Premier at 2050m (6725ft)**

Continue down the dirt road, short-cutting down to the right along a path to a another car park on a tarmac road. Walk down the road, through a forest, and use another short-cut. Afterwards, there is no real option but to stay on the road, passing a forest campsite at Le Planet, at 1850m (6070ft), to reach a village surrounded by meadows.

1hr **Brunissard 1746m (5728ft)** *Gîte d'étape and restaurants; bus to La Chalp, Avrieux, Château-Queyras and Ville-Vieille for a greater range of services*

DAY 20
Brunissard to Ceillac

Distance	25 kilometres (15½ miles)
Total Ascent	1305 metres (4280 feet)
Total Descent	1410 metres (4625 feet)
Time	7 hours 45 minutes
Map	3537 ET
Nature of Terrain	Roads, tracks and forest paths, with a few open slopes. Mostly gently graded, but with some steep descents.
Food and Drink	Restaurants at La Chalp, Château-Queyras and Ceillac.

| **Accommodation** | Plenty at La Chalp. Some off-route at Avrieux, Souliers and Ville-Vieille. Hotel, *gîte* and campsite at Ceillac. |

Leaving Brunissard, views stretch to Col Fromage and almost as far as Col Girardin, so two days of the GR5 are visible. Those wishing to explore Fort Queyras properly should break at that point, even though it is short of halfway. Unfortunately there are no lodgings, but a bus can be used to reach nearby Ville-Vieille. A long, forested valley climbs fairly easily to Col Fromage and the descent to Ceillac is along good paths and tracks.

Follow the main road downhill from **Brunissard** to the neighbouring village of **La Chalp** (hotels, *chambres d'hôte*, *gîte d'étape*, restaurants and bus). Turn left at La Ferme de l'Izoard to follow a road uphill. Turn right at a junction to walk down a road, passing old houses. Turn right at another junction, passing only one house before turning left up a path. The path undulates across a forested slope, with a glimpse down to the village of **Arvieux**. Drop down to a farm road and walk up between the buildings.

1hr 15min Les Maisons 1693m (5554ft) *Water; Arvieux is 20min off-route, for auberge, post office, ATM, shops and*

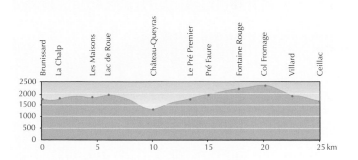

restaurants; bus to Arvieux, Château-Queyras and Ville-Vieille; Maison du Parc, tel 04 92 46 88 94; TIC tel 04 92 46 75 76, www.arvieux.com

Walk straight up a track to pass fields, but watch for a winding path climbing up to the left. Turn right at a junction with another path, then cross a track at a higher level, just to cut out a bend. When the track is joined again, turn right and follow it to a junction close to a small lake.

30min **Lac de Roue 1850m (6070ft)** *Gîte d'étape 30min off-route at Souliers*

Pass the muddy outflow of the lake and follow red/white markers indicating a forest track. Climb a little, avoiding other paths to right and left, then descend gently among pines. Later the path drops steeply, and after passing a cliff-edge viewpoint for Fort Queyras it becomes loose and stony. Zigzag down to a busy road and turn left to follow it, keeping an eye on the traffic while approaching a village.

Mountains reflected in the shallow, vegetated waters of Lac de Roue

1hr 15min Château-Queyras 1384m (4541ft) *Shop, restaurants, post office and campsite; bus to Brunissard, Arvieux and Ville-Vieille; hotel and gîtes d'étape at Ville-Vieille; TIC tel 04 92 46 86 89,* www.chateauvillevieille.com

Fort Queyras

The stump of rock filling the valley was first fortified in 1260. Fortifications were strengthened by Vauban in 1692 and now present an iconic and instantly recognisable picture. Today's visitors can take the château by storm using a *via ferrata*. If the walk is broken at this point, there will be time to enjoy a decent exploration. Tel 04 92 46 86 72, www.fortqueyras.fr.

Walk down a narrow road as signposted, past the *office de tourisme* and *mairie* to reach the church. Turn right, and if time can be spared, visit the Espace Géologique in an old crypt and learn how the Alps were formed. Walk through a car park and cross a bridge over Le Guil Torrent. Climb straight up a steep and stony path to reach a grassy slope, then follow a stony track steeply uphill. ▸ Climb through a pine forest and divert left up to a road. Climb round one bend and walk up to the next bend. Leave the road to follow a path, clipping a higher road bend to climb up to a track junction near a couple of buildings.

From the track there is a view back to Fort Queyras.

1hr Le Pré Premier 1760m (5775ft)

There is a view back to the striking Grand Pic de Rochebrune, and ahead to Pointe de la Selle.

Take the higher track, but later step to the right along a path. The valley appears densely forested with larch, but the path actually wanders from meadow to meadow. ◄ Pass a wooden cabin at **Pré Faure**, at 1950m (6400ft), and keep climbing through larch forest. Follow the river and cross over it, catching a view of Pointe de la Selle again, now revealed as towering twin peaks.

1hr **Fontaine Rouge 2125m (6970ft)** *Water*

Follow a path up a grassy slope where the trees become rather sparse. There are sudden turns to the right, then left (water). Pass an area of pits where gypsum was mined. The path is trodden to white powder as it passes above the appropriately named Ravin de Ruine Blanche. Pines give way to grassy slopes and limestone screes as the path approaches a broad col.

1hr 30min **Col Fromage 2301m (7549ft)** *Shelter; view ahead of snow-streaked Pics de la Font Sancte, but Col Girardin is just out of sight*

Follow a path straight downhill, zigzagging past larches – short-cutting bends is discouraged by fencing. Crumbling dolomitic limestone gives way to crumbling quartzite, so the path is gravelly all the way down. There are fine views from the head of the Vallon du Cristillan to Villard and Ceillac. The path finally lands on a track near a few houses.

45min **Villard 1825m (5990ft)**

Turn right along the track, then, when walking closer to Ceillac, watch for a wooden cross on the left, and follow a path winding down to a road. Turn right down the road and walk straight into the centre of the village.

30min **Ceillac 1639m (5377ft)** *Woodworking centre of the Queyras; hotel, gîte d'étape, campsite, post office, ATM, shops and restaurants; Favier bus to Montdauphin, tel 04 92 45 07 71; TIC tel 04 92 45 05 74*

STAGE 5
CEILLAC TO AURON

The GR5 wanders down to Larche, with views of the Parc National du Mercantour (Day 22)

General Overview Map	IGN 1:100,000 Carte de Promenade 54 Grenoble Gap and 61 Nice Barcelonnette.
Alternative Map	Libris 1:60,000 No 06 Queyras Ubaye (covers route from Montgenèvre to St Étienne de Tinée).

Beyond Ceillac the GR5 leaves the Parc Naturel Régional du Queyras, and the Hautes-Alpes, and enters the Alpes de Haute-Provence as it crosses the Col Girardin (Day 21). The last few peaks that boast obvious permanent snow and ice cover lie nearby. The route descends into a deep valley and has to follow a road. Beyond Fouillouse, the GR5 runs concurrently with the popular GR56, or Tour de l'Ubaye, crossing from one col to another to reach Larche (Day 22), close to the Franco–Italian frontier.

After leaving Larche, walkers enjoy a spectacular trek through the northern part of the scenic and rugged Parc National du Mercantour. The route crosses the steep and rocky Pas de la Cavale, leaving the Alpes de Haute-Provence to enter the Alpes-Maritimes (Day 23). Ahead lies the long and complex Vallée de la Tinée, where the mountains have a habit of generating sudden and sophisticated summer afternoon thunderstorms, so keep an eye on the weather.

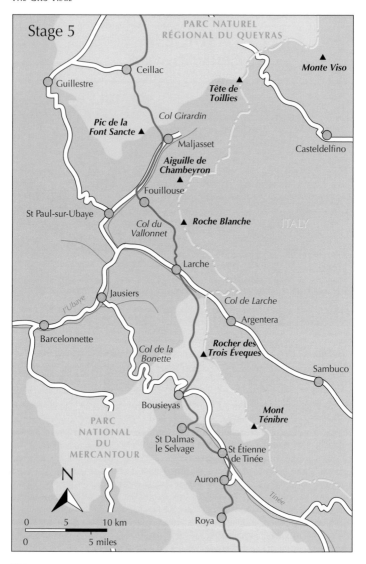

Stage 5

PARC NATUREL
RÉGIONAL DU QUEYRAS

Guillestre

Ceillac

▲ *Monte Viso*

*Tête de
Toillies* ▲

Col Girardin

*Pic de la
Font Sancte* ▲

Maljasset

Casteldelfino

*Aiguille de
Chambeyron*
▲

Fouillouse

St Paul-sur-Ubaye

Col du
Vallonnet

▲ *Roche Blanche*

ITALY

Larche

l'Ubaye

Jausiers

Col de Larche

Argentera

Barcelonnette

Col de la
Bonette

*Rocher des
Trois Éveques* ▲

Sambuco

Bousieyas

*Mont
Ténibre* ▲

PARC
NATIONAL
DU
MERCANTOUR

St Dalmas
le Selvage

St Étienne
de Tinée

Auron

Tinée

N

Roya

| 0 | 5 | 10 km |

| 0 | 5 miles |

Looking back along the GR5 on the final stretch to the top of the Col de la Colombière (Day 24)

The GR5 parts company with the GR56 on the Col de la Colombière (Day 24) and heads down to St Dalmas le Selvage, then over to St Étienne de Tinée. Don't imagine that the route has abandoned the mountains, despite these forays into the valley, since there is still plenty of climbing before the end of the trail on the shore of the Mediterranean.

Either St Étienne de Tinée or Auron makes a fine end to this stage. For those coming or going while covering the GR5 in stages, both towns have regular bus services linking directly with Nice – a name that suggests that the end draws close!

DAY 21
Ceillac to La Barge/Maljasset

Distance	16 kilometres (10 miles)
Total Ascent	1100 metres (3610 feet)
Total Descent	865 metres (2840 feet)
Time	6 hours 45 minutes
Maps	3537 ET and 3637 OT
Nature of Terrain	Steep climb up a forested slope, then easier climbing past a couple of lakes. Another steep climb to a col, then a steep and stony descent into a deep valley.
Food and Drink	Restaurants at Pied du Mélézet and off-route at Maljasset.
Accommodation	Hotel at Pied du Mélézet. *Refuge, gîte d'étape* and *maison d'hôte* off-route at Maljasset.

This is a short day's walk, but it involves steep slopes and crosses one of the highest cols on the GR5. A decision needs to be made on the descent. Either head off-route to Maljasset for food, drink and accommodation, or stay on the GR5 to descend to La Barge. The problem with the latter choice is that there are no services, so a detour may be needed to Maljasset anyway. The only other options involve extending the walk to St Paul-sur-Ubaye or Fouillouse.

Philippe Lamour was the originator of the Parc Naturel Régional du Queyras.

Leave the Place Philippe Lamour in the centre of **Ceillac**. ◀ Go behind the *mairie* and cross a bridge over a river, then follow a narrow road between old buildings. The road leads past two campsites as it heads up through the valley – Les Moutets and Les Mélèzes. Fork right by road after Les Mélèzes to reach a car park.

30min **Pied du Mélézet 1690m (5545ft)** *Hotel and popular waterfall nearby*

Cross a footbridge and climb uphill. The path zigzags up a steep slope of larch, passing brittle outcrops of sedimentary rock, with occasional views back into the valley. The forest is denser at a higher level, then the path climbs alongside the Ruisseau de la Pisse before crossing it at a footbridge. Emerge on a grassy *alpage*, with stunning views of the grey, serrated, snow-streaked peaks of the Crête des Veyres, before reaching a small lake.

2hr Lac Miroir 2214m (7264ft)

The lake, if not disturbed, mirrors the peaks beautifully. Pass the outflow, which drains into a limestone fissure, then cross a slight rise. The path heads downhill, so keep right at a junction to climb again. Pass well to the right of a bergerie and corral at Les Preynasses, in a sparsely forested area. Climb towards a ski piste and follow a path and track uphill beside a *télésiège*. Continue around hummocky moraine to reach another lake and a chapel.

1hr 30min Lac Ste Anne 2415m (7923ft)

There is no outflow, so cross the lowest point near the lake and follow a path up a slope of bouldery moraine. Slopes of lustrous, friable scree lie beyond, sparsely tufted with vegetation, and a path zigzags up to a col.

1hr Col Girardin 2706m (8878ft) *Departmental boundary between Hautes-Alpes and Alpes de Haute-Provence; view*

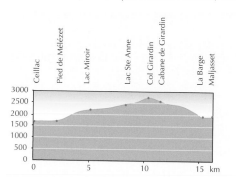

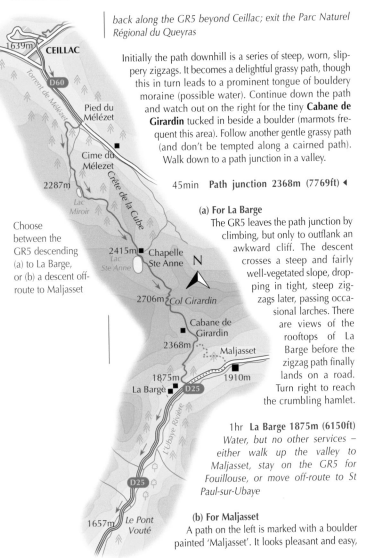

back along the GR5 beyond Ceillac; exit the Parc Naturel Régional du Queyras

Initially the path downhill is a series of steep, worn, slippery zigzags. It becomes a delightful grassy path, though this in turn leads to a prominent tongue of bouldery moraine (possible water). Continue down the path and watch out on the right for the tiny **Cabane de Girardin** tucked in beside a boulder (marmots frequent this area). Follow another gentle grassy path (and don't be tempted along a cairned path). Walk down to a path junction in a valley.

45min **Path junction 2368m (7769ft)** ◄

(a) For La Barge

The GR5 leaves the path junction by climbing, but only to outflank an awkward cliff. The descent crosses a steep and fairly well-vegetated slope, dropping in tight, steep zigzags later, passing occasional larches. There are views of the rooftops of La Barge before the zigzag path finally lands on a road. Turn right to reach the crumbling hamlet.

Choose between the GR5 descending (a) to La Barge, or (b) a descent off-route to Maljasset

1hr **La Barge 1875m (6150ft)**
Water, but no other services – either walk up the valley to Maljasset, stay on the GR5 for Fouillouse, or move off-route to St Paul-sur-Ubaye

(b) For Maljasset

A path on the left is marked with a boulder painted 'Maljasset'. It looks pleasant and easy,

After passing the Cabane de Girardin, walkers can descend either to La Barge or Maljasset

but gradually steepens on a loose and stony slope that needs care. The first sight of Maljasset is almost an aerial view, revealing a huddle of houses and a chapel standing alone in fields. Pass a few larches before finally landing beside the village.

1hr **Maljasset 1905m (6250ft)** *Refuge, gîte d'étape, maison d'hôte, restaurant and shop; Sherpa buses by arrangement, tel 04 92 84 33 33 or 06 03 27 23 98*

DAY 22
La Barge/Maljasset to Larche

Distance	27 kilometres (17 miles)
Total Ascent	1170 metres (3840 feet)
Total Descent	1395 metres (4575 feet)
Time	8 hours 15 minutes
Maps	3537 ET and 3637 OT
Nature of Terrain	A long road-walk, followed by a steep, forested climb and gradual ascent through a valley. Two high cols are linked by a good path and track. A grassy descent leads to Larche.

Food and Drink	Restaurants off-route at St Paul-sur-Ubaye, and at Fouillouse and Larche.
Accommodation	Lodgings off-route at St Paul-sur-Ubaye. *Gîte* at Fouillouse. Hotel, *gîtes* and campsite at Larche.

Lying between the Parc Naturel Régional du Queyras and Parc National du Mercantour, the scenery in these parts is by no means diminished for being excluded from protection. The only drawback is the long road-walk through the Vallon de Maurin, and it takes time for the route to get back into the mountains. Once crossing high cols again, interesting ruined military sites are seen. One fort was built at 2772m (9094ft) on top of the Tête de Viraysse.

Leave **Maljasset** and walk down the road through the Vallon de Maurin, passing a point where the GR5 lands on the road. Continue through a crumbling hamlet.

15min **La Barge 1875m (6150ft)** *Water*

Follow the road down through a forested part of the valley, with views of soaring rocky peaks and **L'Ubaye Rivière** from time to time. Cross a road bridge, then cross another.

1hr **Le Pont Voûté 1656m (5433ft)**

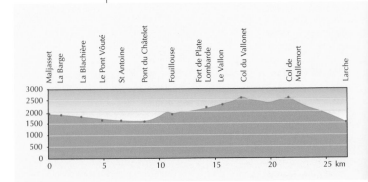

212

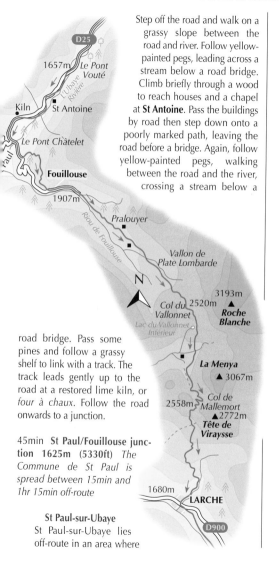

Step off the road and walk on a grassy slope between the road and river. Follow yellow-painted pegs, leading across a stream below a road bridge. Climb briefly through a wood to reach houses and a chapel at **St Antoine**. Pass the buildings by road then step down onto a poorly marked path, leaving the road before a bridge. Again, follow yellow-painted pegs, walking between the road and the river, crossing a stream below a

road bridge. Pass some pines and follow a grassy shelf to link with a track. The track leads gently up to the road at a restored lime kiln, or *four à chaux*. Follow the road onwards to a junction.

45min St Paul/Fouillouse junction 1625m (5330ft) *The Commune de St Paul is spread between 15min and 1hr 15min off-route*

St Paul-sur-Ubaye
St Paul-sur-Ubaye lies off-route in an area where

213

services are sparse. The *commune* comes in several parts, and it may be necessary to walk for over an hour to fulfil a particular need. Heading down the road, the first settlement is La Grande Sérenne (*maison d'hôte* and *café*). Next is Petite Sérenne, followed by Pont de l'Estrech (*chambres d'hôte*). The greatest bulk of services is at St Paul-sur-Ubaye – hotels, *gîte d'étape*, campsite, shop, post office, restaurants and museum; free bus (*navette gratuite*) to Barcelonnette; Sherpa buses by arrangement, tel 04 92 84 33 33 or 06 03 27 23 98; TIC in a roadside hut, tel 04 92 81 03 68, www.ubaye.com.

The bridge was proposed in 1875 as a wooden span, but completed in stone in 1882, arching 27m (89ft) across and 108m (354ft) above L'Ubaye Rivière. It was mined in 1944, but resisted the explosion and was repaired in 1945.

Turn left up a road signposted for Fouillouse. The road has been hacked from rock, and the arch of **Le Pont Châtelet** spans a rocky gorge. ◄ Continue through a tunnel, and after enjoying a view down the Ubaye valley, turn left up a path. Climb steeply towards a ruin, but do not pass it (unless to enjoy one last view of the Vallon de Maurin). Turn right up a winding forest path and keep climbing among pines until a path junction is reached, where there is another fine valley view. Turn right to traverse round the head of a ravine then walk down in loops to a road beside a small village.

1hr **Fouillouse 1907m (6257ft)** *Gîte d'étape and restaurant; Sherpa buses by arrangement*

While walking through Fouillouse, look out for 19th-century water troughs carved out of huge blocks of stone. Larger ones, up to 4m (13ft) long, can be found in the Ubaye valley.

◄ Continue past a chapel (junction of the GR5, GR6 and GR56) and simply follow a track onwards, climbing roughly parallel to a river. Larches proliferate around **Pralouyer**, but don't obscure views, and there are many grassy slopes. Reach a little cabin and turn right to follow a path past the concrete ruin of Fort de Plate Lombarde. The path is gentle and easy, keeping well to the left of a farm building where there may be a large flock of sheep. Climb a little before crossing a footbridge, then climb again, watching for marmots. A steeper climb up a sandstone slope dotted with alpenrose leads to a boulder-strewn col.

2hr **Col du Vallonnet 2520m (8268ft)** *View of Col de Mallemort to the right of the striking peak of La Meyna*

Walk down a gentle path which soon follows a sluggish stream. There are two signposted path junctions – keep right at the first and left at the second, confirming each move by looking for red/white markers. The path crosses bouldery, sheep-grazed moraine to reach a track, which is actually an old military road. Turn left to follow it up to the ruined **Baraquements de Viraysse** (one building is a basic *refuge*/shelter). Follow a well-graded path in sweeping zigzags above the fort to reach a col.

Looking down on the Baraquements de Viraysse from the Col de Mallemort

1hr 15min **Col de Mallemort 2558m (8392ft)** *Option to follow a well-graded zigzag military path up to the ruined Batterie de Viraysse on top of Tête de Viraysse*

Follow a winding path down from the col, which is stony where the grass cover is sparse, but delightful where there is complete grass cover (brief view of Pas de la Cavale ahead). Pass a few larches, and keep straight ahead at two signposted path junctions – Larche is nearly always in view during the descent. The last part of the path is steep and stony, zigzagging down a slope dotted with juniper and other thorn bushes, crossing brittle shale. Join a track that leads easily down beside a stream, then continue along a road into **Larche**.

215

2hr **Larche 1680m (5512ft)** *Hotel, gîtes d'étape, restaurants, post office and nearby campsite/shop*

Larche

There is a long history of travel over Col de Larche (in Italian, Colla della Maddalena), between Provence and the Piémont. Shepherds grazing high *alpages* in the summer drove their flocks to the Piémont before the onset of winter. The establishment of a frontier in the region led to times of strife. The village was destroyed by German and Italian troops in 1944, and has been completely rebuilt. Oddly, the only feature to survive the destruction was the 1914–18 war memorial. Being close to the Parc National du Mercantour, information about the park is available in advance. Free bus (*navette gratuite*) to Barcelonnette; Sherpa buses by arrangement, tel 04 92 84 33 33 or 06 03 27 23 98; TIC tel 04 92 84 33 58 or www.haute-ubaye.com.

DAY 23

Larche to Bousieyas

Distance	21 kilometres (13 miles)
Total Ascent	1240 metres (4070 feet)
Total Descent	1035 metres (3395 feet)
Time	7 hours
Maps	3538 ET and 3639 OT
Nature of Terrain	Roads, tracks and paths climb through a valley, becoming more rugged up to a high col. After a steep and rocky descent a lower grassy col is crossed.
Food and Drink	Campsite restaurant after Larche. Restaurant at Bousieyas.
Accommodation	Campsite after Larche. *Gîte, chambres d'hôte* and basic campsite at Bousieyas.

Leaving Larche the GR5 enters the Parc National du Mercantour in grand style, climbing through the Vallon de Lauzanier. Great slabs of sandstone and limestone hide charming little lakes, then the route crosses the rocky Pas de la Cavale. From this point onwards the GR5 is confined to the large and complex Vallée de la Tinée all the way to Nice. The whole day's walk runs close to the Franco–Italian frontier and old military sites are evident.

Leave **Larche** via the main road in the direction of Italy, but fork right as signposted along a minor road. Pass a campsite (shop and restaurant) and later cross **L'Ubayette Torrent**. The road eventually rises to a car park, often busy with visitors from France and Italy.

1hr 15min **Pont Rouge 1907m (6257ft)** *Enter the Parc National du Mercantour; visitors hand-feed fat marmots at a sign forbidding such activity!*

A track leads into **Val Fourane** where the scenery is impressive. Follow it gently up through the valley, and it narrows and steepens to become a rough and stony path. Tilted slabs of bare sandstone have to be crossed from time to time, and further slabby slopes abound ahead. Climb beside a stream flanked by lush vegetation to reach a fine lake overlooked by a little chapel.

1hr 45min **Lac du Lauzanier 2284m (7493ft)**

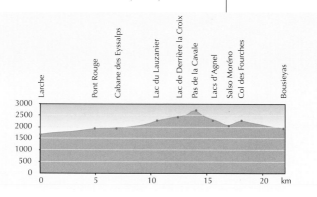

Keep well to the right of the lake to follow a well-worn path further up through the Vallon du Lauzanier, heading towards slabby mountains. Pass a vigorous stream bursting from a spring, then climb beside limestone slabs. Cross a river at a huge boulder and keep climbing. The path splits and rejoins, so either keep left on the GR5, or right to visit nearby **Lac de Derrière la Croix** at 2428m (7966ft). Zigzag uphill, and follow the path from a grassy slope onto boulder scree, which is easy if taken steadily, to reach an impressive rocky col.

Note Take care descending from the col as the limestone is badly fractured and blocks could fall.

1hr 30min **Pas de la Cavale 2671m (8763ft)** *Departmental boundary between Alpes de Haute-Provence and Alpes-Maritimes; view back along the GR5 and ahead to Col de la Colombière, Auron and Mont Mounier* ◀

The path traverses narrow ledges and runs down boulder scree to reach grassy slopes grazed by sheep and goats – looking back, it is impossible to trace the path! The whole area is shaped by unstable geology, with crumbling black shale along Les Roubines Nègres, and crater-like dolines (solution hollows) in the dolomitic limestone near the little Lacs d'Agnel. The gradient eases and the grass may be dotted with delightful pale crocuses. The valley was named **Salso Moréno** when it was occupied by Spanish troops from

Walkers overlook the steep and rugged slopes of the Pas de la Cavale

1744–47. Cross a broad and bouldery streambed around 2100m (6890ft) and pass a **cabin** (shelter). The path later crosses the Ravin de la Tour and climbs up a steep slope to reach a col guarded by concrete casemates (fortifications in which guns were mounted).

1hr 45min **Col des Fourches 2261m (7418ft)**

Follow a grassy track to ruined barracks at the **Camp des Fourches**. Built in the 1890s, the Camp des Fourches housed soldiers known as Les Diables Bleus, who patrolled the border between France and Italy. Halfway through the barracks, turn left to cross a road and continue downhill as marked. A grassy path flanked by sandstone boulders winds downhill. From here there is a view across the valley to the Col de la Colombière. Cross the road again, then later cross it twice in quick succession to cut out a bend. Continue down a grooved path where boulders have been pushed to one side, catching a glimpse of Bousieyas. Step down a series of old terraces and later pass a house, keeping to the right, then turn left down the road. Turn right down a path that leads to stone steps in a tin-roofed hamlet.

45min **Bousieyas 1883m (6178ft)**
Highest hamlet in the Alpes-Maritimes, intended to be inhabited in the summer and abandoned in winter; gîte d'étape, chambres d'hôte, basic campsite and restaurant; Sherpa buses by arrangement, tel 04 92 84 33 33 or 06 03 27 23 98

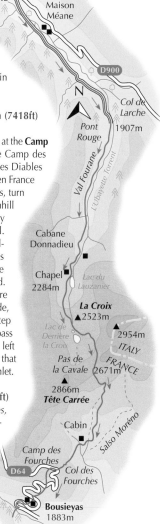

DAY 24

Bousieyas to Auron

Distance	26 kilometres (16 miles)
Total Ascent	1265 metres (4150 feet)
Total Descent	1535 metres (5035 feet)
Time	7 hours
Map	3639 OT
Nature of Terrain	Easy tracks and paths climb to a high col, but the descent is narrow and stony. Easy tracks and paths cross another col, then a steep and stony forest path climbs to Auron.
Food and Drink	Restaurants at St Dalmas le Selvage, St Étienne de Tinée and Auron.
Accommodation	*Gîte* and *chambres d'hôte* at St Dalmas le Selvage. Plenty at St Étienne de Tinée, including campsite. Hotels and campsite at Auron.

Mediterranean influences become pronounced during the day. The Col de la Colombière is high, but the descent to St Dalmas le Selvage features broom, lavender and large, bright-green lizards not seen so far on the GR5. After a gentle traverse of the Col d'Anelle, the descent to St Étienne de Tinée leads deep into the Vallée de la Tinée, which could be very hot in the afternoon. If this is the case, the steep and stony ascent to Auron could be quite tiring.

Leave **Bousieyas** by walking down a road from the church, turning a sharp left bend, then turning sharp right down a track. Cross a bridge over the Tinée Torrent and climb gradually through larch forest, with occasional views back to Bousieyas. Ford the Rio Torrent and keep climbing until the track is almost level and grassy. A path is marked up to the right, zigzagging up the forested slope, crossing the track again and again to emerge from the trees onto a grassy gap at 2123m (6965ft). Follow the track as it climbs easily across

limestone boulder scree, overlooking slopes grazed by
sheep and goats. Avoid a final zigzag by using a short-cut
path straight to a col.

1hr 30min **Col de la Colombière 2237m (7339ft)** *Junction
of GR5 and GR56; view ahead to Mont Mounier*

Leave the track on the col and walk down a winding, stony
path. This narrow path contours across steep slopes or wanders in and out of ravines. Dolomitic limestone gives way to
glistening mica schist. Cabins at **Rochepin** could easily be
passed unnoticed where the path makes a sharp right
turn. ▶ Traverse round more crumbling ravines to land on
dolomitic limestone in the Vallon de la Combe (exit the Parc
National du Mercantour). Feathery clumps of grass and thorny
scrub lend a Mediterranean air to the valley. Continue along
the path, which has been hacked from a limestone cliff further
downhill. Wander down past little terraces and vegetable
plots, then walk straight down a road into a compact village.

From the sharp right
turn there is a brief
glimpse of the church
at St Dalmas le
Selvage deep in the
valley, with the
Massif de Gialorgues
beyond.

1hr 30min **St Dalmas le Selvage 1500m (4920ft)** *Highest
village in the Alpes-Maritimes – 'selvage' is derived from 'syl-
vatica', meaning forested; chambres d'hôte, gîte d'étape,
shop and restaurants; bus by arrangement to St Étienne de
Tinée, tel 08 00 06 01 06; TIC tel 04 93 02 46 40,
www.saintdalmasleselvage.com.*

Leave **St Dalmas le Selvage** by way of the *office de tourisme*

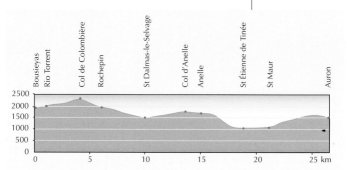

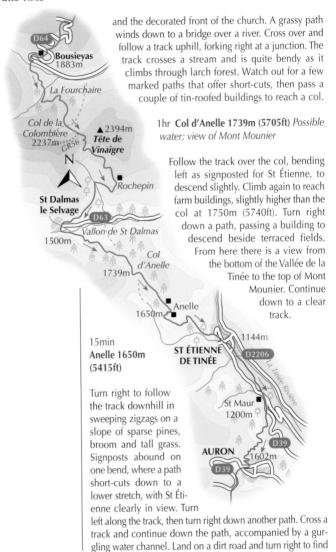

and the decorated front of the church. A grassy path winds down to a bridge over a river. Cross over and follow a track uphill, forking right at a junction. The track crosses a stream and is quite bendy as it climbs through larch forest. Watch out for a few marked paths that offer short-cuts, then pass a couple of tin-roofed buildings to reach a col.

1hr **Col d'Anelle 1739m (5705ft)** *Possible water; view of Mont Mounier*

Follow the track over the col, bending left as signposted for St Étienne, to descend slightly. Climb again to reach farm buildings, slightly higher than the col at 1750m (5740ft). Turn right down a path, passing a building to descend beside terraced fields. From here there is a view from the bottom of the Vallée de la Tinée to the top of Mont Mounier. Continue down to a clear track.

15min
**Anelle 1650m
(5415ft)**

Turn right to follow the track downhill in sweeping zigzags on a slope of sparse pines, broom and tall grass. Signposts abound on one bend, where a path short-cuts down to a lower stretch, with St Étienne clearly in view. Turn left along the track, then turn right down another path. Cross a track and continue down the path, accompanied by a gurgling water channel. Land on a dirt road and turn right to find

222

another path, flanked by box trees, leading down past a couple of houses.

Cross a road twice to avoid a bend, then keep to the left of a house called Le Rocher to walk down a rough, boulder-paved path. Keep straight ahead at a junction, then turn left along a road to reach a chapel. Turn right to reach the Téléphérique Pinatelle, then turn left down the Rue du Val Gelé. Turn right at a chapel and follow the Rue Droite past an orchard. The street narrows as it runs close to the town centre.

1hr **St Étienne de Tinée 1144m (3753ft)** *Fine old town full of five-storey buildings, a large church with a landmark steeple, and several little chapels from the 15th to 18th centuries; all services; TAM buses to Isola, St Sauveur de Tinée,*

Looking back to St Étienne de Tinée from the steep and forested climb towards Auron

223

Valdeblore, Nice and Nice Airport, tel 08 00 06 01 06; Maison du Parc and TIC, tel 04 93 02 41 96, www.auron.com

Follow the Rue Droite onwards through town and out into the country. Keep right at a junction beside a water trough. Walk down and up a road using a green cycle lane. Turn right as signposted for Auron, up a path flanked by walls and trees. Turn right up a track to reach the main road, then left to reach a roundabout and chapel.

30min **St Maur 1200m (3935ft)** *TAM buses to St Étienne, Auron and Nice*

Follow the main road uphill as signposted for Auron, but only as far as can be seen from the roundabout. Step up to the right to follow a narrow path to a track. Turn left to climb steeply up the track, keeping right to climb even more steeply up a broad and stony forest path. Little wayside shrines are passed, and the path drifts to the left across the forested slope. Climb steep zigzags on loose stones, then at a higher level keep right at a path junction to reach a dusty dirt road.

1hr **Dirt road 1700m (5580ft)**

Turn left along the dirt road to link with a tarmac road. This is the winding Chemin du Puy d'Auron, which can be followed all the way down to the *office de tourisme* near the town centre.

15min **Auron 1602m (52556ft)** *Modern ski development with a few old buildings; a popular family sport resort offering plenty of 'activities' in the summer months; all services; TAM buses to St Étienne and Nice, tel 08 00 06 01 06; TIC tel 04 93 23 02 66, www.auron.com*

STAGE 6
AURON TO NICE – GR5

The GR5 works its way up through a forested valley, passing from one village to another (Day 26)

General Overview Map	IGN 1:100,000 Carte de Promenade 61 Nice Barcelonnette.
Alternative Maps	None for this stage.

The southernmost stage of the GR5 is confined within the complex Vallée de la Tinée, named after the Ectinis, a Celtic Ligurian tribe who once occupied the area. However, this final stage is no simple valley walk. There are plenty of mountains, and the route must cross the deep and forested Tinée valley from one side to the other, as well as traversing the rugged Gorges de la Vésubie. However, the mountains are noticeably lower, and throughout this stage the red pantile roofs in the villages and the nature of the vegetation suggest that the Mediterranean is close to hand. Walkers will be straining to catch sight of the sea, and in due course the long trek will end on the shore.

It could be like walking into a furnace, dropping down into the big, brash city of Nice in the height of summer. Alternatively, there might well be afternoon thunderstorms on these last few days, since the heat of the sun, the height of the mountains and the proximity of the sea combine to create unstable conditions. While some walkers

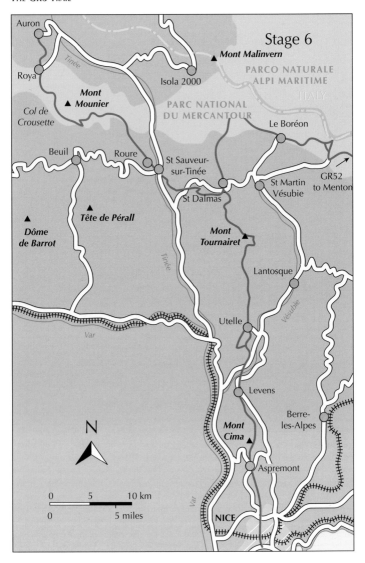

Looking down on St Sauveur sur Tinée, deep in the forested Vallée de la Tinée (Day 26)

may be keen to head straight home, others will wish to spend a couple of days unwinding and exploring, and Nice has plenty of interest for visitors, being a place of both culture and history.

At some point, it is worth climbing onto the Colline du Château to look back towards the Alps, remembering the long and arduous trek that brought you to this place, and maybe wondering if you should have followed the GR52 from St Dalmas to Menton. If you missed out on that spectacular finale, it certainly repays a repeat visit, and is a fine trek in its own right.

A distinctive hump of limestone sits on a rugged col at Le Pertus (Day 27)

DAY 25
Auron to Refuge de Longon

Distance	31 kilometres (19 miles)
Total Ascent	1795 metres (5890 feet)
Total Descent	1460 metres (4790 feet)
Time	9 hours 15 minutes
Maps:	3639 OT 3640 OT and 3641 ET
Nature of Terrain	A forested climb and grassy descent to Roya, then a long climb up a rugged valley to cross the broad flanks of Mont Mounier. After crossing a valley, the route climbs through the Portes de Longon.
Food and Drink	Restaurant at Roya and Refuge de Longon.
Accommodation	*Gîte* at Roya. Refuge de Longon.

This is a long day's walk, and those who are unsure of their ability should adapt the schedule. Anyone who spent a night in St Étienne de Tinée, for example, could spend the following night at Roya, then enjoy an easier walk over to Longon. Mont Mounier, which once bore an observatory and *refuge*, is a broad, exposed, stony mountain. It is the last big mountain on the GR5 and is often caught by the afternoon storms afflicting the Alpes-Maritimes.

Leave **Auron** as signposted beside the *office de tourisme*, passing a small, fenced football pitch. Head for a couple of old buildings and follow a dirt road up to a car park. Exit left and walk gently down to a restaurant. Pass it and keep right to follow a track up beside a golf driving range. Turn left as marked up a steep path into forest. The path becomes convoluted, but is clearly marked and gently graded. Avoid a path down to the left, and keep climbing to pass a viewpoint at Belvédère des Chamois, at 1810m (5938ft). Climb to a broad track – a ski piste – and turn left up it, but leave it as marked and climb roughly parallel along a forest path. Cross the piste at a higher level, then climb until trees give way to a grassy col.

An old wooden cross is passed on the descent from Col du Blainon to the little hamlet of Roya

1hr 30min **Col du Blainon 2014m (6608ft)** *View across the Vallée de la Tinée to high peaks in the Parc National du Mercantour, with Mont Mounier ahead*

Follow a narrow path down past a timber cabin, then pass lots of half-timber, half-stone buildings, many in ruins. Rose bushes flank exhausted terraces, along with clumps of lavender. Cross a bouldery streambed at **Clot Giordan** and climb a little, then fork left at a path junction as signposted for Roya. The path winds down a stony groove, with views of Roya below. Watch for big, bright-green lizards in the undergrowth on the way down to a road. Don't follow the road,

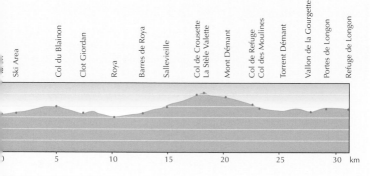

but short-cut down a path and pass between buildings to reach a church.

1hr **Roya 1500m (4920ft)** *Gîte d'étape and restaurant.*

Keep to the right of the church to follow a path downhill. Cross two footbridges over two rivers, at 1465m (4805ft) (enter the Parc National du Mercantour). Zigzag up a forested slope, then climb at a gentler gradient as trees thin out to offer fine valley views. Pass the **Barres de Roya**, where limestone cliffs look like drystone walling. Continue up into a boulder-strewn part of the valley, cross a footbridge and climb to a cabin.

2hr **Cabane de Sallevieille 1955m (6414ft)**

Follow the path carefully through an area of sharp-edged boulders, where the ground is thick with dung from sheep and donkeys, and no grass grows. The path crosses a slight dip on a grassy slope, and later crosses a bouldery streambed. Zigzag uphill to outflank the long cliffs of the **Barre de Sallevieille** (possible tiny water source, easily missed). After passing the cliffs, the path enters a gentle valley with a lush, grassy floor. Cross a thin stream, and while other cliffs are in view, the path climbs grassy slopes and makes an easy traverse of a boulder scree to reach a col.

1hr 30min **Col de Crousette 2480m (8136ft)**

Don't go down the other side of the col,

AURON 1602m

D39

Ravin d'Auron

2014m
Col du Blainon

Clot Giordan

Roya
1500m

Barres de
Roya

Cabane de
Sallevieille
1955m

Barre de
Sallevieille

Col de
Crousette
2480m

Stèle
2587m

Mont
Démant

Le Démant Torrent

1800m

Les Po
de Lon

1810m

Vignols

1982m
Col des Moulines

N

but follow a well-trodden, rough and stony path up across a scree slope. This leads to a small white marble memorial on a high shoulder of Mont Mounier.

15min **La Stèle Valette 2587m (8488ft)** *Wide-ranging view back to the Queyras, and ahead across the Vallée de la Tinée to the Franco–Italian frontier and down to the Mediterranean*

Turn left just before reaching the memorial, walking a short way along the rocky crest before turning right, then turn sharply right to pick up a path downhill. The line of the path is very clear across the rounded slopes of **Mont Démant**, crossing stony ground dotted with sparse clumps of grass, reaching cairns and a signpost. Branch left and note how the limestone bedrock is like paving underfoot. The path winds down in lazy loops to a gentle grassy gap. There is a view from here of Mont Mounier and the awesome Barre Sud du Mounier. Descend to the **Col de Refuge** and briefly leave the national park to pass below a stump of limestone, then re-enter the park on the next grassy col.

Dolomitic limestone forms strange towers of rock high above the hamlet of Vignols

1hr 15min **Col des Moulines 1982m (6499ft)** *View beyond the hamlet of Vignols to the 'hanging valley' of Longon*

Follow a path down across scree slopes, passing a few larches. Drop down to the right along a winding path and cross the **Démant Torrent** at 1810m (5940ft). The path crosses another river nearby, then climbs gently across old grassy terraces. Pass above a long, low cattle shed, the Vacherie de Roubion, and keep below a series of intriguing rocky towers (**NB** strictly no access), where the dolomitic limestone weathers into dramatic landforms. First cross a streambed, then a nearby stream.

45min **Vallon de la Gourgette 1800m (5905ft)** *Vignols is 15min off-route, but has no services*

Climb a zigzag path to cross scree slopes below a cliff. Climb closer to crumbling cliffs and enter the hanging valley, crossing a stream in a ravine. A short ascent leads onto a gentle track, though this peters out in a flat, grassy area overlooked by a chalet, around 1950m (6400ft). Don't be drawn off-course to the chalet, but stay low in the **Portes de Longon**, enjoying easy walking through the grassy valley. Pass a stone pillar (exit the Parc National du Mercantour) and a cattle pond, then let a series of waymark posts lead onwards. The path leads down to an isolated *refuge*.

1hr **Refuge de Longon 1883m (6178ft***) Refuge and restaurant*

DAY 26
Refuge de Longon to St Dalmas

Distance	27 kilometres (17 miles)
Total Ascent	1080 metres (3545 feet)
Total Descent	1675 metres (5495 feet)
Time	7 hours 45 minutes
Map	3641 ET
Nature of Terrain	A long traverse of a deep and forested valley, following good paths and tracks from village to village.
Food and Drink	Restaurants at St Sauveur sur Tinée, Rimplas, La Bolline and St Dalmas.

Accommodation	Hotel, *gîte* and campsite at St Sauveur sur Tinée. Hotel at Rimplas. Hotel and *chambres d'hôte* at La Bolline. *Chambres d'hôte* at La Roche. Hotel, *chambres d'hôte*, *gîtes* and campsite at St Dalmas.

This whole day's walk involves crossing the deep, forested Vallée de la Tinée. The initial descent uses a rugged mule path and gentler forest track. The next part, from Roure to St Sauveur sur Tinée, uses an old mule path pre-dating a long and looping road. The ascent from St Sauveur to Rimplas follows a track that has been hacked from crumbling slate, then old paths and tracks continue from village to village to reach St Dalmas.

Walk down through the valley from the *refuge*, passing the ruins of an old *vacherie*, destroyed by an avalanche, to enter larch forest. ▶ A steep and winding descent leads to a footbridge below a small waterfall. The surrounding rock is sandstone and gritstone, altered by metamorphism. Keep walking down through forest, keeping straight ahead at a path junction, later turning a prominent corner round Crête Autcellier. Continue down across a footbridge over the Ruisseau de l'Arcane, which runs through a ravine cut into soft sandstone. The path cuts across a forested slope, then passes grassy terraces dotted with old cabins, some in ruins.

Watch out for a brief glimpse down the Vallée de la Tinée to La Madone d'Utelle and the distant Mediterranean.

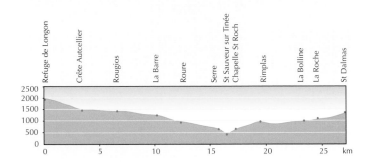

1hr 15min Rougios 1467m (4813ft) *Water*

There is a view of the Mediterranean from the car park.

Turn right as directed at the last cabin and step up to a forest track. Turn left to follow it, with occasional views revealing the depth of the Vallée de la Tinée. The forest track becomes a tarmac road at a small car park. ◄ Step down to the left and follow a path parallel to the road, crossing blocks of purple slate. Cross the road later near a bend (here, a detour right leads to the nearby Arboretum Marcel Kroenlein).

Continue along a rugged, stone-paved path as marked. Pass a few houses, then the path cuts across the road twice to avoid bends. Keep to the left of a small football pitch (water) to walk down to a chapel. Turn left down the road past a house, then right to short-cut down to a lower bend. Drop straight down beside a church, keeping to its left-hand side, to reach the heart of an old village.

1hr 15min Roure 1096m (3596ft) *Gîte détape; bus to St Sauveur de Tinée by arrangement, tel 08 00 06 01 06*

Walk down steps from the church to reach the *mairie*. Walk past the wash-place and turn sharp right down more steps to pass a cog-wheel contraption that once operated a *téléphérique* connecting Roure with St Sauveur. A concrete path leads down past the lowest houses, then a slate-strewn path continues down old terraces to reach a road. Turn right down the road to reach a sharp bend, then drop straight

down a path to zigzag past more terraces, landing on the road at a lower level.

Cross over and continue down the path, which becomes well wooded with oak, chestnut and an occasional fig tree. Zigzag downhill, but watch for a signpost at a junction, and turn left to continue. Cross a concrete water conduit, then cross the road again. Follow the path down to the road, but step to the right to find its continuation. Wind down to cross the road yet again, then walk down one last stretch of path to land on a road beside a graveyard in the Quartier St Blaise. Walk straight ahead to cross a road bridge into town.

The houses of Roure cling to a terraced slope high above the Vallée de la Tinée

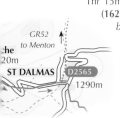

1hr 15min **St Sauveur sur Tinée 496m (1627ft)** *Hotel, gîte d'étape, campsite, bank, post office, shops and restaurants; TAM buses to St Étienne sur Tinée, Auron and Nice, tel 08 00 06 01 06*

Follow the main road straight through town. Immediately on leaving, climb a steep road on the

235

left. The road turns sharply left, then shortly afterwards a path on the right climbs uphill. Pass a bend on the road and climb further, keeping left of the **Chapelle St Roch**. Climb above the chapel to follow the clearest track onwards, past grassy terraces, oak and chestnut.

Wind uphill until the track ends, then continue along a path rising gently across wooded slopes. Another broader track is reached, so keep climbing, enjoying valley views, but beware of the crumbling slate on the left, which has a habit of collapsing. The slate suddenly gives way to quartzite, followed by a series of limestone, sandstone and shale beds. The track itself gives way to a road as it enters a village.

1hr 45min **Rimplas 1016m (3333ft)** *Long-established fortified site, once known as Magdalena, on the Route du Sel, or Salt Route; hotel, restaurant and shop; TRAM buses to St Dalmas and Nice*

The GR5 passes **Rimplas** by road, but it is better to walk through the narrow, stone-paved streets. Leave via the road to pass a chapel, then go down steps on the right and continue straight ahead down a stony path across a rocky slope covered in *maquis*. There is a fine view of the forested **Vallon de Bramatam** and the villages that will be passed later. The path becomes a track, leading to a bend on another track. Head downhill and step to the left before reaching another bend, to follow a narrow path. Descend across a scrubby slope, passing a couple of houses before crossing a narrow stone bridge in a wooded valley.

Reach a road at a hairpin bend and walk downhill. Leave the road at the next bend, stepping to the right of a private track. A narrow path runs along a terrace, then a left turn along another path leads into a wooded valley. Cross a narrow stone bridge and climb to a junction. Turn left up an old cobbled track, passing gnarled chestnuts and hazels in dense woods. The track climbs past orchards, reaching a road end near large buildings. Climb a grassy track to reach a road junction near a church.

1hr 15min **La Bolline 995m (3264ft)** *Hotel, chambres d'hôte, post office, shops, and restaurants; TRAM buses to St Dalmas and Nice*

Climb up the steepest road from the junction, and turn right at a crossroads. Turn left to reach the main road again at the top of a village.

10min **La Roche 1120m (3675ft)** *Chambres d'hôte; TRAM buses to St Dalmas and Nice; TIC tel 04 93 23 25 90* www.colmiane.com

Turn right along the main road, then quickly right again down a minor road. Turn left along a track and follow it uphill to cross the main road twice, as signposted, cutting out lengthy bends. When the main road is reached again, turn right to follow it up to a village.

50min **St Dalmas 1290m (4232ft)** *Hotel, chambres d'hôte, gîtes d'étape, campsite, shops, restaurants and museum; TRAM buses to Nice, tel 08 92 70 12 06.* ▶

There is an option here to switch from the GR5 to the GR52 to finish at Garavan/Menton instead of Nice (see page 254).

DAY 27
St Dalmas to Utelle

Distance	29 kilometres (18 miles)
Total Ascent	1055 metres (3460 feet)
Total Descent	1525 metres (5005 feet)
Time	8 hours
Map	3641 ET
Nature of Terrain	Climb forested and open mountainsides, using paths, tracks and roads later. Rugged paths towards the end are usually well graded, even if they cross steep and rocky slopes.
Food and Drink	Restaurant at Utelle.
Accommodation	Hotel, *gîte* and farm *auberge* at Utelle.

This is a long day's walk, which looks much longer on maps, and there is no way to break the distance. There is road access in the middle, but nowhere to stay.

Most of the climbing comes early in the day and most of the paths and tracks are easy. Even if the mountainsides are steep and rugged, the paths have been well engineered across their flanks and are easy to follow. The hilltop village of Utelle remains hidden until the final descent.

Leave **St Dalmas** by walking up the main road, branching to the right opposite the church, then turning right along the Rue de la Madone. Turn left to find signposts pointing along the Chemin du Col de la Madeleine. Climb a steep and stony track into forest to reach a track junction. Take a path climbing straight up a fairly open slope, then head into dense forest – larches hang heavy with skeins of lichen. Climb through another clearing and turn right at a path junction. Pass a ruined cabin and later drop a little to the forested Col du Varaire at 1710m (5610ft). Keep right to follow the route as marked and signposted, climbing along a winding path in dense forest, to emerge on an open col.

1hr 45min **Col des Deux Caïres 1921m (6302ft)** *View of the Mediterranean and suburbs of Nice*

The GR5 descends a little to cross a grassy slope and small scree slopes, then climbs across a grassy slope above a forest. Climb round a corner on Crête de Serenton. ◄ The path rises across a grassy slope and follows a well-engineered line, turning another corner around 2000m (6560ft) on **Mont**

There is a view from here of Brec d'Utelle, La Madone d'Utelle and Mont Cima.

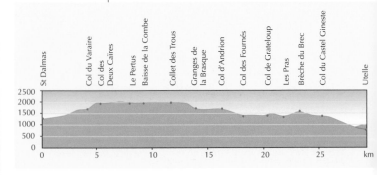

238

Chalancha. Drop to a col at Le Pertus, which is dominated by a huge stump of limestone. Follow the path round the next slope and head down to a lower col.

1hr 15min **Baisse de la Combe 1910 (6266ft)**
The path climbs up across a forested slope, then runs along a crest. Note a transition from limestone to sandstone underfoot, then the path drops downhill a little. Turn left at a signposted junction and zigzag uphill, crossing a shoulder on **Mont Tournairet** to reach a col.

30min **Collet des Trous 1982m (6503ft)**

Immediately after crossing the col, turn left down a grassy track. ▶ Branch right at a waymark post to follow a path down to a bend on a track. Walk down the track, but watch for a right turn down a path to short-cut many bends. Follow the track again, but make a couple more minor short-cuts. Pass a barrier and join a tarmac road near a ruined chapel. Turn right to pass a series of old barracks.

45min **Les Granges de la Brasque 1680m (5510ft)**
Water and nearby dairy farm produce

The road climbs gently to the **Col d'Andrion** at 1690m (5545ft). On reaching a junction between the road and a track, step down to the right. A winding path runs down a forested slope to reach a road. Turn right along the road, but watch for a path down to the left – this leads down to a road bend. Walk down the road, but watch for another path leading down to a lower road bend. Again, walk down the road and watch for

Look out for a brief view of the Mediterranean and suburbs of Nice.

GR52 to Menton

ST DALMAS 1290m

D2565

Les Bosquets

Col des Deux Caïres

2087m ▲*Le Caïre Gros*

Mont ▲*Chalancha* 2102m

Baisse de la Combe 1910m

N

Col du Fort

2086m▲

Mont Tournairet 1680m▲

Les Granges de la Brasque

Col d'Andrion 1690m

D332

Le Mauk 1351m

Col des Fournès

239

a path on the left, this time winding down to a junction of tracks on a col.

1hr 15min Col des Fournés 1351m (4432ft)

Don't follow any of the tracks, but step straight up onto a path marked and signposted as the GR5. This becomes an old forest track, which climbs gently and reverts to a path. Emerge on a stony slope covered in juniper, box and lavender to see the dome of Brec d'Utelle ahead. Enter forest again and roughly contour across a gentle col.

45min Col de Grateloup 1412m (4633ft)

Continue along the forest path to emerge on a grassy slope at **Les Pras**. Branch right at a vague, grassy path junction, signposted for Utelle. Head back into forest with a juniper and box understorey, then climb steeply up grassy terraces reverting to forest. Cut across a steep and rocky slope to reach a rocky col at Le Petit Brec. The path winds steeply uphill, like stone steps, then climbs a well-built ramp up a cliff face. Cross a rocky gap close to the summit of Brec d'Utelle.

The GR5 climbs up a rough and rocky path to reach the Brèche du Brec

30min Brèche du Brec 1520m (4990ft) *View back to Mont Mounier and ahead to the Mediterranean and suburbs of Nice*

Turn a corner on bare limestone and zigzag down a stony path into a forest to reach a col at 1370m (4495ft). Keep right to pass through the forest, briefly crossing a slope with open views. Emerge on a well-defined crest with more views towards the sea, and make a sharp left turn at a path junction. Descend across a steep and rugged slope, even slicing across cliffs. (A couple of narrow stretches, formerly protected by chains, have footbridges to carry the path onwards.) Despite the steepness of the slope, the path heads gently and easily to a col.

30min Col du Castel Gineste 1220m (4003ft) *View back to Mont Mounier and ahead to La Madone d'Utelle*

Look back to Castel Gineste on the descent, which is surrounded by tiered cliffs. The path becomes more rugged underfoot, passing through mixed woods on a steep and rocky slope. There are a glimpses of Utelle when the path turns prominent corners. Later, the village is seen to much better effect, huddled on its hilltop, as the path zigzags down crumbling layers of rock under sparse pines. A signposted path junction is reached. (**Note** A variant route turns right for La Madone d'Utelle – see page 243, variant route.) Turn left to walk down to a concrete road, then cross over a tarmac road to the left of a hotel. The road leads straight into the centre of a fine old village.

45min Utelle 821m (2694ft) *Hilltop village fortified against Saracen raiders; hotel, gîte d'étape, farm auberge, post office, shop and restaurants*

DAY 28

Utelle to Aspremont

Distance	25 or 28 kilometres (15½ or 17½ miles)
Total Ascent	900 or 1205 metres (2950 or 3955 feet)
Total Descent	1220 or 1525 metres (4000 or 5005 feet)
Time	6 hours 45 minutes or 7 hours 45 minutes
Maps	3741 ET and 3742 OT
Food and Drink	Bar near Pont du Cros. Restaurants at Levens, Ste Claire and Aspremont.
Accommodation	Hotels near Levens and at Aspremont.

There are two ways out of Utelle. The main route follows a partly paved path across limestone slopes, passing areas of oaks and pines, with bushy juniper, box and aromatic shrubs. A variant route climbs to the pilgrim church of La Madone d'Utelle, then descends to rejoin the main route.

After dropping into the Gorges de la Vésubie, the lowest point reached on the GR5, a steep climb leads to the fortified hilltop village of Levens, and later to the fortified hilltop village of Aspremont.

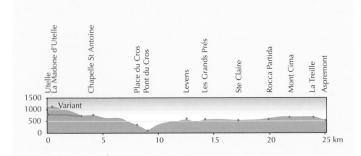

Main Route

Leave the central Place de la Republique in **Utelle**, following the Rue Emile Passeronie, which ends with a flight of steps down to a footbridge. The path is narrow as it climbs, then enjoys views into a deep valley. Rough-paved surfaces and steps lead gently down across a steep limestone slope dotted with box, juniper and evergreen oaks. Cross a small stone bridge in a valley to pass through woods, where old terraces are full of oaks and chestnuts. The path climbs a little then descends to a chapel.

1hr **Chapelle St Antoine 673m (2208ft)**
Dating from 1686, the chapel is open and serves as a shelter – a button inside starts the 'chant of the month'

Variant Route

Leave **Utelle** by backtracking a little along the main GR5 route. Reach a signpost and turn left to follow a path flashed with yellow paint. Pass through a little gap and cross a crumbling slope sparsely planted with pines. Pass just below a col that has a road tunnel bored beneath it, then climb gently round a forested valley head to reach a track junction. Don't follow any track, but climb a rough and stony path marked by cairns. Climb through mixed woods and open slopes, zigzagging up across bands of crumbly shale and limestone. The path broadens, but is rough and stony. Turn left at a junction to reach a road bend, then turn right to follow the road. Another right turn reveals a zigzag path on a forested slope. Cross the road at a higher level, then zigzag up to the road one last time. Turn left to reach a church.

1hr **La Madone d'Utelle 1176m (3858ft)** *Pilgrim church, refuge and restaurant; nearby viewpoint with view from Mont Mounier to Nice*

243

Walk up the road from the church and watch for a signpost on the left. A path hacked from limestone continues down bare and broken rock dotted with juniper, box and thorny scrub. Cross a track and continue down the path, flashed with yellow paint, and follow a grassy track across the broad Col d'Ambellarte at 967m (3173ft), heading for tall pines.

Leave the col using a path, signposted for Chapelle St Antoine, through mixed woods. Pass a couple of ruined buildings while stepping down a series of overgrown terraces, enjoying occasional valley views. Cross a rib of limestone and zigzag down through increasingly dense and thorny scrub, guarding against brambles and wild rose.

When a path junction is reached, turn right to rejoin and follow the main GR5 through woods. Old terraces are full of oaks and chestnuts. The path climbs a little then descends to a chapel.

The GR5 cuts across limestone cliffs, following the course of an old mule track

1hr Chapelle St Antoine 673m (2208ft) *Dating from 1686, the chapel is open and serves as a shelter – a button inside starts the 'chant of the month'*

Follow a terrace through an oak wood, then zigzag down round the Vallon de la Rosièra, passing pines, evergreen oak, juniper, broom and other scrub. The path contours across a cliff, then descends in zigzags, always with fine valley views, though becoming more wooded. Fork left down a stony path, passing olive terraces to reach a chapel.

1hr **Cros d'Utelle 330m (1085ft)** *Water*

Pass left of the chapel and go underneath part of a house called L'Auberge. Walk down steps and watch for markers to avoid a long and bendy road. Cross the road to continue downhill as the path gets rougher near the bottom. Reach a junction with a main road deep in the **Gorges de la Vésubie**.

15min **Pont du Cros 180m (590ft)** *Nearby bar; TRAM bus to Nice, tel 08 92 70 12 06*

Walk down from the main road to cross a graceful stone arch bridge. Climb a winding path, crossing the Canal de Vésubie where it runs through a tunnel. Zigzag uphill among pines, juniper, box and guelder rose. Follow a concrete road uphill a little, but leave it using a path on the left to reach a tarmac road. Cross over and follow a concrete track up to a house. Keep left to walk along an olive terrace, pass above a small quarry, then follow a road to a crossroads. ▶ Turn left, then walk up a road flanked by 'no entry' signs, which is the Avenue Maréchal Foch.

At the crossroads there are restaurants and a shop, and the Ligne d'Azur bus to Nice.

1hr 15min **Levens 550m (1805ft)** *5min off-route; Bank with ATM, post office, shops and restaurants; TIC tel 04 93 79 71 00, www.levenstourisme.com*

Turn left down the Chemin des Valettes, a road that becomes a zigzag stone-paved track. Go straight along the Avenue Charles David. Turn left at the end and walk past an olive mill to a road bend. A path on the right leads up to a main road. Turn right to follow the road between tall houses, then drop down a path on the right. Cross an old stone bridge and turn left to walk among back gardens. Turn left along the Chemin du Vignal, then right along the Route de St Blaise to

Les Grands Prés are fields surrounded by forested hills near the village of Levens

walk beside the wide grassy meadow of **Les Grands Prés** (hotels and Ligne d'Azur bus to Nice nearby).

Towards the end of the meadow watch for a gap on the right, beside house number 684. Follow a path up a slope bearing a few pines, then turn left to cross a shoulder covered in oaks. Take care to follow the marked route straight past old terraces, as there are other paths. Cross a gentle gap covered in pines at 584m (1916ft), where there is a view of the Mediterranean. Walk down past a stone ruin to reach a path junction. Turn left and rise across a slope of pines, passing below an olive terrace. Walk down steps to reach a road.

1hr **Sainte Claire 520m (1705ft)** *Restaurant; Ligne d'Azur bus to Nice and Levens*

Turn right to walk away from the village, keeping straight ahead at a road junction. The road rises, bends and falls gently on a slope of oaks. Turn left up a forest track, the Piste de Rocca Partida. Pass evergreen oaks and a few pines to reach a sign on a col.

45min Rocca Partida 564m (1850ft)

Turn right along a path that heads into trees, taking care passing a split cliff where boulder conglomerate is unstable. If you are worried, stay on the forest track, since the path and track meet at a complex junction on a gap at 609m (1998ft). Climb as marked, straight up a crest of conglomerate bearing pine trees. Cross a slight hump to reach a path junction at 708m (2323ft), where the GR5 heads left. ▶

The path contours easily across slopes of pine and broom, with fine valley views. Turn left along a battered road, the Piste du Mont Cima, to pass a barrier. Turn left down a track and quickly step up to the right. Follow a limestone path down past broom, juniper and evergreen oaks, with Aspremont in view below. Turn left a short way down a road, then turn right down a path to another road, the Route de la Cima. Walk down to a viewpoint at the Place des Salettes. Turn right down the Montée du Commandant Gérome, where tarmac gives way to a track, then walk down the Avenue Caravadossi.

1hr 30min Aspremont 500m (1640ft) *Hotels, restaurants, post office and shop; Ligne d'Azur bus to Nice, tel 08 10 06 10 06*

Aspremont
Around the year 900 many people took to the hills to avoid Saracen raiding parties along the coast. Aspremont, one of several easily defended sites, was known from 1062. Ludovic Macquesan fortified Aspremont in 1432, while Napoleon I burnt the defences in 1810. High in the village the Place du Château can be visited outside school hours (it is used as a school playground).

The turning to the right is flashed yellow for Mont Cima, and recommended for its fine views.

DAY 29

Aspremont to Nice

Distance	13 kilometres (8 miles)
Total Ascent	210 metres (690ft)
Total Descent	720 metres (2360ft)
Time	4 hours 15 minutes
Map	3742 OT
Food and Drink	Plenty of restaurants in Nice.
Accommodation	Plenty in Nice.

This is an easy day, but it can feel very hot after so long on high mountains. The arid slopes of Mont Chauve are followed by a gradual descent. The city of Nice is full of distractions and well worth exploring in detail. The GR5, for some bizarre reason, officially finishes abruptly in a busy square nowhere near the sea. Most walkers will want to finish on the Mediterranean, and the route description below takes you all the way.

Leave **Aspremont** by walking a short way down a road from a car park, as signposted for Nice. Steps down to the right reveal the Chemin de la Vallière, which is a path running parallel to the road, joining it again on a bend. Walk up the Chemin du Campoun, a narrow road giving way to a track.

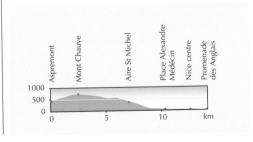

Turn right as signposted for the GR5 (**note** junction with the GR51 along the Balcons de la Méditerranée). Walk up a path on a slope of burnt pines. The way is stony as it climbs a slope covered in broom, passing a ruin at **Fondalin**. Roughly contour across the slopes of **Mont Chauve**, at almost 700m (2295ft), reaching a wide track on a gentle gap.

Looking back towards Mont Chauve, which is the last rugged hillside traversed by the GR5

45min Les Morgues 670m (2200ft)

The wide track ends abruptly, and a pleasant path runs easily along the broomy flanks of Crête de Graus, descending gently and passing beneath a pylon line to reach a gap at 499m (1637ft), where a tin hut stands near old terraces. Cistus and broom grow on broken limestone and the path passes another pylon line. A rough and rocky stretch passes an old stone ruin among deciduous and evergreen oaks. Follow the path down to a pylon and turn right, then later turn left at a path junction. Walk down through scrub and pass through an olive grove among pines and cypress. A tarmac path leads to steps (water) and a road. Walk down the road to a reach mini-roundabout.

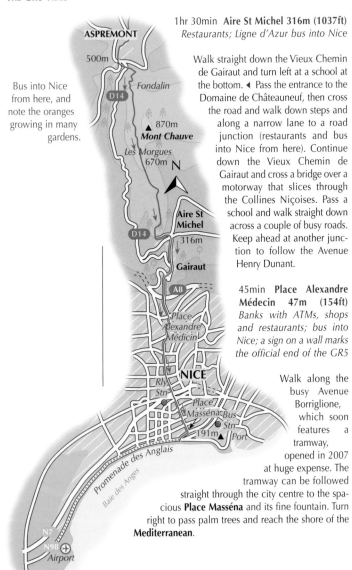

ASPREMONT

500m

Fondalin

Bus into Nice from here, and note the oranges growing in many gardens.

D14

870m
▲ *Mont Chauve*

Les Morgues 670m

N

Aire St Michel

D14

316m

Gairaut

A8

Place Alexandre Médicin

NICE

Rly Stn

Place Masséna Bus Stn

191m▲ Port

Promenade des Anglais

Baie des Anges

N7

N98
Airport

1hr 30min Aire St Michel 316m (1037ft)
Restaurants; Ligne d'Azur bus into Nice

Walk straight down the Vieux Chemin de Gairaut and turn left at a school at the bottom. ◄ Pass the entrance to the Domaine de Châteauneuf, then cross the road and walk down steps and along a narrow lane to a road junction (restaurants and bus into Nice from here). Continue down the Vieux Chemin de Gairaut and cross a bridge over a motorway that slices through the Collines Niçoises. Pass a school and walk straight down across a couple of busy roads. Keep ahead at another junction to follow the Avenue Henry Dunant.

45min Place Alexandre Médecin 47m (154ft)
Banks with ATMs, shops and restaurants; bus into Nice; a sign on a wall marks the official end of the GR5

Walk along the busy Avenue Borriglione, which soon features a tramway, opened in 2007 at huge expense. The tramway can be followed straight through the city centre to the spacious **Place Masséna** and its fine fountain. Turn right to pass palm trees and reach the shore of the **Mediterranean**.

1hr 15min **Promenade des Anglais 0m (0ft)** *Sea level!*

Dip your feet in the sea at the Plage Beau Rivage and you can declare your trek along the GR5 well and truly complete. Congratulations!

Nice

Nice (or 'Nissa' in the local dialect) is the fifth largest city in France, so no justice can be done to it in limited space. The name derives from 'Nikaia', which was a Phocian/Greek trading post in the third century BC. Start exploring where the city was founded, on the Colline du Château. Celtic Ligurians occupied and fortified the hill, and their settlement was Romanised in early Christian times. A medieval town crowned the hill, where the ruins of the 11th-century Cathedral of Ste Marie can be inspected. Nice was once under the authority of Provence, but from 1388 it came under the authority of Savoie. It was a stoutly defended citadel in the 16th century, with a rampart protecting the lower part of town, now known as Vieux-Nice. Louis XIV had the defences dismantled in 1706, following the French occupation of the city during the War of the Spanish Succession. The hill was abandoned and used as a cemetery from 1783, then later converted to a park.

The Colline du Château and Vieux-Nice are flanked on the east by a bustling port, referred to as Le Port, where ferries sail to Corsica. On the west the new city sprawl is referred to as Nice-Ville, which contains the bulk of services and facilites – easily the fullest range on the whole GR5. The main bus station, or Gare Routière, is close to Vieux-Nice, while the Gare SNCF, or railway station, is centrally located in Nice-Ville. The TIC is next to the Gare SNCF, tel 08 92 70 74 07, www.nicetourism.com.

The newly paved Place de Masséna is a fine open space in the heart of the city of Nice

Getting Away from Nice

Anyone who has trekked across the Alps would have no problem with flat city pavements. The railway station, or Gare SNCF, and bus station, or Gare Routière, are only a few minutes' walk from the Promenade des Anglais, and even the Aéroport Nice Côte d'Azur is little more than an hour or so on foot along the promenade, if you want to save the bus fare!

Local Bus Ligne d'Azur, tel 08 10 06 10 06, www.lignedazur.com, operates bus services to and from the Gare SNCF and Gare Routière, but few operate to both, so the easiest method is to change at the intermediate Station Jean-Claude Bermond. To reach the airport, use either the number 98 bus every 20 minutes from the Gare SNCF, or the number 99 bus every 30 minutes from the Gare Routière. The best way to deal with bus travel is to buy a day pass that offers cheap and unlimited transport on all Ligne d'Azur buses.

Long-distance Bus Eurolines (www.eurolines.com) offers services from Nice to London, as well as to other destinations all over Europe. Coaches operate to and from the gloomy Gare Routière. A service offered by VFD (www.vfd.fr) links Nice with Grenoble and Geneva.

Train Check out timetables for the French railway system on www.ter-sncf.com. One timetable offers links between Nice and Geneva via Grenoble.

Air The Aéroport Nice Côte d'Azur has plenty of budget flights to and from Britain, as well as other destinations. The cheapest deals are available with companies such as Easyjet (www.easyjet.com). Air France (www.airfrance.com), the national carrier, offers scheduled flights, as do many other carriers. For airport information tel 08 20 42 33 33, www.nice.aeroport.fr.

Ferry In the summer months a leisurely departure from Nice is possible by ferry. Services operate to Monaco for onward connections along the Rivièra. Adventurous walkers who wish to extend their experience beyond the GR5 can catch a ferry from Nice to Calvi and walk the celebrated GR20 through the mountains of Corsica! (See *GR20: Corsica*, by Paddy Dillon, Cicerone Press.)

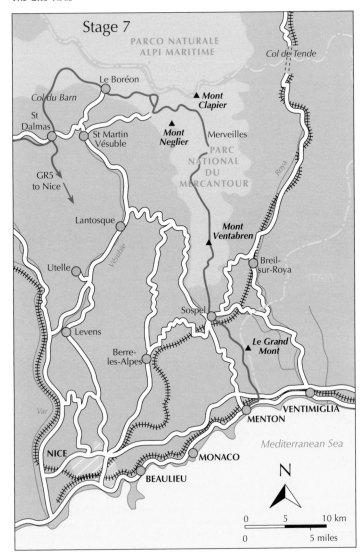

Stage 7

STAGE 7
St Dalmas to Garavan/Menton – GR52

The Lac de Trécolpas sits in a scenic hollow below the rugged Pas des Ladres (Day 28)

General Overview Map	IGN 1:100,000 Carte de Promenade 61 Nice Barcelonnette.
Alternative Maps	None for this stage.

The GR5 ends with relative ease in the city of Nice, while the GR52 from St Dalmas to Menton offers a longer and more mountainous conclusion to the long trek through the Alps. It passes through a splendidly rugged part of the Parc National du Mercantour, where steep and rocky mountains are flanked by slopes of huge boulders. Wildlife abounds, and large animals such as *bouquetin* and *chamois* will often tolerate close approaches. There are wolves in the area too, though these are seldom seen, being extremely shy of human contact after centuries of persecution.

One of the most remarkable places along the GR52 is the Vallée des Merveilles, where Bronze Age artists hammered thousands of rock carvings, or petroglyphs, onto glacially polished rock faces. There is a long day's walk from the Vallée des Merveilles to Sospel (Day 30) completely without services, where food and water need to be carried, but apart from that the route has a good level of services, despite seeming wild and remote.

Looking across the Lac du Trem shortly after leaving the Refuge des Merveilles (Day 30)

The final descent from the mountains to the Mediterranean is steep and rugged, unlike the gentler GR5 plodding along the city streets in Nice. However, once the seashore is reached, the walk through the Alps is over, and unless walkers have made plans to stay longer in the area, all that remains is to head home.

If the GR52 is used to complete the traverse of the Alps, it will doubtless remain one of the enduring highlights of the entire trek. If walkers intend heading home by way of a flight from Nice, there might be time to explore the city before leaving, which is in any case only a short journey by bus or train from Menton.

One of the few rock carvings that can be approached without a guide in the Vallée des Merveilles (Day 29)

DAY 27

St Dalmas to Le Boréon

Distance	22 kilometres (13½ miles)
Total Ascent	1450 metres (4760 feet)
Total Descent	1265 metres (4150 feet)
Time	8 hours
Maps:	3641 ET and 3741 OT
Nature of Terrain	A forested ascent leads to rugged slopes and a high col. A rough descent, then easier paths and tracks through forested valleys, ending with a road-walk.
Food and Drink	Restaurants at Le Boréon.
Accommodation	Hotels and *gîte* at Le Boréon.

The GR52 starts by climbing steadily north to cross the Col du Barn and enter the Parc National du Mercantour – views of the mountains along the Franco–Italian frontier are stunning. The route runs from one forested valley to another, crossing the Col de Salèse to reach the hamlet of Le Boréon. At this point, any extra time could be spent exploring the wolf reserve at Alpha (wolves are present in the wild, but highly unlikely to be spotted).

Leave **St Dalmas** by following a road opposite the *alimentation*, called Chemin des Barches. This passes a car park and later bends right, so keep straight ahead up a track and a path, until a left turn leads up to a road junction. Turn right towards a bridge, but turn left just before it to follow a path up through the Vallon de la Chanaria. The riverbed is usually dry and the valley sides are forested. Follow the path away from the riverbed, up a more open sloping tongue of land, passing the ruined Granges de la Chanaria. Pass a water trough, where the path levels out a bit, then it climbs a bouldery, forested slope. The path winds about as it crosses a couple of clear-felled slopes, before crossing a track near a cabin.

The view from the Col du Barn looks straight into the rugged heart of the Parc National du Mercantour

1hr 30min **Plan de la Gourra 1850m (6070ft)**

Climb uphill to clip a road bend, then climb again to cross the road at a higher level. Cross a shoulder offering fine views of a forested valley, with Rimplas seen in the distance. Pass beneath limestone cliffs, then zigzag up to the road near a car park. Don't go to the car park, but climb to join a well-worn path used by motorists. The path zigzags up to a col.

1hr 30min **Col de Veillos 2194m (7198ft)**

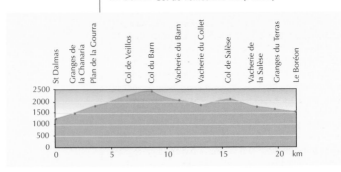

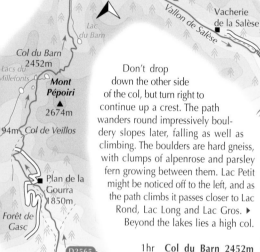

Don't drop down the other side of the col, but turn right to continue up a crest. The path wanders round impressively bouldery slopes later, falling as well as climbing. The boulders are hard gneiss, with clumps of alpenrose and parsley fern growing between them. Lac Petit might be noticed off to the left, and as the path climbs it passes closer to Lac Rond, Lac Long and Lac Gros. ▶ Beyond the lakes lies a high col.

These small lakes are collectively known as the Lacs du Millefonts.

1hr Col du Barn 2452m (8045ft) *Enter the Parc National du Mercantour, with fine views of the mountains*

The path down from the col is rough, stony and convoluted as it negotiates steep and bouldery slopes. Forest gradually becomes established, and the ground cover includes alpenrose, juniper and bilberry. Cross three footbridges and note the ruined Vacherie du Barn off to the right. Walk through a clearing in the forest, then later cross another footbridge. The path leads close to another *vacherie*, but turns right to reach a junction of tracks nearby.

1hr 30min Vacherie du Collet 1842m (6043ft)

Don't follow any of the tracks, but walk along a grassy path as marked. This later climbs back onto the track and follows

it gently up through forest. Watch for a cabin and a pond on the left, then later turn left along a lesser track as marked. This becomes a path climbing back towards the main forest track. Turn left, then right, to follow another stretch of path up to a col where the ground has been trodden to white dust.

45min **Col de Salèse 2031m (6663ft)**

Turn right to cross the col and walk down a stretch of concrete to reach a sharp bend. Drop downhill to follow a gritty, dusty forest path. Clip the forest road further downhill, but stay on the rugged path. This eventually passes the **Vacherie de la Salèse** and reaches a car park. Just before the car park, turn right to cross a footbridge.

The route runs through a series of forested valleys, starting with a descent to the Vacherie du Collet

1hr **Parking de Salèse 1670m (5480ft)**

The path is a mess at first, but improves as it heads downstream. Eventually a signpost points left to a footbridge, where a zigzag path climbs a forested slope to a road. Turn right to follow the road gently downhill, passing crumbling granite, with views of the valley and a reservoir. The GR52 turns left up a road signposted for a *gîte d'étape*, but a nearby path allows hotels to be reached beside a reservoir.

45min **Le Boréon 1475m (4840ft)** *Hotels, gîte d'étape and restaurants; Alpha, tel 04 93 02 33 69, www.alpha-loup.com; wolves have been present in the wild since 1992, having crossed from Italy, but are rarely spotted*

DAY 28

Le Boréon to Refuge de Nice

Distance	18 or 20 kilometres (11 or 12½ miles)
Total Ascent	1815 or 1915 metres (5955 or 6290 feet)
Total Descent	1060 or 1160 metres (3480 or 3805 feet)
Time	7 hours 15 minutes or 8 hours
Map	3741 OT
Nature of Terrain	Forest paths at first, then rough and stony over the Pas des Ladres. Very steep and bouldery over the Pas de Mont Colomb.
Food and Drink	La Madone de Fenestre and Refuge de Nice.
Accommodation	Refuge de la Madone de Fenestre and Refuge de Nice.

The GR52 climbs through a forested valley to a charming lake, then reaches the rugged Pas des Ladres. The route runs so close to the Franco–Italian frontier that many detour to peep through the Col de Fenestre into the Parco Naturale Alpi Maritime. Walkers can stop at the Refuge de la Madone de Fenestre, while those who continue over the Pas de Mont Colomb to the Refuge de Nice should note that the ground is very steep and bouldery.

Leave the *gîte d'étape* at **Le Boréon** by following a road uphill, but only to a bend. Keep straight ahead to follow a path to a higher part of the road. Keep climbing and use rough stone steps to reach a path junction. Turn right and climb to another junction, then turn right again, crossing footbridges over two streams. Contour easily across a forested slope, listening for wolves howling on the Alpha reserve below. When the path forks, keep right to head down towards **Le Boréon Torrent**, but turn left away from the river.

45min **Le Boréon Torrent 1650m (5415ft)**

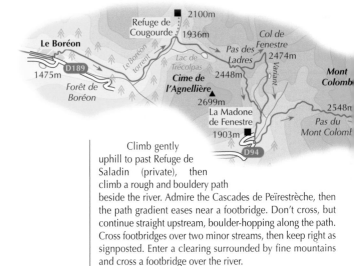

Climb gently
uphill to past Refuge de
Saladin (private), then
climb a rough and bouldery path
beside the river. Admire the Cascades de Peïrestrèche, then
the path gradient eases near a footbridge. Don't cross, but
continue straight upstream, boulder-hopping along the path.
Cross footbridges over two minor streams, then keep right as
signposted. Enter a clearing surrounded by fine mountains
and cross a footbridge over the river.

Detour off-route
before the footbridge
to the Refuge de
Cougourde in 30min

45min **Footbridge 1936m (6352ft)** ◀

Climb up a forested slope and follow a paved path up to a
junction (left offers another detour off-route to the Refuge de
Cougourde in 30min). Turn right and keep climbing, often
steep and stony, levelling out as a lovely lake is reached.

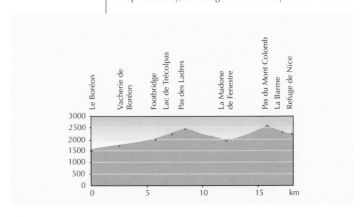

30min Lac de Trécolpas 2150m (7055ft)

The GR52 keeps to the left-hand side of the lake and climbs again. The path is steep and zigzags up a bouldery slope to reach a high col, where the main route turns right, and the variant route to the Col de Fenestre heads left (see below).

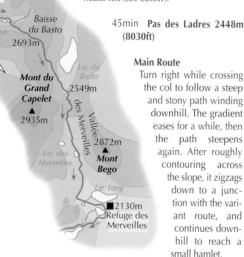

45min Pas des Ladres 2448m (8030ft)

Main Route
Turn right while crossing the col to follow a steep and stony path winding downhill. The gradient eases for a while, then the path steepens again. After roughly contouring across the slope, it zigzags down to a junction with the variant route, and continues downhill to reach a small hamlet.

1hr La Madone de Fenestre 1903m (6243ft) *Pilgrim church, refuge and restaurant*

Variant Route

Turn left while crossing the col to follow a path up a rocky slope, then down a stretch hammered from the rock. Climb again on boulder scree to reach a junction, then turn left and zigzag a short way uphill to reach a rugged col.

30min Col de Fenestre 2474m (8117ft) *Italian – Colle di Finestra; Franco–Italian frontier and boundary between Parc National du Mercantour and Parco Naturale Alpi Maritime*

Drop back down to the path junction, and keep left to descend as signposted for La Madone de Fenestre. The convoluted path crosses bare rock and boulders, passing Lac de Fenestre. Continue downhill, but look to the left to view the later ascent of the Pas de Mont Colomb. The path winds downhill, passing a junction with the main GR52 route and continuing downhill to reach a small hamlet.

1hr 30min **La Madone de Fenestre 1903m (6243ft)** *Pilgrim church, refuge and restaurant*

Walk down across a wet hillside to cross a wooden bridge over a river at the Vacherie de la Madone. Turn left to follow a path climbing steeply upstream, passing sparse pines and grazing cows. Swing right towards the rugged slopes of Caire de la Madone, then swing left to cross a bouldery slope. Watch for red/white markers, which show the easiest way, especially when a short 'hands-on' scramble is required. The route passes bouldery hollows that may contain pools of water – look for *chamois* and *bouquetin* grazing grassy areas. The path climbs one last, loose, awkward slope of boulders to reach a narrow, rocky col.

2hr 15min **Pas du Mont Colomb 2548m (8360ft)** *Distinctive col with a huge stump of rock, or gendarme, in the middle*

The GR52 climbs round the bouldery slopes of Caire de la Madone to reach the Pas du Mont Colomb

The GR52 keeps to the right of the *gendarme,* but an equally steep and rocky path lies left – note how the rock crumbles, and this weakness formed the col. A tightly winding path leads down onto a tongue of boulders. Watch carefully for markers and cairns. Another steep and rugged path continues downhill, reaching a junction with a path above a river.

40min **La Barme 2150m (7055ft)**

Turn left and follow the path uphill to join an old construction track beside **Lac de la Fous**, which is a reservoir. Walk beyond the head of the reservoir and cross a footbridge, then climb stone steps to reach a *refuge.*

20min   **Refuge de Nice 2232m (7323ft)** *Refuge and restaurant*

DAY 29
Refuge de Nice to Refuge des Merveilles

Distance	11 kilometres (6½ miles)
Total Ascent	685 metres (2250 feet)
Total Descent	785 metres (2575 feet)
Time	5 hours
Map	3741 OT
Nature of Terrain	Steep, rocky and bouldery slopes are traversed across two cols, followed by a descent through the bouldery Vallée des Merveilles.
Food and Drink	Refuge des Merveilles.
Accommodation	Refuge des Merveilles.

This is a short day's walk, but it takes time because the ground is so steep, rocky and bouldery. The scenery is astounding, and the mountains contain several small natural lakes as well as reservoirs. If arriving early at the Refuge des Merveilles, join an archaeological tour to visit interesting rock carvings. There are over 36,000 of them, so only a small selection can be seen. (It is forbidden to explore without a guide, as the area is very sensitive.) See page 263 for map.

A path leaves the **Refuge de Nice** and quickly climbs over a slight rise to reach a valley where a footbridge spans a stream. Climb again, following a path that is steep at first, but levels out, becoming rough, rocky and bouldery as it climbs again. An easy stretch passes a lake in a bouldery hollow.

30min **Lac Niré 2353m (7720ft)**

The way ahead passes a couple of small lakes, which can dry out in summer, though patches of grass tend to remain green and offer good grazing for *chamois* and *bouquetin*. Climb another rocky, bouldery slope, keeping an eye open for red/white markers revealing the best course. Stop and admire wonderful mountain views on the ascent. A crunchy, worn, stony path finally leads to a col.

1h15 **Baisse du Basto 2693m (8835ft)**

Cross the col and follow a path down a bouldery slope, passing well to the right of a little lake among rock and boulders. Watch carefully for red/white markers and cairns, as the path

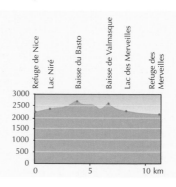

The Lac du Basto is seen to good effect on the way to the Baisse du Valmasque

crosses plenty more boulders. ▶ A junction of paths is reached, and the GR52 turns right to follow a well-trodden zigzag path uphill. Huge boulders of gneiss are mixed with distinctive boulders of volcanic breccia, fallen from peaks on the right. The path crosses another col.

There are views down the valley of the dammed Lac du Basto, which looks pleasant when full.

2h **Baisse de Valmasque 2549m (8363ft)** *Splendid view down the rugged Vallée des Merveilles*

A convoluted path leads down a steep and rugged slope, littered with boulders of volcanic breccia and conglomerate. One stretch of path is level and easy, then there are plenty more boulders on the way to **Lac des Merveilles**. ▶ The valley is usually busy with visitors, many on guided tours round a series of rock carvings on glacially polished rocks. If you do not wish to join a tour, then you must stay on the GR5, except where signposts allow visits to specific sites. The path later runs level and easy, passing within sight of little Lac Mouton. One final zigzag path leads down smooth rocks to a *refuge* above **Lac Long Superior**.

Be aware that the Vallée des Merveilles is a protected archaeological site, and if you are using trekking poles, you must pack them away.

1hr 15min **Refuge des Merveilles 2130m (6990ft)** *Refuge and restaurant; starting point for popular guided* *archaeological tours exploring Bronze Age petroglyphs; interesting information panels bolted to nearby rock outcrops*

DAY 30
Refuge des Merveilles to Sospel

Distance	31 kilometres (19 miles)
Total Ascent	820 metres (2690 feet)
Total Descent	2600 metres (8530 feet)
Time	8 hours 45 minutes
Maps:	3741 OT and 3741 ET
Food and Drink	Plenty at Sospel.
Accommodation	Plenty at Sospel.

This is a long day's walk, but gradients and paths are easier than on previous days, and the latter half is entirely downhill. Water is available at only one point and is not guaranteed, and there is nowhere to eat or stay until Sospel is reached. The route leaves the Parc National du Mercantour and follows a long ridge, while eyes strain to catch a glimpse of the Mediterranean. The interesting old town of Sospel remains hidden almost until the end.

Leave the **Refuge des Merveilles** by walking back up the smooth rocks, then turn left as marked and signposted. The GR52 climbs and keeps left of the dam of Lac Fourca. Follow only the marked path alongside the reservoir, avoiding others, and weaving easily past outcrops and boulders. The path swings right to pass a cliff, exploiting a natural breach. Climb a little further, then dip down to pass between Lac du Trem and the dam of **Lac de la Muta**. Climb alongside the latter, still weaving around outcrops and boulders. A grassy slope leads up to a signpost at Lacs du Diable. Turn left and an easy climb leads to a col.

1hr 15min **Pas du Diable 2430m (7972ft)** *Exit the Parc National du Mercantour*

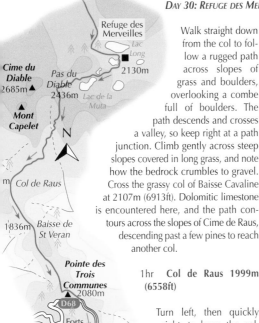

Walk straight down from the col to follow a rugged path across slopes of grass and boulders, overlooking a combe full of boulders. The path descends and crosses a valley, so keep right at a path junction. Climb gently across steep slopes covered in long grass, and note how the bedrock crumbles to gravel. Cross the grassy col of Baisse Cavaline at 2107m (6913ft). Dolomitic limestone is encountered here, and the path contours across the slopes of Cime de Raus, descending past a few pines to reach another col.

1hr **Col de Raus 1999m (6558ft)**

Turn left, then quickly right, to leave the col, following a clear and obvious path across the steep, grassy slopes of Cime de Tuor. A gentle downhill traverse leads to another col at **Baisse de St Veran**, at 1836m (6024ft). Follow a broad, sweeping, zigzag path up what appears to be a pyramidal peak, passing concrete ruins. The path becomes a track – an old military road – climbing gradually, then steepening as it approaches a hill crowned by a fort. Turn left to make a short detour up to the fort.

1hr 15min **L'Authion 2080m (6825ft)** *The Redoute de la Pointe des Trois Communes was an important site for the defence of the Alpes-Maritimes*

Just beyond the turning for the fort, a path leads left down a grassy slope to reach a road bend. Turn left to follow the road, with ruined barracks to the left and the Vacherie de l'Authion down to the right. Watch for the access track rising from the *vacherie*, and a path is marked nearby, heading right from the road, steeply down through a valley, to a lower bend on the same road, around 1760m (5775ft). Water may be available here, but is not guaranteed.

Turn left up the road to reach a bend, and keep straight ahead along a forest track. When a signpost is reached, leave the track to climb up a grassy path on the left, passing close to the top of **Mont Giagiabella**. The path rejoins the track at a higher level, but is more pleasant underfoot. Follow a level stretch of the track, then take another path up to the left, levelling out on a grassy, flowery slope with only a few pines dotted around. The path joins the track again on a col.

1hr 15min Baisse de Ventabren 1862m (6109ft)

Continue straight ahead along a path, cutting easily across the steep slope of **Pointe de Ventabren**, which is covered in clumps of long grass. A prominent track cuts across the next col, Baisse de la Déa, at 1750m (5740ft). The path switches to the other flank of the ridge, becoming a little more rugged on the steep slopes of **Cime de la Gonella**. Pass through a patch of forest where the ground has been worn to dust by sheep seeking shade. Roughly contour round the slopes of **Mangiabo**, then forest cover gives way to a pleasant grassy shoulder on Tête de Gais,

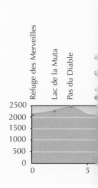

where the path turns sharply left to descend through deciduous woodland and cross another col.

1hr 45min **Baisse de la Linière 1342m (4403ft)**

Walk down through woods as marked, and continue along a broad path on a well-defined crest where pines and bushy

Walkers follow the path away from the Baisse de la Déa, continuing gently down beside Cime de la Gonella

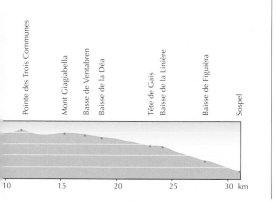

scrub allow occasional views of the valleys alongside. Drop down a winding, stony path through mixed woodlands to reach a road.

1hr Baisse de Figuièra 750m (2460ft)

Cross the road and turn right down a path featuring well-engineered zigzags, leading down to a lower part of the road. Turn left to reach a junction on a prominent bend, then step down onto a track cutting across a slope of ivy-clad oaks. Wind downhill among pines, then go straight ahead through mixed woods. There are valley views throughout, but Sospel remains hidden until the end. Walk straight down a road, the Chemin de Cantamerlou, to reach a school. Go straight down steps called the Montée du Serret, then straight down to a river. Turn left to reach the Vieux Pont and cross the river.

1hr 15min Sospel 350m (1150ft) *All services*

Sospel

Settled since Neolithic times, Sospel avoids the worst heat of Mediterranean summers, and the cold of Alpine winters. It was a notable stage on the Route du Sel (or Salt Route), from Nice to the Piémont, from the 13th century. Traders crossing the Vieux Pont paid a toll, and the peak trading period was the 18th century. Explorations reveal old ramparts and a *donjon* keep. The 16th-century church of Sainte Croix was associated with the Pénitents Blancs. The Cathedral of St Michel, full of Baroque art, dates from 1762, and is one of the grandest in the Alpes-Maritimes. It is flanked by the Chapelle des Pénitents Rouges and Chapelle des Pénitents Gris. Mont Agaisen looms over Sospel, and is crowned with military structures dating from the 1930s, associated with border disputes with Italy. There is a full range of services, including trains to Menton and Nice, and TAM buses to Menton, tel 08 00 06 01 06. TIC tel 04 93 04 15 80, www.sospel-tourisme.com.

DAY 31

Sospel to Garavan/Menton

Distance	20 kilometres (12½ miles)
Total Ascent	1170 metres (3840 feet)
Total Descent	1520 metres (4990 feet)
Time	7hr 15min
Maps	3741 ET and 3742 OT
Nature of Terrain	A forested ascent is followed by a fairly easy walk from col to col. After a final climb, a steep and stony descent ends on an urban coast.
Food and Drink	Plenty at Garavan and Menton.
Accommodation	Plenty at Garavan and Menton.

This is the last day on the GR52. A long and well-wooded climb from Sospel gives way to an easy walk from one col to another, with glimpses of the Mediterranean. After climbing to a final col, a long and stony descent offers occasional views of Menton, but this last stage is very steep and requires careful route-finding. All that remains is to dip a boot ceremonially in the Mediterranean, then figure out how to head home.

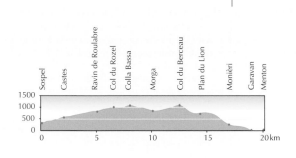

Leave **Sospel** by the road signposted 'Menton par le Col de
Castillon'. Cross a railway and later, when the road turns
round a building, short-cut up steps behind the building
instead. Cross the road and climb up another road, which
later becomes a track. A gentle ascent leads through mixed
forest. Watch for a marker post on the right, where a rough,
stone-paved path short-cuts to a higher bend on the track
near the ruins of **Castes**. Keep straight ahead, then keep left
at a later track junction. Almost immediately, a rugged path
climbs to the right to reach a signposted junction.

1hr **L'Albaréa 638m (2093ft)**

Fork right and follow a path past a ruin, heading further up
through the forest, reaching a shoulder offering fine views
(water). Follow the path gently down into the well-wooded
Ravin de Roulabre before climbing more and more steeply.
Chestnut and holly give way to pines and holly, reaching a
junction of paths and tracks on a col.

1hr 15min **Col du Razet 1032m (3386ft)** *View of the
Mediterranean*

Cross the col before turning left as marked and signposted,
walking gently through an old coppice wood. Pass through a
scrubby sheep-grazing area, with Le Grand Mont in view
ahead. The path climbs through dense pines to reach a track
and sheep pens on another col.

30min
Colla Bassa
1107m
(3632ft) ▸

Le Grand Mont (in
Italian, 'Gramondo')
is a fine viewpoint
on the Franco–
Italian frontier, and
can be climbed by a
detour

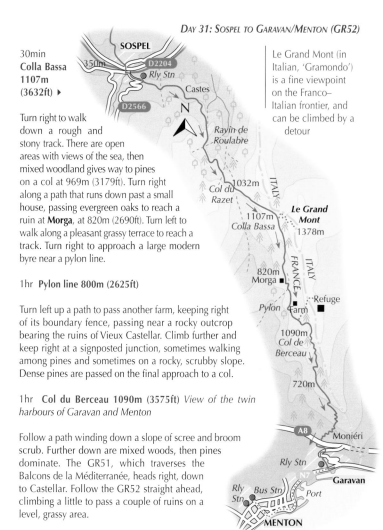

Turn right to walk
down a rough and
stony track. There are open
areas with views of the sea, then
mixed woodland gives way to pines
on a col at 969m (3179ft). Turn right
along a path that runs down past a small
house, passing evergreen oaks to reach a
ruin at **Morga**, at 820m (2690ft). Turn left to
walk along a pleasant grassy terrace to reach a
track. Turn right to approach a large modern
byre near a pylon line.

1hr **Pylon line 800m (2625ft)**

Turn left up a path to pass another farm, keeping right
of its boundary fence, passing near a rocky outcrop
bearing the ruins of Vieux Castellar. Climb further and
keep right at a signposted junction, sometimes walking
among pines and sometimes on a rocky, scrubby slope.
Dense pines are passed on the final approach to a col.

1hr   **Col du Berceau 1090m (3575ft)** *View of the twin
harbours of Garavan and Menton*

Follow a path winding down a slope of scree and broom
scrub. Further down are mixed woods, then pines
dominate. The GR51, which traverses the
Balcons de la Méditerranée, heads right, down
to Castellar. Follow the GR52 straight ahead,
climbing a little to pass a couple of ruins on a
level, grassy area.

45min **Plan du Lion 720m (2360ft)**

The path climbs a little, then a signpost points left to Mont
Carpano (10min detour allows a fine view into Italy). Keep

right to stay on the GR52, which runs downhill and steepens as it passes sparse pines, evergreen oak, broom, guelder rose and aromatic scrub. At a track junction at **Granges St Paul**, at 460m (1510ft), step down from a ruin and go down a steep and rugged path on a slope of pines. Dense parasol pines feature further downhill, before the path lands on a road.

1hr **Moniéri 280m (920ft)** *Take care with route-finding on the final descent, to avoid being drawn onto lengthy loop roads*

Cross the road and walk steeply down to another road. Turn right to walk down this, the Chemin Bella Vista, then turn sharp left to follow another road under the busy A8. Climb for a while, later turning right down a steep concrete road, then turn left down a path to drop to a road end. Walk down the road, round a bend, then turn left after passing Villa Cristina, to short-cut down a path.

Cross the road and drop down a path nearby. Turn right down a road and pass beneath two arches. Do not pass the house called Bethsaïda, but turn right down steps. Cross a road and continue down more steps, passing under a railway bridge at the bottom. Technically, the GR52 turns right to finish at the railway station, but you should walk down the Avenue Katherine Mansfield to finish by the **Mediterranean**.

45min **Garavan 0m (0ft)** *Sea level!*

A tiny scrap of a beach can be found to the left of the harbour, with a couple of free showers for sweaty bodies. Walking any further in that direction quickly leads into Italy. The long Alpine trek is over. Congratulations!

Garavan/Menton

These two settlements merge into one resort, and it is well worth strolling from Garavan to Menton. Old Menton, huddled on a hill once crowned by a château, was from 1346 until 1861 a possession of the Grimaldis of Monaco. The landmark Basilica of St Michel dates from the 17th century. Visit the Cimitière du Vieux Château, marveling at the vari-

A tiny, rugged beach can be reached just to one side of the harbour at Garavan

ety interred there: princes and peasants, exiles and ex-pats, some from countries that no longer exist. Rugby fans should search for the grave of William Webb-Ellis, founder of the sport.

'Menton – ma Ville est un Jardin', proclaims the local tourism authority, and the area abounds in exotic gardens, while the main streets are planted with palms and oranges. The Musée Jean Cocteau is housed in a bastion on the sea wall, and the Promenade du Soleil can be followed, as can shady shopping streets. When the time comes to leave, head inland from the Casino for the rail and bus stations. A full range of services is available, mostly in the new town – TIC tel 04 92 41 76 76, www.menton.fr.

Getting Away from Garavan/Menton Local Bus

Communauté de la Riviera Française is the local bus operator. Several buses link Garavan and Menton, the latter having the main bus station, or Gare Routière. This is located close to the Gare SNCF, or railway station.

Long-distance Bus Rapides Côte d'Azur run expensive daily express services at hourly intervals from Menton to Monaco and Nice. The full journey to the Nice Côte d'Azur Airport takes one hour. Pick up a timetable from the bus station or TIC, or tel 04 97 00 07 00, www.rca.tm.fr. Slower and cheaper TAM buses run every 15 or 20 minutes, winding along the coast, stopping frequently between Menton, Monaco and Nice, without serving the airport. The full journey time is 90 minutes. Tel 04 93 85 64 44, www.rca.tm.fr.

Train Trains stop hourly at Garavan SNCF station, running to Menton and stopping at all stations to Nice, taking less than an hour for the full journey. Speedier half-hourly services can be caught at Menton SNCF station – connections at Nice link with the rest of the French rail network. Those who prefer to leave via Italy can take a train across the border to Ventimiglia ('Vintimille' in French). Timetables and information are easily obtained at stations, or can be checked on www.ter-sncf.com.

Air The Aéroport Nice Côte d'Azur has plenty of budget flights to and from Britain, as well as other destinations. The cheapest deals are available with companies such as Easyjet (www.easyjet.com). Air France (www.airfrance.com), the national carrier, offers scheduled flights, as do many other carriers. For airport information tel 08 20 42 33 33, www.nice.aeroport.fr.

Ferry In the summer months a leisurely departure from Menton is possible by ferry. Services operate to Monaco and St Jean-Cap Ferrat. Ferries from Monaco operate to Nice. Check details with tourist information centres along the Riviera.

Nice If visiting Nice before returning home, basic information about the city and its services can be found on pages 250–53.

APPENDIX 1

Route Summary – North to South

Time	Place	Services
Direct Route		
0hr 00min	St Gingolph	All services, TIC, trains, buses, ferries
1hr 30min	Novel	*Chambres d'hôte*
0hr 45min	La Planche	
1hr 30min	Chalets de Neuteu	Shelter, water
0hr 30min	Col de Bise	
0hr 45min	Chalets de Bise	*Refuge*, restaurants
1hr 00min	Pas de la Bosse	
1hr 00min	Chalets de Chevenne	Water
0hr 30min	Chapelle d'Abondance	All services, TIC, buses
Main Route		
0hr 00min	Thonon-les-Bains	All services, TIC, trains, buses, ferries
0hr 30min	Bridge over Bypass	
0hr 30min	Repos de l'Aigle	
1hr 00min	Armoy	Hotel, shops, buses

Time	Place	Services
0hr 45min	Les Jossières	
1hr 00min	Reyvroz	Cafés
0hr 45min	Bioge	Bar/restaurant, buses
0hr 45min	La Plantaz	
0hr 30min	Les Clouz	
0hr 15min	Outskirts of Vinzier	Campsite, PO, bar, supermarket, café, ATM, buses
1hr 00min	Le Cret – for Chevenoz	*Gîte*, shop, bar, buses, 30min off-route
0hr 30min	Sur les Trables	
1hr 00min	Le Grand Chesnay	Water
0hr 45min	Les Boeufs	
1hr 30min	Tête des Fieux	
0hr 30min	Lac de la Case	
1hr 00min	Col de Pavis	
0hr 30min	Col de Bise	
0hr 45min	Chalets de Bise	*Refuge*, restaurants
1hr 00min	Pas de la Bosse	
1hr 00min	Chalets de Chevenne	Water
0hr 30min	Chapelle d'Abondance	All services, TIC, buses

Time	Place	Services
1hr 15min	Sur Bayard	
1hr 00min	Chalet des Crottes	*Refuge* 1hr 15min off-route
0hr 45min	Chalet de la Torrens	
0hr 45min	Les Mattes	
1hr 30min	Lenlevay	Water
1hr 15min	Col de Bassachaux	*Refuge*, restaurant
1hr 30min	Refuge de Chésery	*Refuge*, restaurant
0hr 45min	Chaux Palin	*Gîte*, restaurant
0hr 55min	Lapisa	*Buvette*
0hr 10min	La Pierre	*Gîte*, restaurant
0hr 10min	La Poyat	
0hr 45min	Col de Coux	
0hr 45min	Torrent de Chardonnière	*Refuge* off-route
1hr 15min	Col de la Golèse	*Refuge*, restaurant
1hr 00min	Les Allamands	Water
0hr 45min	Le Chevreret	
0hr 15min	Samoëns	All services, TIC, buses
1hr 00min	Pont du Perret	Water, buses
1hr 00min	Pont des Nants	Selvagny and Sixt-Fer-à-Cheval off-route – all services
0hr 50min	Cascade du Rouguet	Restaurant
0hr 20min	Chalet de Lignon	Restaurant

Time	Place	Services
1hr 00min	Cascade de la Sauffaz	
1hr 00min	Collet d'Anterne	
0hr 30min	Chalets d'Anterne	*Refuge*, restaurant
1hr 10min	Lac d'Anterne	
0hr 40min	Col d'Anterne	
0hr 30min	Refuge Moède Anterne	*Refuge*, restaurant
0hr 45min	Pont d'Arlevé	
2hr 15min	Col du Brévent	
0hr 45min	Le Brévent	Restaurant, *téléphérique* to Chamonix
0hr 45min	Refuge de Bellachat	*Refuge*, restaurant
1hr 00min	Merlet	Wildlife park, restaurant, off-route
1hr 30min	Les Houches	All services, TIC, trains, buses
1hr 45min	Col de Voza	Hotel, café/bar, tramway
0hr 10min	Refuge de Fioux	*Gîte*, restaurant
0hr 35min	Bionnassay	*Auberge/gîte*, café
0hr 45min	Champel	*Gîte*, water
1hr 00min	Tresse	Hotel, restaurant, buses
1hr 00min	Les Contamines-Montjoie	All services, TIC, buses

Time	Place	Services
Variant Route		
0hr 00min	Col de Voza	Hotel, café/bar, tramway
0hr 45min	Passarelle de Glacier	
0hr 45min	Col de Tricot	
1hr 00min	Chalets de Miage	*Refuge*, restaurant
0hr 30min	Chalets du Truc	*Refuge*, restaurant
1hr 15min	Les Contamines-Montjoie	All services, TIC, buses
Main Route		
0hr 00min	Les Contamines-Montjoie	All services, TIC, buses
1hr 00min	Notre Dame de la Gorge	Restaurant
0hr 30min	Chalet de Nant Borrant	*Refuge*, restaurant
1hr 00min	Refuge de la Balme	*Refuge*, restaurant
0hr 45min	Plan Jovet	
1hr 30min	Col du Bonhomme	Shelter
0hr 45min	Croix du Bonhomme	*Refuge*, restaurant, Les Chapieux off-route
1hr 15min	Col de la Sauce	

Time	Place	Services
0hr 30min	Chalet Bel-Air	
0hr 45min	Plan de la Lai	*Refuge*, restaurant, nearby gite
0hr 40min	La Petite Berge	
0hr 50min	Lavachay	
0hr 45min	Presset	
1hr 30min	Col du Bresson	*Refuge* 20min off-route
1hr 00min	Refuge de la Balme	*Refuge*, restaurant
2hr 00min	Les Fours	
0hr 30min	Valezan	*Auberge, gite, restaurant*
0hr 45min	Bellentre	Bar/shop, post office
0hr 10min	Pont de Bellentre	
Variant Route		
0hr 00min	Pont de Bellentre	
1hr 00min	Landry	Hotel, restaurant, shop, bar, campsite, trains, buses
1hr 30min	Moulin	Peisey 15min off-route, buses
Main Route		
0hr 00min	Pont de Bellentre	

Time	Place	Services
0hr 30min	Pas de la Tovière	
1hr 30min	Val d'Isère	All services, TIC, buses
2hr 00min	Main Road	
1hr 30min	Col de l'Iseran	Restaurant
0hr 30min	Pont de la Neige	
0hr 45min	La Lenta	Option to descend to Bonneval to link with GR5E in 1hr
1hr 00min	Les Roches	
0hr 45min	Le Vallon	Possible *gîte d'alpage*
0hr 45min	Ruisseau du Pis	
0hr 15min	Bessans	All services except bank. TIC, buses, link with GR5E
1hr 00min	Le Chalp	Nearby campsite
0hr 30min	Le Collet	Water
1hr 45min	Refuge de Vallonbrun	*Refuge*, restaurant
0hr 45min	Plan de la Cha	
1hr 15min	Refuge du Cuchet	Unstaffed *refuge* with kitchen – own supplies needed
0hr 45min	Pré Valliant	
1hr 00min	La Turra	
1hr 45min	Bellecombe	Buses
0hr 30min	Refuge de Plan du Lac	*Refuge*, restaurant, buses

Time	Place	Services
1hr 00min	Montorlin	Water
0hr 15min	Montchavin	Hotels, shops, PO, ATM, restaurants, TIC
0hr 30min	La Jacottaz	
1hr 00min	Moulin	Peisey 15min off-route, buses
0hr 40min	Palais de la Mine	*Gîte* and restaurant nearby
0hr 10min	Les Lanches	*Buvette*, buses
0hr 10min	Chalet-Refuge de Rosuel	*Refuge*, restaurant, buses
1hr 45min	Path Junction	Option to walk direct to Refuge d'Entre-le-Lac
0hr 30min	Chalets de la Plagne	
0hr 25min	Path Junction	
0hr 15min	Refuge d'Entre-le-Lac	*Refuge*, restaurant
0hr 25min	Path Junction	
1hr 30min	Refuge du Col du Palet	*Refuge*, restaurant
0hr 05min	Col du Palet	
0hr 30min	Tichot Télésiège	
0hr 15min	Croix de Lognan	Short-cut via Val Claret to link with GR55
0hr 30min	Tignes-le-Lac	All services, TIC, buses, link with GR55

Time	Place	Services
0hr 30min	La Renaudière	Buses, nearby *refuge*, restaurant and link with GR55
1hr 00min	Mont de la Para	
1hr 00min	Lacs des Lozières	
1hr 00min	Ruiseau de Miribel	
1hr 00min	Refuge de l'Arpont	*Refuge*, restaurant
1hr 00min	Le Mont	
0hr 45min	Montafia Dessus	
1hr 45min	La Loza	
1hr 00min	La Turra	
1hr 00min	Le Montana	Hotel, *refuge*, restaurant, *télésiège* to Aussois
0hr 20min	Refuge de Plan Sec	*Refuge*, restaurant, just off-route
0hr 20min	Refuge de la Fournache	*Refuge*, restaurant, just off-route
0hr 20min	Pont de la Sétéria	
1hr 30min	Col du Barbier	
1hr 30min	Chalets de l'Orgère	*Refuges*, restaurants, 10min off-route
0hr 30min	Pierre Brune	Water, short-cut to Modane in 2hr
0hr 30min	Polset	Water, *chalet d'alpage*, restaurant off-route

Time	Place	Services
1hr 15min	Track Junction	
0hr 30min	Loutraz	
0hr 15min	Modane/Fourneaux	All services, TIC, trains, buses
GR55 Variant		
0hr 00min	Tignes-le-Lac	All services, TIC, buses, link with GR5
0hr 30min	Val Claret	All services, TIC, buses, link with GR5
2hr 00min	Col de la Leisse	
1hr 30min	Refuge de la Leisse	*Refuge*, restaurant
1hr 15min	Pont de la Croé Vie	
0hr 30min	Refuge d'Entre Deux Eaux	*Refuge*, restaurant, nearby *gîte*, link with GR5 in 15min
0hr 20min	Pont de la Croé Vie	
0hr 45min	Blockhouse	
1hr 15min	Refuge Col de la Vanoise	*Refuge*, restaurant
0hr 30min	Lac des Vaches	
0hr 30min	Refuge les Barmettes	*Refuge*, restaurant
0hr 45min	Les Fontanettes	Restaurant
0hr 30min	Pralognan-la-Vanoise	All services, TIC, buses
0hr 45min	Pont de Gerlon	

Time	Place	Services
0hr 20min	Les Prioux	*Refuge*, restaurant
0hr 45min	Refuge du Roc de la Pêche	*Refuge*, restaurant
2hr 15min	Refuge de Péclet-Polset	*Refuge*, restaurant
1hr 00min	Col de Chavière	
0hr 45min	Path Junction	Option to descend to Refuge de l'Orgère in 1hr 15min
1hr 00min	Polset	Water, *chalet d'alpage*, restaurant off-route
1hr 15min	Track Junction	
0hr 30min	Loutraz	
0hr 15min	Modane/Fourneaux	All services, TIC, trains, buses

GR5E Variant

Time	Place	Services
0hr 00min	Tralenta/Bonneval-sur-Arc	GR5E, hotels, *refuge*, PO, shops, restaurants, TIC, bus
1hr 30min	Le Villaron	*Gîte*, water
0hr 45min	Bessans	All services except bank. TIC, buses, link with GR5

Time	Place	Services
0hr 45min	Les Chardonnettes	Nearby campsite
1hr 00min	Chantelouve d'en Haut	
1hr 00min	Lanslevillard	All services, TIC, buses
0hr 30min	Lanslebourg-Mont Cenis	All services, TIC, buses
1hr 30min	Termignon	All services except bank; TIC, buses
0hr 45min	Sollières-Envers	Campsite
1hr 15min	Le Verney	*Boulangerie/patisserie*, buses
0hr 15min	Bramans	Hotel/restaurant, *gîte*, campsite, shop, PO, buses
0hr 15min	Croix du Mollard	
1hr 00min	Fort Marie-Thérèse	Restaurant, buses
1hr 00min	La Norma	ATM, shops, restaurants, TIC, buses by arrangement
0hr 45min	Modane-Pâquier	Link with GR5 main route
0hr 15min	Modane/Fourneaux	All services, TIC, trains, buses

Time	Place	Services
Main Route		
0hr 00min	Modane/Fourneaux	All services, TIC, trains, buses
0hr 15min	Modane-Pâquier	Link with GR5E
2hr 00min	Notre Dame du Charmaix	
0hr 15min	Valfréjus	Hotels, *gîte*, PO, ATM, shops, restaurants
1hr 30min	Le Lavoir	
2hr 00min	Refuge du Thabor	*Refuge*, restaurant
0hr 15min	Col de la Vallée Étroite	
1hr 15min	Pont de la Fonderie	
0hr 45min	Granges de la V Étroite	*Refuges*, restaurants
1hr 30min	Col des Thures	
0hr 30min	Path Junction	Junction of GR5 and GR5B
0hr 45min	Chalet Forestière	
0hr 30min	Chapelle des Ames	Junction of GR5 and GR5C
1hr 00min	Plampinet	*Auberges, chambres d'hôte, restaurants, buses*
GR5B Variant		
0hr 00min	Path Junction	Junction of GR5 and GR5B

Time	Place	Services
1hr 00min	Col de l'Échelle	Buses
0hr 30min	La Mauvais Pas	Buses
2hr 15min	Col de Pertusa	
0hr 45min	Track junction	Junction of GR5 and GR5B
GR5C Variant		
0hr 00min	Chapelle des Ames	Junction of GR5 and GR5C
2hr 00min	Lac de Cristol	
0hr 45min	Porte de Cristol	
0hr 45min	Col de Granon	Café
0hr 30min	Col de Barteaux	Variant available to Serre des Aigles
1hr 45min	Serre des Aigles	
1hr 15min	Croix de Toulouse	
0hr 45min	Fort des Salettes	
0hr 15min	Cité Vauban	All services, being part of Briançon
0hr 30min	Briançon	All services, TIC, trains, buses
Main Route		
0hr 00min	Plampinet	*Auberges, chambres d'hôte, restaurants, buses*
1hr 45min	Chalets des Acles	

Time	Place	Services
1hr 45min	Col de Dormillouse	
0hr 30min	Col de la Lauze	
0hr 45min	Vallon des Baisses	
1hr 15min	Montgenèvre	All services, TIC, buses
0hr 15min	Golf Course	
1hr 00min	Track Junction	*Vachette, gîte,* campsite, buses, 10min off-route
0hr 45min	L'Envers du Fontenil	Le Fontenil, *gîte,* 5min off-route
0hr 15min	Pont d'Asfeld	
0hr 30min	Briançon	All services, TIC, trains, buses
0hr 15min	Pont de Cervières	
1hr 00min	Sachas	Villard St Pancrace, *gîte,* PO, restaurant, 10min off-route
		Buvette
1hr 30min	Chalets des Ayes	
1hr 15min	Chalets Vers le Col	Basic unstaffed *refuge;* own supplies needed
0hr 45min	Col des Ayes	
0hr 45min	Pra Premier	
1hr 00min	Brunissard	*Gîte,* restaurants, buses

Time	Place	Services
0hr 15min	La Chalp	Hotels, *chambres d'hôte,* restaurants, buses
1hr 00min	Les Maisons	Water
0hr 30min	Lac de Roue	*Gîte,* 30min off-route at Souliers
1hr 15min	Château-Queyras	Shop, restaurants, PO, campsite, TIC, buses
1hr 00min	Le Pré Premier	Water
1hr 00min	Fontaine Rouge	Water
1hr 30min	Col Fromage	Shelter
0hr 45min	Villard	
0hr 30min	Ceillac	All services except bank. TIC, buses
0hr 30min	Pied du Mélezet	Hotel, restaurant
2hr 00min	Lac Miroir	
1hr 30min	Lac Ste Anne	
1hr 00min	Col Girardin	
0hr 45min	Path Junction	Option to descend off-route to Maljasset for lodgings
1hr 00min	La Barge	Water, buses by arrangement
1hr 00min	Le Pont Vouté	

Time	Place	Services
0hr 45min	Road Junction	All services 15min–1hr 15min off-route at St Paul
1hr 00min	Fouillouse	*Gîte*, restaurant, buses by arrangement
2hr 00min	Col du Vallonet	
1hr 15min	Col de Mallemort	
2hr 00min	Larche	Hotel, *gîtes*, restaurants, PO, campsite/shop, buses
1hr 15min	Pont Rouge	
1hr 45min	Lac du Lauzanier	
1hr 30min	Pas de la Cavale	
1hr 45min	Col des Fourches	
0hr 45min	Bousieyas	*Gîte, chambres d'hôte*, restaurant, campsite
1hr 30min	Col de la Colombière	
1hr 30min	St Dalmas le Selvage	*Gîte, chambres d'hôte*, shop, restaurants, TIC
1hr 00min	Col d'Anelle	Possible water
0hr 15min	Anelle	
1hr 00min	St Étienne de Tinée	All services, TIC, buses
0hr 30min	St Maur	Buses
1hr 00min	Dirt Road	
0hr 15min	Auron	All services, TIC, buses
1hr 30min	Col du Blainon	
1hr 00min	Roya	*Gîte*, restaurant
2hr 00min	Cabane de Sallevieille	
1hr 30min	Col de Crousette	
0hr 15min	La Stèle Valette	
1hr 15min	Col des Moulines	
0hr 45min	Vallon de la Gourgette	
1hr 00min	Refuge de Longon	*Refuge*, restaurant
1hr 15min	Rougios	Water
1hr 15min	Roure	*Gîte*, buses by arrangement
1hr 15min	St Sauveur de Tinée	Hotel, *gîte*, camp site, bank, PO, shop, restaurants, buses
1hr 45min	Rimplas	Hotel, restaurant, shop, buses
1hr 15min	La Bolline	Hotel, *chambres d'hôte*, PO, shops, restaurants, buses
0hr 10min	La Roche	*Chambres d'hôte*, TIC, buses

Time	Place	Services
0hr 50min	St Dalmas	Hotel, *chambres*, *gîtes*, campsite, shops, restaurants, bus
1hr 45min	Col des Deux Caires	
1hr 15min	Baisse de la Combe	
0hr 30min	Collet des Trous	
0hr 45min	Granges de la Brasque	Water, nearby dairy farm produce
1hr 15min	Col des Fournés	
0hr 45min	Col de Grateloup	
0hr 30min	Brèche du Brec	
0hr 30min	Col du Castel Gineste	
0hr 45min	Utelle	Hotel, *gîte*, shop, restaurants

Variant Route

Time	Place	Services
0hr 00min	Utelle	Hotel, *gîte*, shop, restaurants
1hr 00min	La Madone d'Utelle	*Refuge*, restaurant
1hr 00min	Chapelle St Antoine	Shelter

Main Route

Time	Place	Services
0hr 00min	Utelle	Hotel, *gîte*, shop, restaurants

Time	Place	Services
1hr 00min	Chapelle St Antoine	Shelter
1hr 00min	Cros d'Utelle	Water
0hr 15min	Pont du Cros	Bar, buses
1hr 15min	Levens	Bank, ATM, PO, shops, restaurants, TIC, buses
0hr 30min	Les Grands Pres	Hotels, buses
0hr 30min	Ste Claire	Restaurant, buses
0hr 45min	Rocca Partida	
1hr 30min	Aspremont	Hotels, restaurants, PO, shop, buses
0hr 45min	Les Morgues	
1hr 30min	Aire St Michel	Hotel, restaurants, buses
0hr 45min	Place Alexandre Médecin	Banks, ATMs, shops, restaurants, buses
1hr 15min	Promenade des Anglais	Nice – all services, TIC, trains, buses, airport, end of GR5

GR52 Variant

Time	Place	Services
0hr 00min	St Dalmas	Hotel, *chambres*, *gîtes*, campsite, shops, restaurants, bus

Time	Place	Services
1hr 30min	Plan de la Gourra	
1hr 30min	Col de Veillos	
1hr 00min	Col du Barn	
1hr 30min	Vacherie du Collet	
0hr 45min	Col de Salèse	
1hr 00min	Parking de Salèse	
0hr 45min	Le Boréon	Hotels, *gîte*, restaurants
0hr 45min	Le Boréon Torrent	
0hr 45min	Footbridge	*Refuge* 30min off-route
1hr 30min	Lac de Trécolpas	
0hr 45min	Pas des Ladres	Variant route to Col de Fenestre in 30min
1hr 00min	La Madone de Fenestre	*Refuge*, restaurant
2hr 15min	Pas du Mont Colomb	
0hr 40min	La Barme	
0hr 20min	Refuge de Nice	*Refuge*, restaurant
0hr 30min	Lac Niré	
1hr 15min	Baisse du Basto	
2hr 00min	Baisse de Valmasque	

Time	Place	Services
1hr 15min	Refuge des Merveilles	*Refuge*, restaurant
1hr 15min	Pas du Diable	
1hr 00min	Col de Raus	
1hr 15min	L'Authion	
0hr 25min	Road Bend	Possible water
0hr 50min	Baisse de Ventabren	
1hr 45min	Baisse de la Linière	
1hr 00min	Baisse de Figuièra	
1hr 15min	Sospel	All services, TIC, trains, buses
1hr 00min	L'Albarea	
1hr 15min	Col du Razet	
0hr 30min	Colla Bassa	
1hr 00min	Pylon Line	
1hr 00min	Col du Berceau	
0hr 45min	Plan du Lion	
1hr 00min	Moniéri	
0hr 45min	Garavan/Menton	All services, TIC, trains, buses, end of GR55

APPENDIX 2
Route Summary – South to North

Time	Place	Services
0hr 00min	Promenade des Anglais	Nice – all services, TIC, trains, bus, airport, start of GR5
1hr 45min	Place Alexandre Médecin	Banks, ATMs, shops, restaurants, buses
1hr 00min	Aire St Michel	Hotel, restaurants, buses
1hr 45min	Les Morgues	
0hr 30min	Aspremont	Hotels, restaurants, PO, shop, buses
1hr 30min	Rocca Partida	
0hr 45min	Ste Claire	Restaurant, buses
0hr 30min	Les Grands Pres	Hotels, buses
0hr 30min	Levens	Bank, ATM, PO, shops, restaurants, TIC, buses
1hr 00min	Pont du Cros	Bar, buses
0hr 30min	Cros d'Utelle	Water
1hr 15min	Chapelle St Antoine	Shelter
1hr 15min	Utelle	Hotel, *gîte*, shop, restaurants

Time	Place	Services
Variant Route		
0hr 00min	Chapelle St Antoine	Shelter
1hr 15min	La Madone d'Utelle	*Refuge*, restaurant
0hr 45min	Utelle	Hotel, *gîte*, shop, restaurants
Main Route		
0hr 00min	Utelle	Hotel, *gîte*, shop, restaurants
1hr 15min	Col du Castel Gineste	
1hr 15min	Brèche du Brec	
0hr 30min	Col de Grateloup	
0hr 45min	Col des Fournés	
1hr 30min	Granges de la Brasque	Water, nearby dairy farm produce
1hr 00min	Collet des Trous	
0hr 30min	Baisse de la Combe	
1hr 15min	Col des Deux Caïres	
0hr 45min	St Dalmas	Hotel, *chambres*, *gîtes*, campsite, shops, restaurants, bus

Time	Place	Services
GR52 Variant		
0hr 00min	Garavan/Menton	All services, TIC, trains, buses, start of GR52
1hr 00min	Moniéri	
1hr 15min	Plan du Lion	
1hr 00min	Col du Berceau	
0hr 45min	Pylon Line	
1hr 15min	Colla Bassa	
0hr 30min	Col du Razet	
0hr 00min	L'Albarea	
0hr 45min	Sospel	All services, TIC, trains, buses
1hr 30min	Baisse de Figuièra	
1hr 30min	Baisse de la Linière	
2hr 30min	Baisse de Ventabren	
1hr 00min	Road Bend	Possible water
0hr 30min	L'Authion	
0hr 00min	Col de Raus	
1hr 15min	Pas du Diable	
1hr 00min	Baisse des Merveilles	Refuge, restaurant
1hr 30min	Baisse de Valmasque	
1hr 30min	Baisse du Basto	
0hr 25min	Lac Niré	
0hr 50min	Refuge de Nice	Refuge, restaurant
0hr 15min	La Barme	
1hr 00min	Pas du Mont Colomb	

Time	Place	Services
1hr 30min	La Madone de Fenestre	Refuge, restaurant, variant route to Col de Fenestre 2hr
1hr 45min	Pas des Ladres	
0hr 35min	Lac de Trécolpas	
0hr 25min	Footbridge	Refuge 30min off-route
0hr 35min	Le Boréon Torrent	
0hr 45min	Le Boréon	Hotels, gîte, restaurants
1hr 00min	Parking de Salèse	
1hr 15min	Col de Salèse	
0hr 30min	Vacherie du Collet	
2hr 00min	Col du Barn	
0hr 45min	Col de Veillos	
0hr 50min	Plan de la Gourra	
0hr 50min	St Dalmas	Hotel, chambres, gîtes, campsite, shops, restaurants, bus
Main Route		
0hr 00min	St Dalmas	Hotel, chambres, gîtes, campsite, shops, restaurants, bus

Time	Place	Services
0hr 45min	La Roche	*Chambres d'hôte*, TIC, buses
0hr 10min	La Bolline	Hotel, *chambres d'hôte*, PO, shops, restaurants, buses
1hr 15min	Rimplas	Hotel, restaurant, shop, buses
1hr 15min	St Sauveur de Tinée	Hotel, *gîte*, camp site, bank, PO, shop, restaurants, buses
1hr 45min	Roure	*Gîte*, buses by arrangement
1hr 30min	Rougios	Water
1hr 30min	Refuge de Longon	*Refuge*, restaurant
0hr 45min	Vallon de la Gourgette	
1hr 00min	Col des Moulines	
2hr 00min	La Stèle Valette	
0hr 15min	Col de Crousette	
1hr 15min	Cabane de Sallevieille	
1hr 45min	Roya	*Gîte*, restaurant
1hr 45min	Col du Blainon	
1hr 00min	Auron	All services, TIC, buses
0hr 15min	Dirt Road	
0hr 30min	St Maur	Buses
0hr 30min	St Étienne de Tinée	All services, TIC, buses

Time	Place	Services
1hr 45min	Anelle	
0hr 15min	Col d'Anelle	Possible water
0hr 45min	St Dalmas le Selvage	*Gîte, chambres d'hôte*, shop, restaurants, TIC
2hr 00min	Col de la Colombière	
1hr 15min	Bousieyas	*Gîte, chambres d'hôte*, restaurant, campsite
1hr 00min	Col des Fourches	
2hr 00min	Pas de la Cavale	
1hr 15min	Lac du Lauzanier	
1hr 30min	Pont Rouge	
1hr 15min	Larche	Hotel, *gîtes*, restaurants, PO, campsite/shop, buses
3hr 00min	Col de Mallemort	
1hr 15min	Col du Vallonet	
1hr 30min	Fouillouse	*Gîte*, restaurant, buses by arrangement
0hr 45min	Road Junction	All services 15min–1hr 15min off-route at St Paul
1hr 00min	Le Pont Vouté	
1hr 00min	La Barge	Water, buses by arrangement

Time	Place	Services	Time	Place	Services
1hr 30min	Path Junction	Option to descend off-route to Maljasset for lodgings	0hr 30min	Chalets Vers le Col	Basic unstaffed *refuge;* own supplies needed
1hr 15min	Col Girardin		1hr 00min	Chalets des Ayes	*Buvette*
0hr 45min	Lac Ste Anne		1hr 15min	Sachas	Villard St Pancrace, *gîte,* PO, restaurant, 10min off-route
1hr 00min	Lac Miroir				
1hr 30min	Pied du Mélezet	Hotel, restaurant			
0hr 30min	Ceillac	All services except bank; TIC, buses	1hr 00min	Pont de Cervières	
			0hr 15min	Briançon	All services, TIC, trains, buses
0hr 40min	Villard				
1hr 20min	Col Fromage	Shelter	0hr 40min	Pont d'Asfeld	
1hr 20min	Fontaine Rouge	Water	0hr 15min	L'Envers du Fontenil	Le Fontenil, *gîte,* 5min off-route
0hr 45min	Le Pré Premier				
0hr 45min	Château-Queyras	Shop, restaurants, PO, campsite, TIC, buses	0hr 45min	Track Junction	*Vachette, gîte,* camp site, buses, 10min off-route
1hr 45min	Lac de Roue	*Gîte* 30min off-route at Souliers	1hr 15min	Golf Course	
			0hr 15min	Montgenèvre	All services, TIC, buses
0hr 20min	Les Maisons	Water			
1hr 00min	La Chalp	Hotels, *chambres d'hôte,* restaurants, buses	1hr 30min	Vallon des Baisses	
			1hr 00min	Col de la Lauze	
			0hr 30min	Col de Dormillouse	
0hr 15min	Brunissard	*Gîte,* restaurants, buses	1hr 20min	Chalets des Acles	
			1hr 20min	Plampinet	*Auberges, chambres d'hôte,* restaurants, buses
1hr 15min	Pra Premier				
1hr 00min	Col des Ayes				

293

Time	Place	Services
Main Route		
0hr 00min	Plampinet	*Auberges, chambres d'hôte*, restaurants, buses
1hr 10min	Chapelle des Ames	Junction of GR5 and GR5C
0hr 40min	Chalet Forestière	
1hr 00min	Path Junction	Junction of GR5 and GR5B
0hr 30min	Col des Thures	
1hr 15min	Granges de la V Étroite	*Refuges*, restaurants
1hr 00min	Pont de la Fonderie	
1hr 45min	Col de la Vallée Étroite	
0hr 15min	Refuge du Thabor	*Refuge*, restaurant
1hr 30min	Le Lavoir	
1hr 00min	Valfréjus	Hotels, *gîte*, PO, ATM, shops, restaurants
0hr 15min	Notre Dame du Charmaix	
1hr 30min	Modane-Pâquier	Link with GR5E
0hr 15min	Modane/Fourneaux	All services, TIC, trains, buses
GR5E Variant		
0hr 00min	Modane/Fourneaux	All services, TIC, trains, buses

Time	Place	Services
GR5C Variant		
0hr 00min	Briançon	All services, TIC, trains, buses
0hr 40min	Cité Vauban	All services, being part of Briançon
0hr 20min	Fort des Salettes	
1hr 00min	Croix de Toulouse	
1hr 45min	Serre des Aigles	
1hr 45min	Col de Barteaux	Variant available to Serre des Aigles
0hr 30min	Col de Granon	Café
0hr 45min	Porte de Cristol	
0hr 30min	Lac de Cristol	
1hr 30min	Chapelle des Ames	Junction of GR5 and GR5C
GR5B Variant		
0hr 00min	Track junction	Junction of GR5 and GR5B
1hr 00min	Col de Pertusa	Buses
2hr 00min	La Mauvais Pas	Buses
0hr 30min	Col de l'Échelle	
1hr 15min	Path Junction	Junction of GR5 and GR5B

Time	Place	Services
0hr 15min	Modane-Pâquier	Link with GR5E
1hr 15min	La Norma	ATM, shops, restaurants, TIC, buses by arrangement
0hr 45min	Fort Marie-Thérèse	Restaurant, buses
1hr 00min	Croix du Mollard	
0hr 15min gîte,	Bramans	Hotel/restaurant, campsite, shop, PO, buses
0hr 15min	Le Verney	*Boulangerie/patisserie*, buses
1hr 15min	Sollières-Envers	Campsite
0hr 45min	Termignon	All services except bank; TIC, buses
1hr 45min	Lanslebourg-Mont Cenis	All services, TIC, buses
0hr 30min	Lanslevillard	All services, TIC, buses
1hr 15min	Chantelouve d'en Haut	
0hr 45min	Les Chardonnettes	Nearby campsite
0hr 45min	Bessans	All services except bank; TIC, buses, link with GR5
0hr 45min	Le Villaron	*Gîte*, water

Time	Place	Services
1hr 45min	Tralenta/Bonneval-sur-Arc	GR5E, hotels, *refuge*, PO, shops, restaurants, TIC, buses
GR55 Variant		
0hr 00min	Modane/Fourneaux	All services, TIC, trains, buses
0hr 15min	Loutraz	
0hr 45min	Track Junction	
1hr 30min	Polset	Water, *chalet d'alpage*, restaurant off-route
1hr 30min	Path Junction	Option to descend to Refuge de l'Orgère in 1hr 15min
1hr 00min	Col de Chavière	
0hr 50min	Refuge de Péclet-Polset	*Refuge*, restaurant
1hr 45min	Refuge du Roc de la Pêche	
0hr 35min	Les Prioux	*Refuge*, restaurant
0hr 20min	Pont de Gerlon	*Refuge*, restaurant
0hr 30min	Pralognan-la-Vanoise	All services, TIC, buses

295

Time	Place	Services
0hr 50min	Les Fontanettes	Restaurant
1hr 25min	Refuge les Barmettes	*Refuge*, restaurant
0hr 45min	Lac des Vaches	
0hr 45min	Refuge Col de la Vanoise	*Refuge*, restaurant
1hr 00min	Blockhouse	
0hr 30min	Pont de la Croé Vie	
0hr 30min	Refuge d'Entre Deux Eaux	*Refuge*, restaurant, nearby *gîte*, link with GR5
0hr 30min	Pont de la Croé Vie	
1hr 30min	Refuge de la Leisse	*Refuge*, restaurant
1hr 45min	Col de la Leisse	
1hr 30min	Val Claret	All services, TIC, buses, link with GR5
0hr 30min	Tignes-le-Lac	All services, TIC, buses, link with GR5
Main Route		
0hr 00min	Modane/Fourneaux	All services, TIC, trains, buses
0hr 15min	Loutraz	
0hr 45min	Track Junction	Short-cut to Pierre Brune in 1hr 30min

Time	Place	Services
1hr 30min	Polset	Water, *chalet d'alpage*, restaurant off-route
0hr 30min	Pierre Brune	Water
0hr 30min	Chalets de l'Orgère	*Refuges*, restaurants, 10min off-route
2hr 00min	Col du Barbier	
1hr 15min	Pont de la Sétéria	
0hr 30min	Refuge de la Fournache	*Refuge*, restaurant, just off-route
0hr 20min	Refuge de Plan Sec	*Refuge*, restaurant, just off-route
0hr 20min	Le Montana	Hotel, *refuge*, restaurant, *télésiège* to Aussois
1hr 15min	La Turra	
1hr 15min	La Loza	
1hr 30min	Montafia Dessus	
0hr 40min	Le Mont	
1hr 00min	Refuge de l'Arpont	*Refuge*, restaurant
1hr 15min	Ruisseau de Miribel	
1hr 00min	Lacs des Lozières	
1hr 00min	Mont de la Para	
0hr 45min	La Renaudière	Buses, nearby *refuge*, restaurant and link with GR55
0hr 45min	Refuge de Plan du Lac	*Refuge*, restaurant, buses

Time	Place	Services
0hr 20min	Tignes-le-Lac	All services, TIC, buses, link with GR55
0hr 40min	Croix de Lognan	Short-cut via Val Claret to link with GR55
0hr 20min	Tichot Télésiège	
0hr 40min	Col du Palet	
0hr 05min	Refuge du Col du Palet	*Refuge*, restaurant
1hr 15min	Path Junction	
0hr 15min	Refuge d'Entre-le-Lac	*Refuge*, restaurant; option to short-cut down the valley
0hr 25min	Path Junction	
0hr 20min	Chalets de la Plagne	
0hr 25min	Path Junction	
1hr 15min	Chalet-Refuge de Rosuel	*Refuge*, restaurant, buses
0hr 10min	Les Lanches	*Buvette*, buses
0hr 10min	Palais de la Mine	*Gîte* and restaurant nearby
0hr 30min	Moulin	Peisey 15min off-route, buses
1hr 30min	La Jacottaz	
0hr 20min	Montchavin	Hotels, shops, PO, ATM, restaurants, TIC

Time	Place	Services
0hr 30min	Bellecombe	Buses
1hr 30min	La Turra	
0hr 45min	Pré Valliant	
1hr 00min	Refuge du Cuchet	Unstaffed *refuge* with kitchen – own supplies needed
1hr 30min	Plan de la Cha	
0hr 30min	Refuge de Vallonbrun	*Refuge*, restaurant
1hr 15min	Le Collet	Water
0hr 30min	Le Chalp	Nearby campsite
1hr 00min	Bessans	All services except bank. TIC, buses, link with GR5E
0hr 15min	Ruisseau du Pis	
1hr 15min	Le Vallon	Possible *gîte d'alpage*
0hr 45min	Les Roches	
0hr 45min	La Lenta	Option to descend to Bonneval to link with GR5E in 1hr
1hr 15min	Pont de la Neige	
0hr 45min	Col de l'Iseran	Restaurant
1hr 15min	Main Road	
1hr 30min	Val d'Isère	All services, TIC, buses
2hr 00min	Pas de la Tovière	

Time	Place	Services
0hr 10min	Montorlin	Water
0hr 45min	Pont de Bellentre	

Variant Route

Time	Place	Services
0hr 00min	Moulin	Peisey 15min off-route, buses
1hr 15min	Landry	Hotel, restaurant, shop, bar, campsite, trains, buses
1hr 00min	Pont de Bellentre	

Main Route

Time	Place	Services
0hr 00min	Pont de Bellentre	
0hr 15min	Bellentre	Bar/shop, PO
1hr 15min	Valezan	Auberge, gîte, restaurant
0hr 45min	Les Fours	
2hr 30min	Refuge de la Balme	Refuge, restaurant
1hr 30min	Col du Bresson	Refuge 20min off-route
1hr 00min	Presset	
0hr 40min	Lavachay	
1hr 00min	La Petite Berge	

Time	Place	Services
0hr 30min	Plan de la Lai	Refuge, restaurant, nearby gîte
1hr 00min	Chalet Bel-Air	
0hr 45min	Col de la Sauce	
1hr 30min	Croix du Bonhomme	Refuge, restaurant, Les Chapieux off-route
0hr 40min	Col du Bonhomme	Shelter
1hr 00min	Plan Jovet	
0hr 30min	Refuge de la Balme	Refuge, restaurant
0hr 45min	Chalet de Nant Borrant	Refuge, restaurant
0hr 20min	Notre Dame de la Gorge	Restaurant
1hr 00min	Les Contamines-Montjoie	All services, TIC, buses

Variant Route

Time	Place	Services
0hr 00min	Les Contamines-Montjoie	All services, TIC, buses
1hr 30min	Chalets du Truc	Refuge, restaurant
0hr 30min	Chalets de Miage	Refuge, restaurant
1hr 30min	Col de Tricot	
0hr 30min	Passerelle de Glacier	
0hr 40min	Col de Voza	Hotel, café/bar, tramway

Time	Place	Services
Main Route		
0hr 00min	Les Contamines-Montjoie	All services, TIC, buses
1hr 00min	Tresse	Hotel, restaurant, buses
1hr 15min	Champel	*Gîte*, water
1hr 00min	Bionnassay	*Auberge/gîte*, café
0hr 45min	Refuge de Fioux	*Gîte d'étape*, restaurant
0hr 15min	Col de Voza	Hotel, café/bar, tramway
1hr 15min	Les Houches	All services, TIC, trains, buses
2hr 00min	Merlet	Wildlife park, restaurant, off-route
1hr 45min	Refuge de Bellachat	*Refuge*, restaurant
1hr 15min	Le Brévent	Restaurant, *téléphérique* to Chamonix
0hr 45min	Col du Brévent	
1hr 45min	Pont d'Arlevé	
1hr 15min	Refuge Moëde Anterne	*Refuge*, restaurant
0hr 45min	Col d'Anterne	
0hr 30min	Lac d'Anterne	

Time	Place	Services
1hr 00min	Chalets d'Anterne	*Refuge*, restaurant
0hr 30min	Collet d'Anterne	
0hr 45min	Cascade de la Sauffaz	
0hr 45min	Chalet de Lignon	Restaurant
0hr 15min	Cascade du Rouguet	Restaurant
0hr 40min	Pont des Nants	Selvagny and Sixt-Fer-à-Cheval off-route
1hr 00min	Pont du Perret	Water, buses
1hr 00min	Samoëns	All services, TIC, buses
0hr 15min	Le Chevreret	
1hr 00min	Les Allamands	Water
1hr 30min	Col de la Golèse	*Refuge*, restaurant
1hr 00min	Torrent de Chardonnière	*Refuge* off-route
1hr 15min	Col de Coux	
0hr 30min	La Poyat	
0hr 10min	La Pierre	*Gîte*, restaurant
0hr 15min	Lapisa	*Buvette*
0hr 50min	Chaux Palin	*Gîte*, restaurant
1hr 00min	Refuge de Chésery	*Refuge*, restaurant
1hr 15min	Col de Bassachaux	*Refuge*, restaurant
1hr 00min	Lenlevay	Water
2hr 00min	Les Mattes	
0hr 30min	Chalet de la Torrens	
0hr 30min	Chalet des Crottes	*Refuge* 1hr 15min off-route

Time	Place	Services
0hr 40min	Sur Bayard	
1hr 00min	Chapelle d'Abondance	All services, TIC, buses
0hr 40min	Chalets de Chevenne	Water
1hr 30min	Pas de la Bosse	
0hr 45min	Chalets de Bise	*Refuge*, restaurants
1hr 15min	Col de Bise	
0hr 30min	Col de Pavis	
0hr 45min	Lac de la Case	
0hr 45min	Tête des Fieux	
1hr 15min	Les Boeufs	
0hr 45min	Le Grand Chesnay	Water
0hr 45min	Sur les Trables	
0hr 20min	Le Cret – for Chevenoz	*Gîte*, shop, bar, buses, 30min off-route
0hr 50min	Outskirts of Vinzier	Campsite, PO, bar, supermarket, café, ATM, buses
0hr 15min	Les Clouz	
0hr 20min	La Plantaz	
0hr 30min	Bioge	Bar/restaurant, buses

Time	Place	Services
1hr 15min	Reyvroz	Cafés
1hr 00min	Les Jossières	
0hr 45min	Armoy	Hotel, shops, buses
1hr 00min	Repos de l'Aigle	
0hr 30min	Bridge over Bypass	
0hr 30min	Thonon-les-Bains	All services, TIC, trains, buses, ferries, end of GR5

Main Route

Time	Place	Services
0hr 00min	Chapelle d'Abondance	All services, TIC, buses
0hr 40min	Chalets de Chevenne	Water
1hr 30min	Pas de la Bosse	
0hr 45min	Chalets de Bise	*Refuge*, restaurants
1hr 15min	Col de Bise	
0hr 20min	Chalets de Neuteu	Shelter, water
1hr 15min	La Planche	
0hr 30min	Novel	Hotel, *chambres d'hôte*, restaurants
1hr 10min	St Gingolph	All services, TIC, trains, buses, ferries, end of GR5

APPENDIX 3
Accommodation List

STAGE 1 LAC LEMAN TO LES HOUCHES

Indoor accommodation is listed, including *refuges*, *gîtes d'étape*, *chambres d'hôte* and hotels, in locations where there are only a few options available. In towns and villages where several options are available, the local TIC telephone number is given, where staff will assist you with making a choice. Only a few off-route options are listed, and only in places where they might prove useful. Be wary of booking too far in advance, since a spell of bad weather could result in you having to change all your onward plans. Don't assume that the place with the most beds is the place you should be heading. It might be full, while the little place nearby might be almost empty!

Day 1 St Gingolph to La Chapelle d'Abondance
St Gingolph Hotels; TIC tel 024 481 84 31
Novel Gîte/Chambres Le Franco Suisse, tel 04 50 76 73 74
Chalets de Bise Refuge de Bise, tel 04 50 73 11 73
La Chapelle d'Abondance Les Routards du Monde, tel 04 50 73 52 51; Gîte Au Gai Soleil, tel 04 50 73 50 35; Chalet Bellevue, tel 04 50 73 51 37; hotels; TIC tel 04 50 73 51 41

Day 1 Thonon-les-Bains to Chevenoz
Thonon-les-Bains Hotels; TIC tel 04 40 71 55 55
Armoy Hotel Echo des Montagnes, tel 04 50 73 94 55
Chevenoz Gîte l'Autan, tel 04 50 72 20 33

Day 2 Chevenoz to La Chapelle d'Abondance
Dent d'Oche Refuge de la Dent d'Oche, tel 04 50 73 62 45
Chalets de Bise Refuge de Bise, tel 04 50 73 11 73
La Chapelle d'Abondance Les Routards du Monde, tel 04 50 73 52 51; Gîte Au Gai Soleil, tel 04 50 73 50 35; Chalet Bellevue, tel 04 50 73 51 37; hotels, TIC tel 04 50 73 51 41

Day 3 La Chapelle d'Abondance to Chésery
Trébentaz Refuge de Trébentaz, tel 04 50 73 26 17
Col de Bassachaux Refuge de Bassachaux, tel 04 50 73 31 97
Col de Chésery Refuge de Chésery, tel 024 479 35 11

Day 4 Chésery to Samoëns
Chaux Palin Gîte de Chaupalin, tel 024 477 26 16
Lapisa Gîte d'alpage La Pisa, tel 024 479 36 43

La Pierre Gîte d'alpage La Pierre, tel 024 479 31 32
Chardonnière Refuge de Chardonnière, tel 04 50 90 11 40
Col de la Golèse Refuge de la Golèse, tel 04 50 90 59 53
Samoëns Gîte les Moulins, tel 04 50 34 95 69; Gîte Les Couadzous, tel 04 50 34 41 62;
    hotels; TIC tel 04 50 34 40 28

Day 5 Samoëns to Refuge de Moëde Anterne
Sixt-Fer-à-Cheval Hotels, TIC tel 04 50 34 49 36
Selvagny Auberge de Salvagny, tel 04 50 34 47 64
Chalets d'Anterne Refuge Alfred Wills, tel 06 70 63 12 45
Moëde-Anterne Refuge de Moëde-Anterne, tel 04 50 93 60 43

Day 6 Refuge de Moëde Anterne to Les Houches
Bellachat Refuge de Bellachat, tel 04 50 53 43 23
Les Houches Hotels, TIC tel 04 50 55 50 62

STAGE 2 LES HOUCHES TO LANDRY

Day 7 Les Houches to Les Contamines (main)
Col de Voza Hotel Gîte Le Prarion, tel 04 50 54 40 07
Fioux Refuge du Fioux, tel 04 50 93 52 43
Bionnassay Auberge de Bionnassay, tel 04 50 93 45 23
Champel Gîte du Champel, tel 04 50 47 77 55
Tresse Le Relais du Mont Blanc, tel 04 50 47 02 08
Les Contamines Chalet du CAF, tel 04 50 47 00 88; Chalet du Mont Joye, tel 04 50 93
    20 22; hotels, TIC tel 04 50 47 01 58

Day 7 Les Houches to Les Contamines (variant)
Col de Voza Hotel Gîte Le Prarion, tel 04 50 54 40 07
Chalets de Miage Refuge de Miage, tel 04 50 93 22 91
Chalets du Truc Auberge du Truc, tel 04 50 93 12 48
Les Contamines Chalet du CAF, tel 04 50 47 00 88; Chalet du Mont Joye, tel 04 50
    93 20 22; hotels, TIC tel 04 50 47 01 58

Day 8 Les Contamines to Plan de la Lai
Le Pontet Gîte du Pontet, tel 04 50 47 04 04
Nant Borrant Chalet Refuge de Nant Borrant, tel 04 50 47 03 57
La Balme Refuge de la Balme, tel 04 50 47 03 54
Bonhomme Refuge de la Croix du Bonhomme, tel 04 79 07 05 28
Plan de la Lai Refuge du Plan de la Lai, tel 04 79 89 07 78
Les Chapieux (off-route) Refuge de la Nova, tel 04 79 89 07 15

Curved boilerplate slabs of limestone are seen along the flanks of Les Terres Maudites above Chardonnière (Day 4)

Day 9 Plan de la Lai to Landry
Plan de la Lai Gîte d'alpage Plan de Mya, tel 06 08 46 03 10
Presset (off-route) Refuge du Presset, tel 06 87 54 09 18
La Balme Refuge de la Balme, tel 04 79 09 70 62
Valezan Auberge de Valezan, tel 04 79 07 22 13
Landry Hotel le Bon Acceuil, tel 04 79 07 08 79

STAGE 3 LANDRY TO MODANE GR5 MAIN ROUTE

Day 10 Landry to Refuge d'Entre-le-Lac
Montchavin Hotels, TIC tel 04 79 07 82 82
Peisey Hotels, TIC tel 04 79 07 88 67
Pont Baudin Gîte Les Glières, tel 04 79 07 92 65.
Rosuel Chalet-Refuge de Rosuel, tel 04 79 07 94 03
Entre-le-Lac Refuge d'Entre-le-Lac, tel 04 79 04 20 44

Day 11 Refuge d'Entre-le-Lac to Val d'Isère
Col du Palet Refuge du Col du Palet, tel 04 79 07 91 47
Tignes-le-Lac Hotels, TIC tel 04 79 40 04 40
Val d'Isère Hotels, TIC tel 04 79 06 06 60

Day 12 Val d'Isère to Bessans
Bonneval-sur-Arc (off-route) see under GR5E
Le Vallon Possible *alpage* lodging
Bessans Gîte le Petit Bonheur, tel 04 79 05 06 71; hotels, TIC tel 04 79 05 96 52

Day 13 Bessans to Refuge du Plan du Lac
Vallonbrun Refuge de Vallonbrun, tel 04 79 05 93 93
Le Cuchet Refuge du Cuchet, unstaffed
Plan du Lac Refuge du Plan du Lac, tel 04 79 20 50 85

Day 14 Refuge du Plan du Lac to Le Montana
Entre Deux Eaux (off-route) Refuge d'Entre Deux Eaux, tel 04 79 05 27 13;
    Alpage Christine Richard
L'Arpont Refuge de l'Arpont, tel 04 79 20 51 51
Le Montana Hotel Refuge Le Montana, tel 04 79 20 31 47

Day 15 Le Montana to Modane/Fourneaux
Plan Sec Refuge de Plan Sec, tel 04 79 20 31 31
Fournache Refuge de la Fournache, tel 04 79 20 35 48
Chalets de l'Orgère Refuge de l'Aiguille Doran, tel 06 80 72 46 63; Refuge de
    l'Orgère, tel 04 79 05 11 65

Polset Chalet d'alpage de Polset, tel 04 79 05 00 22
Fourneaux Hotels. TIC, tel 04 79 05 28 58 (NB None at Modane)

GR55 HIGH LEVEL VARIANT

Day 11 Refuge d'Entre-le-Lac to Refuge d'Entre Deux Eaux
Col du Palet Refuge du Col du Palet, tel 04 79 07 91 47
Val Claret Hotels; TIC, tel 04 79 40 04 40
La Leisse Refuge de la Leisse, tel 04 79 05 45 33
Entre Deux Eaux (off-route) Refuge d'Entre Deux Eaux, tel 04 79 05 27 13;
    Alpage Christine Richard

Day 12 Refuge d'Entre Deux Eaux to Roc de la Pêche
Col de la Vanoise Refuge du Col de la Vanoise, tel 04 79 08 25 23
Les Barmettes Refuge les Barmettes, tel 04 79 08 75 64
Pralognan-la-Vanoise Hotels, TIC tel 04 79 08 79 08
Les Prioux Refuge le Repoju, tel 04 79 08 73 79
Roc de la Pêche Refuge du Roc de la Pêche, tel 04 79 08 79 75

Day 13 Roc de la Pêche to Modane/Fourneaux
Péclet-Polset Refuge de Péclet-Polset, tel 04 79 08 72 13
Polset Chalet d'alpage de Polset, tel 04 79 05 00 22
Fourneaux Hotels, TIC tel 04 79 05 28 58 (NB None at Modane)

GR5E LOW LEVEL VARIANT

Day 13 Bonneval-sur-Arc to Lanslevillard
Bonneval-sur-Arc Refuge du Club Alpin Française, tel 04 79 05 83 78; hotels, TIC tel
    04 79 05 95 95
Le Villaron Gîte la Batisse, tel 04 79 05 95 84
Bessans Gîte le Petit Bonheur, tel 04 79 05 06 71; hotels, TIC tel 04 79 05 96 52
Lanslevillard Hotels, TIC tel 04 79 05 99 15

Day 14 Lanslevillard to Bramans
Lanslebourg-Mont Cenis Hotels, TIC tel 04 79 05 23 66
Termignon Gîte La Para, tel 04 79 20 51 45; hotels, TIC tel 04 79 20 51 67
Bramans Hotel/gîte Les Glaciers, tel 04 79 05 08 73

Day 15 Bramans to Modane/Fourneaux
Fourneaux Hotels, TIC tel 04 79 05 28 58 (NB None at Modane)

While traversing towards the Col du Granon, there are fine views of the Ecrins across the valley (Day 18a GR5C)

STAGE 4 MODANE TO CEILLAC

Day 16 Modane/Fourneaux to Refuge de Thabor
Valfréjus Gîte Les Tavernes, tel 04 79 05 16 41; hotels, TIC tel 04 79 05 33 83
Mont Thabor Refuge du Thabor, tel 04 79 20 32 13

Day 17 Refuge de Thabor to Plampinet (GR5)
Granges de la Vallée Étroite Rifugio i Re Magi, tel 012296451; Rifugio Tre Alpini, tel 0122902071
Névache (off-route) Hotels, TIC tel 04 92 20 02 20
Plampinet Gîte Auberge La Cleïda, tel 04 92 21 32 48; Auberge de la Clarée, tel 04 92 21 37 71

Day 17 GR5B, La Vallée Étroite to Plampinet (Variant)
Plampinet Gîte Auberge La Cleïda, tel 04 92 21 32 48; Auberge de la Clarée, tel 04 92 21 37 71

Day 18 Plampinet to Briançon (GR5)
Montgenèvre Hotels, TIC tel 04 92 21 52 52
Les Alberts Gîte Auberge La Maïta, tel 04 92 20 29 72
Vachette Gîte Le Duranceau, tel 04 92 21 19 57
Le Fontenil Gîte Le Petit Phoque, tel 04 92 20 07 27
Briançon Hotels, TIC tel 04 92 21 08 50

Day 18 GR5C, Névache to Briançon (Variant)
Névache Hotels. TIC tel 04 92 20 02 20
Briançon Hotels. TIC tel 04 92 21 08 50

Day 19 Briançon to Brunissard
Villar St Pancrace Gîte du Barracan, tel 04 92 21 27 79
Chalets de Vers le Col Basic unstaffed *refuge*
Brunissard Gîte Les Bons Enfants, tel 04 92 46 73 85

Day 20 Brunissard to Ceillac
La Chalp Hotels, TIC tel 04 92 46 75 7
Ville-Vieille (off-route) Hotels, TIC tel 04 92 46 86 89
Ceillac Gîte Les Baladins, tel 04 92 45 00 23. Hotel Les Veyres, tel 04 92 45 01 91; TIC tel 04 92 45 05 74

STAGE 5 CEILLAC TO AURON

Day 21 Ceillac to La Barge/Maljasset
Pied du Mélézet Hotel La Cascade, tel 04 92 45 05 92

Maljasset Refuge du Club Alpin Française, tel 04 92 84 34 04; Gîte Auberge La Cure, tel 04 92 84 31 15; Maison d'hôte, tel 04 92 84 37 64

Day 22 La Barge/Maljasset to Larche
St Paul sur Ubaye (off-route) Hotels, TIC tel 04 92 81 03 68
Fouillouse Gîte Auberge Les Granges, tel 04 92 84 31 16
Larche Gîte Le Refuge, tel 04 92 84 30 80; Gîte Auberge du Lauzanier, tel 04 92 84 35 93; Hotel au Relais d'Italie, tel 04 92 84 31 32; TIC tel 04 92 84 33 58

Day 23 Larche to Bousieyas
Bousieyas Gîte de Bousieyas, tel 04 93 02 42 20

Day 24 Bousieyas to Auron
St Dalmas le Selvage Gîte d'étape, tel 04 93 02 44 61; TIC tel 04 93 02 46 40
St Étienne de Tinée Gîte Le Corboran, tel 04 93 02 49 36; hotels, TIC tel 04 93 02 41 96
Auron Hotels, TIC tel 04 93 23 02 66

STAGE 6 AURON TO NICE
Day 25 Auron to Refuge de Longon
Roya Gîte Ma Vieille École, tel 04 93 03 43 05
Longon Refuge de Longon, tel 04 93 02 83 99

Day 26 Refuge de Longon to St Dalmas
Roure Gîte La Chèvrerie, tel 04 93 02 83 99
St Sauveur sur Tinée Gîte d'étape, tel 04 93 02 03 20; hotels
Rimplas Hostellerie de Rimplas, tel 04 93 02 86 80
La Bolline Hotel de Valdeblore, tel 04 93 03 28 53; Chambres d'hôte Le Welcome, tel 06 86 79 46 99
La Roche TIC tel 04 93 23 25 90
St Dalmas Gîte Les Marmottes, tel 04 93 02 89 04; Gîte Rando Sport Nature, tel 04 93 02 82 86; Hotel Les Mures, tel 04 93 23 24 60

Day 27 St Dalmas to Utelle
Utelle Gîte Municipal, tel 04 93 03 17 01; Hotel Bellevue, tel 04 93 03 17 19; Auberge Ferme Les Merinos, tel 04 93 03 18 39

Day 28 Utelle to Aspremont
La Madone d'Utelle Hostellerie du Sanctuaire, tel 04 93 03 19 44
Levens Hotels, TIC tel 04 93 79 71 00
Aspremont Relais St Jean, tel 04 93 08 00 66; Hostellerie d'Aspremont, tel 04 93 08 00 05

Clumps of long, feathery grass lend a Mediterranean air to the route as it drops to St Étienne de Tinée (Day 24)

Day 29 Aspremont to Nice
Nice Hotels, TIC tel 08 92 70 74 07

STAGE 7 GR52, ST DALMAS TO GARAVAN/MENTON

Day 27 St Dalmas to Le Boréon
Le Boréon Gîte du Boréon, tel 04 93 03 27 27; Hotel Le Boréon, tel 04 93 03 20 35;
    Hotel Le Cavalet, tel 04 93 03 21 46

Day 28 Le Boréon to Refuge de Nice
Cougourde (off-route) Refuge de Cougourde, tel 04 93 03 26 00
La Madone de Fenestre Refuge du Club Alpin Française, tel 04 93 02 83 19
Lac de la Fous Refuge de Nice, tel 06 61 97 59 38

Day 29 Refuge de Nice to Refuge des Merveilles
Vallée des Merveilles Refuge des Merveilles, tel 04 93 04 64 64

Day 30 Refuge des Merveilles to Sospel
Sospel Gîte Le Mercantour, tel 04 93 04 00 99; hotels. TIC tel 04 93 04 15 80

Day 31 Sospel to Garavan/Menton
Garavan/Menton Hotels, TIC tel 04 92 41 76 76

APPENDIX 4
Basic French for the GR5

ARRIVAL IN FRANCE

Hello!/good evening/how are you?	*Bonjour!/bonsoir/ça va?*
Where can I get a taxi?	*Où puis-je trouver un taxi?*
Take me to…	*Conduisez-moi à…*
…the railway station/the hotel/this address	*…la gare/l'hôtel/cette adresse*
How much is it?	*Combien est-ce?*
Where is the bus stop/train station?	*Où se trouve l'arrêt du bus/la gare?*
Tourist information office	*L'office de tourisme/syndicate d'initiative*
Post office/grocery	*La poste/alimentation*
I'd like a single/ eturn ticket to…	*Je voudrais un billet aller simple/aller-retour à…*
Can I have a timetable?	*Puis je avoir un horaire?*
Information/open/closed	*Reseignements/ouvert/fermé*

STAYING THE NIGHT

Rooms available/no vacancies	*Chambres libres/complet*
I'd like a single/double room	*Je voudrais une chambre pour une personne/deux personnes*
How much does it cost per night?	*Quel est le prix par nuit?*
How much does it cost for bed and breakfast?	*Quel est le prix avec petit déjeuner?*
Is there hot water/a toilet/a shower?	*Y a-t-il l'eau chaude/une toilette /un douche?*
Where is the dining room/bar?	*Où est la salle à manger/bar?*

WALKING THE GR5

Where is the GR5?	*Où est le GR5?* (pronounced 'jair sank')
The path/the waymarks/rucksack	*Le sentier/les balisés/sac à dos*
Where are you going?	*Vous allez où?*
I'm going to…	*Je vais à…*
Right/left/straight ahead	*À droit/à gauche/tout droit*
Can you show me on the map?	*Est-ce que vous pouver me le montrer sur la carte?*
Camping/fire prohibited	*Camping/feu interdit*

AT THE *REFUGE*

Guardian	*Gardien* (male)/*gardienne* (female)
Can I stay in the refuge?	*Puis-je reste dans le refuge?*
Dormitory/bed/sleeping bag	*dortoir/lit/sac à couchage*
Can I camp here?	*Puis-je camper ici?*
Tent/camping space/campsite	*Tente/emplacement/aire de bivouac*
Where are the toilets/showers?	*Où sont les toilettes/douches?*
Can I have a meal/a beer/breakfast?	*Puis-je avoir un repas/une bière/ petit déjeuner?*
What is the weather forecast for tomorrow?	*Quel est le météo demain?*
Hot/cold/rain/snow/storm/mist	*Chaud/froid/pluie/neige/orage/brouillard*

WHEN IT ALL GOES WRONG

Help me!	*Aidez-moi!*
I feel sick	*Je suis malade*
There has been an accident	*Il y a eu un accident*

LAST RESORT

I don't understand	*Je ne comprends pas*
Do you speak English?	*Parlez-vous anglais?*

LAZY WALKER'S FRENCH

Bonjour, merci and s'il vous plaît will get you a long way!

Hello *Bonjour!* (A standard greeting, which is useful everywhere you go. For instance, on entering a *refuge* or bar, greet all present with this single word.)

Please, a bed/a meal/a beer *S'il vous plaît, un lit un repas/une bière* (The simplest and politest way of dealing with requests and needs.)

How much? Thank you! *Combien? Merci!* (Keep it polite and simple!)

Goodbye *Au revoir*; see you later *a tout à l'heure* (as English 'toodle-loo!').

NB The bigger the word is in English, the more likely the French word is to be similar!

COMMON FOOD AND DRINK TERMS

French	English	French	English
Ail	Garlic	*Jus d'orange*	Orange juice
Beurre	Butter	*Legumes*	Vegetables
Bière	Beer	*Lentilles*	Lentils
Boissons (froid/chaud)	Drinks (cold/hot)	*Miel*	Honey
Café/café au lait	Black/white coffee	*Oeufs*	Eggs
Champignons	Mushrooms	*Omelette*	Omelette
Charcuterie	Cured meats served cold	*Pain (chaud)*	Bread (hot)
Châtaigne	Chestnut, used in main courses and desserts	*Panini* Filled bread rolls, often toasted	
Chocolat	Chocolate	*Pâté*	Paté
Confiture	Jam	*Pâtes*	Pasta
Crudities Chopped raw vegetables or salad		*Pomme de terre*	Potato
		Poisson	Fish
Flan	Egg custard dessert	*Poulet*	Chicken
Frites	Chips	*Riz*	Rice
Fromage	Cheese	*Rôti*	Roast
Gâteau	Cake	*Saucisson*	Sausage
Haricots	Beans	*Sel*	Salt
Huile	Oil	*Sucre*	Sugar
Jambon	Ham	*Thé/thé au lait*	Black/white tea
		Thon	Tuna
		Vin blanc/rouge	White/red wine

APPENDIX 5
Topographical Glossary

French	English
Aiguille	Needle-like peak
Balme	Cave
Blanc/blanche	White
Bois	Wood
Clap/clapier	Boulders
Col	Gap/saddle
Combe	High dry valley
Crête	Ridge/crest
Croix	Cross/crucifix
Estive	Summer pasture
Forêt	Forest
Grand/grande	Large/big
Lac	Lake
Malpas/mauvais pas	Bad step
Mont/montagne	Mountain

French	English
Noir/noire	Black
Pas	Steep-sided col
Petit/petite	Little/small
Plagne/plan	Plain/plateau
Pointe	Peak
Rivière	River
Roc/rocher	Rock
Rouge	Red
Ruisseau	Stream
Sentier	Path
Sommet	Summit
Source	Spring
Val/vallée	Valley
Vert/verte	Green

NOTES

LISTING OF CICERONE GUIDES

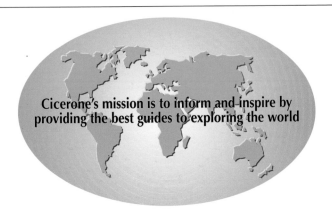

Cicerone's mission is to inform and inspire by providing the best guides to exploring the world

Since its foundation over 30 years ago, Cicerone has specialised in publishing guidebooks and has built a reputation for quality and reliability. It now publishes nearly 300 guides to the major destinations for outdoor enthusiasts, including Europe, UK and the rest of the world.

Written by leading and committed specialists, Cicerone guides are recognised as the most authoritative. They are full of information, maps and illustrations so that the user can plan and complete a successful and safe trip or expedition – be it a long face climb, a walk over Lakeland fells, an alpine traverse, a Himalayan trek or a ramble in the countryside.

With a thorough introduction to assist planning, clear diagrams, maps and colour photographs to illustrate the terrain and route, and accurate and detailed text, Cicerone guides are designed for ease of use and access to the information.

If the facts on the ground change, or there is any aspect of a guide that you think we can improve, we are always delighted to hear from you.

Cicerone Press
2 Police Square Milnthorpe Cumbria LA7 7PY
Tel:01539 562 069   Fax:01539 563 417
e-mail:info@cicerone.co.uk   web:www.cicerone.co.uk

CICERONE